American Small-Town
Fiction, 1940–1960

American Small-Town Fiction, 1940–1960
A Critical Study

NATHANAEL T. BOOTH

McFarland & Company, Inc., Publishers
Jefferson, North Carolina

ISBN (print) 978-1-4766-7274-8
ISBN (ebook) 978-1-4766-3572-9

LIBRARY OF CONGRESS CATALOGUING DATA ARE AVAILABLE

BRITISH LIBRARY CATALOGUING DATA ARE AVAILABLE

© 2019 Nathanael T. Booth. All rights reserved

No part of this book may be reproduced or transmitted in any form or by any means, electronic or mechanical, including photocopying or recording, or by any information storage and retrieval system, without permission in writing from the publisher.

Front cover: Postcard of the business district in Forty Fort, Pennsylvania, circa 1945 (Mebane Greeting Card Company)

Manufactured in the United States of America

*McFarland & Company, Inc., Publishers
Box 611, Jefferson, North Carolina 28640
www.mcfarlandpub.com*

To Teressa Conley Booth
My Special Angel

Acknowledgments

 I would not have been able to write his book without the assistance of many people along the way. First, of course, I owe thanks to Randy Booth, my father, and to my late mother Teressa, both of whom supported me during the long years of my education. I am grateful to Frederick Whiting, who directed my dissertation at the University of Alabama, as well as the members of my committee: Philip Beidler, Nikhil Bilwakesh, Trudier Harris, and Richard Megraw. I owe thanks, too, to my colleagues and friends who not only put up with my rantings but were willing to look at the manuscript and give me feedback: Matthew Kelley, Matthew Wells, Stephanie Parker, Erik Kline, William Murray, Geoffrey Emerson, and Caitlan Sumner. Without the help of all of these people, I could never have produced this book.
 Thanks to the administration and faculty at Huazhong University of Science and Technology in Wuhan, China, for their support and encouragement as I turned my dissertation into a book. Special gratitude is also owed to the publishers at McFarland, particularly Layla Milholen, who worked closely with me as I revised this manuscript for publication, as well as to my two anonymous reviewers at McFarland (I do not know you, but your work is on each page the same as mine).
 Extra-special thanks to Ethan, who puts up with my obsessions.

Table of Contents

Acknowledgments vi
Preface 1
Introduction 5

ONE   Columbus on the Platform: The Train Station   25
TWO   "The Crisis of Individuation": The Schoolhouse   42
THREE   The Small-Town *Bildungsroman*: The Malt Shop   61
FOUR   No Town Is an Island: Main Street and the Town Square   82
FIVE   False Transcendence: The Movie Theater   98
SIX   Good God, Bad God: The Church   114
SEVEN   Fortunate Fall: The Courthouse   135
EIGHT   Transcending Division: The Outskirts   152
NINE   In This Garden of Death: The Graveyard   175

Epilogue: The Train, Again 185
Chapter Notes 191
Bibliography 201
Index 207

Preface

This project came to me, as such projects do, by accident. I intended to write my dissertation (of which this book is an expansion) on detective fiction during World War II. That project would have focused on Ellery Queen and William Faulkner, with a side glance to the now-forgotten detective stories of noted scholar Hugh Holman. As I was preparing myself for research, I noticed that all the detective stories I was considering were set in small towns, which led me to ask what, exactly, a small town symbolizes for America in an age of crisis. My research led ultimately to Henry Bellamann's 1940 novel *Kings Row*, a book whose emotional intensity—and emphatic queerness—spoke to me on a level that I did not quite anticipate. In a moment, my entire project was turned on its head and the book which was initially supposed to focus on crime fiction became something else entirely.

As I discovered while researching, the critical literature on small-town fiction is quite small; Ima Honaker Herron's *The Small Town in American Literature*, published in 1939, was the last full-scale study of the topic. Since then, there has been no exhaustive treatment of literary small towns, though Ryan Poll makes an important contribution to the field his slim volume *Main Street and Empire*. I am indebted to Poll for his basic theoretical framework, though, as will be seen, I diverge from his analysis in key ways. Other studies, such as Richard V. Francaviglia's *Main Street Revisited: Time, Space, and Image Building in Small-Town* and Miles Orvell's *The Death and Life of Main Street: Small Towns in American Memory, Space, and Community*, examine different facets of the small-town myth. But none of them, I noticed, attempted to finish what Herron began—to provide a detailed and exhaustive history of small-town fiction *since* World War II. This lapse is curious; the small town is foundational to America's self-fashioning, and there seems to be a broad consensus as to what that self-fashioning represents, but little attention is paid to the actual texts that *create* that self-image.

This book is in some ways an attempt to correct that imbalance. My period is narrow—roughly 1940–1960—and cannot pretend to the expansive range Herron provides in her study. Instead, I focus on a handful of novels that might be classified as "middlebrow." This decision was the result of both inclination and choice. I was once told by a professor whom I admire very much that I "like trash." He meant it as a compliment, and I took it as such. My bias is toward forgotten works. Insofar as cultural detritus can give us insight into the society that produced it, such work should never be discarded. I do not mean to imply the books I examine here are bad. Some of them are; if I spend the rest of my life without ever reading another book by James Gould Cozzens, I will die a happy man. But most of these books are unjustly forgotten. The two-man writing team known as Ellery Queen constituted one of the most important figures in American detective fiction for much of the twentieth century, and his (their) appearance here is part of an attempt to re-insert him into the discourse surrounding American crime fiction. As for Henry Bellamann, whose *Kings Row* was such an influence on the direction of this study, he is an undeniable artist and his novel is a marvelous and strange concoction, half fever-dream and half wish-fulfillment.

I have in mind two potential audiences for this book. The first is academics who, like me, are interested in the workings of the American imagination. In the pages that follow I consider several novels and story collections from a narrow period of time and under several lenses. For these readers, the logic of this study's construction will prove helpful. Scholars interested in race, gender, and sexuality can pay special attention to my chapter on the outskirts, for instance, where they will find me arguing that these three modes of social exclusion often stand in, during the time period, for a broader sense of isolation and loneliness. Scholars of American religious thought will find that I have heavily used Paul Tillich as a way of explaining small-town fiction's treatment of God and the divine in my chapter on the church. And so on. Though my primary interest is in the texts themselves, I have tried to implement as much scholarly apparatus as possible while still maintaining the integrity of each chapter.

My second intended audience is much less well-defined. I intend this book for those of us who find ourselves late in the second decade of the twenty-first century looking about and blinking in surprise and terror. It may do us good to remember that the American myth has always included two equally-real Americas: the America of Walt Whitman, full of hope and sanity, and the America of Alan Ginsberg—a terrifying figure which, Moloch-like, eats its young. It is useless to say "this is not who we are" because both are, equally, who we are. And the American small-town narrative is unblinking in reminding us of this fact. Not simply a nostalgic portrait of a bygone era, this fiction (which identifies the local with the national) will not allow us to pretend that America has ever been anything but a deeply conflicted, unjust, lonely place. But neither does it leave us to despair. For the burden of small-town literature is that this is *not how it has to be*. Even the blandest small-town story contains a protest and a promise—a protest against the alienation of the modern world and a promise that this alienation can be transcended by moving *through* it rather than back to a dead past.

All criticism is autobiography. I wrote the first draft of book in the final years of my graduate education and completed it during the first year of my teaching career. And I produced it in a time of great uncertainty for America. My argument is that the small town offered writers the opportunity to examine, to critique, and to explore the tensions facing America during the years of World War II as well as those immediately following it. The book is structured around a series of landmarks, locations that occur constantly in small-town fiction and which provide insight into the anxieties of the time: religion, race, sexuality.... As I continued to write and revise, it became clear to me that the concerns of my authors mirrored concerns very much in the air in America, particularly during the election of 2016. The struggles and tensions that we experience today are not novel; they have their roots in a long, long past—and part of that past is the anxiety that gripped the nation during and following World War II. If my research can contribute to a little-analyzed field, it can also provide insights into contemporary American society. It can, perhaps, show how thinkers in the past dealt with precisely the same anxieties that we experience today. Thus, I offer this book both as a study and as an incantation against the worst impulses of America.

Introduction

In William A. Wellman's 1947 movie *Magic Town*, Jimmy Stewart plays a statistician named Rip Smith who is elated to discover the existence of a small town named Grandview, a town whose demographics perfectly replicate America itself—the same percentage of Democrats, of Republicans, and of undecided voters. Smith assumes that polling this town will allow him as a researcher to take the "grand view" of America (the name of the town speaks to this idea, just as the title of the movie suggests that there is something altogether unreal about the fantasy presented to viewers). Eagerly, Smith visits Grandview posing as an insurance salesman in order to poll the town on matters of national importance. He is (as he claims when disembarking from the train) a new Columbus, (re)discovering America. If Smith ever had any objectivity, however, he loses it when he falls in love with Mary Peterson (Jane Wyman), the local newspaper editor. He also begins coaching the basketball team for the local school. In short order, Smith becomes an integral part of small-town life rather than an onlooker. Eventually, Peterman discovers Smith's real intentions and angrily publishes an article exposing him.

This exposure triggers events that show Grandview to be less idyllic than Smith at first assumes. Indeed, Grandview's response suggests that the small town is a complex mixture of boosterism and genuine heart. At first, the citizens are horrified that they are essentially objects of curiosity to the wider world. But as Grandview becomes more famous throughout the United States, it eagerly assumes its role as the most average small town in America. The formerly quiet, serene community is transformed into a carnival. Economic boom-times have come at last and the townsfolk arrange to build a civic center and a new high school. Ironically, of course, this is the most typically American move the town could make; as Hugh Kenner has observed, "American genius" is often indiscernible from hucksterism,[1] and the citizens of Grandview, no less than Smith himself, are incorrigible hucksters. However, as Smith has warned repeatedly, once the citizens of Grandview know of their special status as America's most typical small town, their responses to surveys become worthless. The results of the first major study conducted in Grandview—on the question of whether a woman could be president—is out of step with the larger United States because now, instead of being merely typical, the citizens are attempting to give the "correct" response. Grandview becomes a laughing-stock. The economic boom-time ends and the small town becomes a ghost town. It is only when Smith convinces the townsfolk to work together that they regain the community the boom-times took from them. The townspeople band together and overcome the disaster that has befallen them—confirming Grandview's position as a thoroughly average American town.

This movie encapsulates the pattern of small-town fiction in the years during and following World War II. Far from being merely laudatory, *Miracle Town* expresses tremendous ambivalence about its subject. The film's plot may be taken as a foretaste of this book's central argument, which is that small towns stage the loss of innocence and an attempt to move through that loss, to transcend it, through a mode of imagination that I call redemptive nostalgia. Redemptive nostalgia is a remembering of the past with the goal of remaking the present. As such, it is less concerned with escape than other forms of nostalgia. Certainly, seen from the outside, Grandview seems like a bucolic enough escape from modern city life. The city-dweller Smith praises the lazy pace of life in the town, for instance, but his perspective is warped. Town native Mary Peterman sees, perhaps, just as clearly when she strains against the small-minded provincialism of the village elders. This is the choice *Magic Town* dramatizes: naïve faith in village life versus weary cynicism about its provinciality. Within the argument of the film, both views are correct. The ease with which the town embraces boosterism suggests that the crass world of commerce is not one that is *alien* to the town, except insofar as it is unattainable; given the chance, Grandview is willing to sell itself—and its opinions—to the highest bidder. The movie encourages viewers to accept both viewpoints as correct: the small town *is* provincial, narrow, closed; on the other hand, it is a reservoir of untapped creative potential for anyone who wishes to build a better world. These traits are precisely what makes it typically American.

This mixture of affection and irony is central to understanding the way in which the small town functions as an imagined version of America itself. The small town in American literature and thought may seem to the casual glance to promote an idealized vision of the nation. As such, offering a definition of even so concrete-seeming a concept as the "small town" is difficult. For the small town in American thought is not a matter of demographics—that is, it is not a matter of how many people actually live in the town. Rather, the small town is a cluster of symbols. Often, it is spoken of in terms echoed by Smith in *Magic Town*. Shaded streets, immaculate lawns. A town square where the old men lounge in front of the courthouse and smoke, discussing politics and the faults of the younger generation. Children at play. These signifiers denote a casual, relaxed life, a kind of pastoral existence freed from the pressures of modernity. The small town is idyllic, the home to young adventurers like Tom Sawyer, Archie Andrews, and the Hardy Boys. The implication of these clusters of symbols seems to be that America's truest form is the small town. As such, critics have tended to suspect small-town mythology of harboring a deep-seated reactionary streak. Multiple scholars have asserted that the small town re-presents America to itself as a kind of idealized state. If, as per Benedict Anderson's *Imagined Communities*, the nation "is an imagined political community—and imagined as both inherently limited and sovereign,"[2] then the small town is that imagined community made flesh and dwelling among its citizens. Ryan Poll, in his book *Main Street and Empire*, argues that the small town functions in the United States as a concrete (rather than abstract) version of the national imaginary. Poll says that "the small town [...] is an imagined community that is central to the United States' imagined community."[3] Poll's analysis of the function of the small town in American thought is perceptive:

> The small town ideologically stages an authentic and autonomous American space, culture, history, and identity. This nation form instantiates a cultural logic in which a small town's community is the nation's community, a small town's history is a nation's history, and a small town's epistemic regime is a nation's epistemic regime. To recognize the small town as a nation form changes the way we read popular literary, cultural, and political texts that focus on small towns.[4]

The loop is self-reinforcing: the national imaginary creates the small town in order to present itself to itself; having seen that presentation, it then conforms to that self-presentation more closely than ever. Ironically, perhaps, there is constant anxiety about the continued death of the small town. Indeed, the idea of the dying small town is central to this self-imagination. For Poll, the small town is always vanishing under the influence of modernity, and so offers an idea-space through which the American imagination can mystify the realities of global capitalism and American imperialism. Thus, the small town must always be set apart from the rest of America in some way, isolated as a residue of the real, true America. Importantly, this imagined small town bears no relation to actual small towns except insofar as the actual gradually adopts aspects of the imaginary. Similarly, Richard V. Francaviglia, in his book *Main Street Revisited*, argues that "[o]n Main Street—according to the shared mythology, at least—the honest merchant, the hardworking townsfolk, and an accessible community government are all found in close proximity to one another."[5] Miles Orvell says that "while [the small town] has served as a microcosm of America on many occasions, it has also served, as in [...] post–World War II films, as the epitome of the backwater," and therefore as a symbol of a space that is safe from the pressures of the wider world.[6] In these readings, small towns can be thought of as harbors or refuges.

This binary choice, like the one offered in *Magic Town*, is reductive. One need not assume that there are only two choices in terms of small-town presentation, the realistic or the ideological. Such an assumption inevitably leads to the conclusion that, since no small towns exist in precisely the way they do in fiction, these communities must be comforting fantasies. In fact, the small-town fantasy is often far from comforting. Even in so optimistic a film as *Magic Town*, the view of the community is split. Midcentury small-town literature virtually never confirms the supposition that the town is an idyllic escape. As I will show in this book, depictions of the American small town do not merely elide or cover the workings of American imperialism, as Poll and (implicitly) Orvell assert, offering a fantasy of escape to a simpler time; nor do they offer a wholly realistic or naturalistic picture of the Union. Small-town fiction, particularly in the years during and following World War II, uses nostalgia to critique existing inequalities and anxieties. This double vision provides a model for studying the increasing alienation of American life. For the purposes of this study, I refer to this body of writing as midcentury small-town literature, with the acknowledgment that the period I consider—1940–1960—is fairly constricted. This literature is at one and the same time escapist and realistic. It is, in fact, realistic precisely because of the element of escapism. Following World War II, America entered a stage of new prosperity and this prosperity brought with it attendant anxieties. Worries about both conformity and the isolation of the individual were raised in studies such as Riesman's *The Lonely Crowd* (1950). The 1950s are often seen as a time of tremendous pressure and conformity. However, Wyn Wachhorst, expressing his own dissatisfaction with what he calls a "countercultural myth," argues that "it was an introspective era of innovation and creativity, the seedtime of the sixties."[7] As always, America during the 1940s and '50s presents a paradox: both regressive and progressive, and possibly progressive precisely because it is regressive.

Midcentury small-town literature, modeling America to itself, examines national tensions and anxieties through a structure of redemptive nostalgia and irony. The uses of nostalgia in the literature are complex. In addition to deadening the responses, nostalgia can also serve as a tool for social change (transcendence, redemption). Such a suggestion is contrary to some accounts of nostalgia. In her book *On Longing*, Susan Stewart speaks of nostalgia as a "social disease" (like gonorrhea, presumably) and says that it is "a sadness without an object, a sadness that creates a longing that of necessity is inauthentic because it does not take part in lived experience" since "the past it seeks has never existed except as narrative, and hence, always absent, that past continually threatens to reproduce itself as a felt lack."[8] The distrust of nostalgia here is palpable, and it is (tellingly) rooted in a distrust of narrative itself. Because nostalgia exists within, arises from, narrative, then (Stewart suggests) it can never be anything other than "inauthentic," false, and ultimately damaging. Philosophically, the idea that an experience which is not lived is therefore inauthentic is, of course, suspect; that I have not lived the life of the Other does not mean that my empathy with them is inauthentic (whatever we mean by authenticity in the first place). Ultimately, what Stewart's project would accomplish is the end of narrative itself, since all narratives are by their nature inauthentic (indeed, all putting of all things into words, including this book, is inauthentic because words cannot approach the Thing Itself). In terms of the literature, the idea that nostalgia has no object is also curious. Certainly, Ray Bradbury has an object when he distills his childhood into *Dandelion Wine* (1957) and, as I will assert in this study, other authors who deal in nostalgia during the 1940s and '50s certainly do have an object beyond pining for the purportedly good old days.

Redemptive nostalgia looks back in order to move forward. Stewart rightly emphasizes that nostalgia is narrative characterized by longing. In contrast to her somewhat distrustful characterization, I might suggest that nostalgia is dangerous precisely because it speaks to a lack, not a falsely-narrativized, ideologically-created lack (at least, not entirely) but a deep existential breach. Other critics have made similar claims. In her study *Reclaiming Nostalgia: Longing for Nature in American Literature*, Jennifer K. Ladino argues that "nostalgia works as a productive force—an individual emotional experience, a source of collective consciousness, or a narrative catalyst" that can be deployed for progressive ends.[9] Accordingly, Ladino suggests that "a surprising amount of American fiction envisions nostalgia as a disruptive, productive, even progressive force."[10] The nostalgia Ladino locates in representations of nature can also be applied to the small town (an imaginative geography which, as I will discuss, intersects with nature in key ways). The nostalgic small town signifies a lack precisely because it does not—and cannot—fill that lack. Even the most anti-nostalgic authors under consideration here—Henry Bellamann, who had no love for the town that gave birth to *Kings Row* (1940) or his heir-apparent Grace Metalious in *Peyton Place* (1956)—are nostalgic in this sense. Both Bellamann and Metalious rage against the fact that the small town fails to provide the security that it should. The process of reading these books is a process of disillusionment, a coming-to-grips with the fact that the small town (and, implicitly, America itself) is fallen. And an awareness of that fallen state is intended as a demand for change, for redemption, for transcendence. Nostalgia for the lost-but-imagined past becomes a means of escape, to be sure, but also a means of remaking the present. This recrafting is seen in the hundreds of Main Streets around the United States, which (as Francanviglia shows) have been transformed into idyllic settings that they never where in actual dirt-and-dung-spattered history.

The ever-present irony associated with nostalgic memories of the small town is a direct inheritance from the movement called the Revolt from the Village. However, the approach used during the 1940s and '50s is different from Revolt writing in key ways. Whatever the vision of the small community in popular consciousness, small towns in Revolt literature are places where individuals find themselves fundamentally alienated. In works such as *Spoon River Anthology* (1915) and *Winesburg, Ohio* (1919), the residents of the village are imagined as living encysted lives, lives cut off from each other even after death. For Revolt authors there is no redemption unless (like George Willard in *Winesburg*) that redemption is found in escape (and even then, George's escape is tempered by the fact that he implicitly becomes the old writer from "The Book of the Grotesques"—that is, he leaves the small town only to replicate it on the page). Sinclair Lewis' *Main Street* (1920) dramatizes the protagonist Carol Kennecott's repeated attempts to escape from or redeem her town of Gopher Prairie before finally succumbing to what her friend Guy Pollock calls "the village virus."[11] There is no hope, there is no escape, in the cyclical fiction of Sinclair Lewis.

In midcentury small-town fiction, escape *is* offered—a development which sets them apart from their predecessors in the Revolt. And the mode of that escape is transcendence—a working through nostalgia into a better world. In *Magic Town*, Rip Smith reunites Grandview, and the mechanic for this reunification is found in personal contact (the final shot of *Magic Town* is Stewart and Jane Wyman touching hands). Far from being pessimistic about escape, these authors suggest that some form of redemption—even if it is only tentative and ironic—is not only desirable but possible. This redemption does not obviate the tensions and anxieties existing within the small town; Smith and Peterman touch hands, but that contact does not eliminate the fact that Grandview is a town of hucksters. The end of the movie—the end of *any* narrative—does not obviate its middle. Midcentury small-town fiction could, thus, be thought of as an amalgamation of the Revolt writers and the Regionalists. Robert L. Dorman's *Revolt of the Provinces* charts the rise and fall of the Regionalist movement in America, arguing that the Regionalists "confronted not only the disintegrative crisis brought on by the 'acids of modernity,' but also [...] the Great Depression [...] and the rise of totalitarianism abroad."[12] Accordingly, these Regionalists hoped "to reclaim the myths and ideals that had been abandoned and 'dispersed' during the centuries-long march of Americans across the continent and into modernity."[13] In making this attempt, the Regionalists and the Revolt writers speak with one voice; as Mark Buechsel argues in *Sacred Land*, the Midwestern Modernists—which included Revolt writer Sherwood Anderson—were in fact very much concerned with "the interrelated phenomena of Puritanism and materialism/industrialism."[14] Midcentury small-town narratives continue the demystifying actions of Lewis, Masters, and Anderson. They also continued the activities of the Regionalists, who "believed that the materials for cultural reconstruction must be found at home."[15] Though Dorman claims that "the *nationalizing* requirements of wartime"[16] put an end to the Regionalist quest for authenticity, in fact these requirements led to a re-statement of that same quest in broader terms. The result was a fusion of the Regionalists with the Revolt and the creation of midcentury small town fiction. This fusion leads to foregrounding of the cycle of fall and redemption that characterizes midcentury small-town fiction.

The cycle of fall and redemption is not a new one to literature, but within small town fiction of the midcentury it becomes a dominating symbol. The Eden-myth forms the core of small-town literature during the years I am considering. The small town is envisioned as a kind of paradise, but a paradise whose point is that it no longer exists—that, indeed, it never existed. As in *Kings Row* and *Peyton Place*, the most common realization of protagonists in these novels is that the façade of Paradise is precisely that—a false front concealing deep-set rot. The fall that takes place is not a fall into sin by the community but the recognition (and real-ization) of death and ambiguity within the life of the protagonist. The metaphor of the fall stages a recognition of the fundamental ambiguity of life within a world in which competing interests may seem equally valid. When the protagonist enters this world, he or she falls from the innocence of believing in a single unitary good. Thus, in James Gould Cozzens' *The Just and the Unjust* (1942), the protagonist learns that there is no ideal solution to the tension between Law and Mercy. Fallenness also betokens a state of alienation. The fallen individual has been distanced from other people, from God (or, more abstractly, the Tillichian Ground of Being), and from him- or herself. This condition of alienation is manifested in loneliness.

Loneliness is, of course, a central fact of the human experience; "obligatorily gregarious," humans desire contact with others in order to maintain social well-being.[17] Ben Lazare Mijuskovic goes so far as to say that "the thoughts as well as the actions of all men can be interpreted as a desire to avoid the feeling of existential, human isolation."[18] My contention here is that the literature of the small town is fundamentally about this isolation. Existential separation is uniquely inflected (but not uniquely *inflicted*) by the time period I have chosen to focus on. The War and the Bomb cast a pall over the possibility of human existence. Furthermore, with the rise of city- and-suburban existence, of Riesman's lonely crowd, people seem increasingly alienated from each other. Though the small town may seem to offer the chance to escape into a comforting community, it does not. Conformity or dissolution are the law of the land, even in its hamlets. Far from representing a state of communal unity, the small town becomes an island made up of islands—a symbolically separated world in which existentially separated humans live and move and have their being.

This presupposition means that my approach to small-town literature is fundamentally different from most previous studies. I have mentioned that Poll's analysis is perceptive but incomplete in fundamental ways. Because he is so committed to challenging and deconstructing the small-town myth, his methodology becomes one of positing universal assumptions and then demonstrating from American literature that this perception mystifies or occludes the workings of American imperialism. That is to say, all of the evidence he adduces is calculated to disprove a thesis whose existence he never seems to feel the need to prove. I choose to confine generalizations regarding the small town to the texts I discuss, with minimal recourse to universal assumptions. By taking this methodological approach, I will demonstrate that the business of small town fiction is much more complicated than such a suspicious reading as Poll's would allow. Where Poll sees the small town as working to mystify America's status as an imperial power, I argue that it offers a *model* by which American ideas and ideals can be tested and reconciled and in which the fundamental alienation of the common person—the condition of modernity, to be sure, but also of humanity itself—can be explored.

I am using the word "model" here in a particular sense. Though in common use "model" can mean something like "standard" or "ideal," a more accurate definition in this context would be "test-case." It is in this sense that small towns are models of America. Thus, by introducing stressors into that model, authors work through the tensions latent in American life during the period. Thus, I treat the small town in American literature in precisely the way Stewart's statistician treats Grandview in *Magic Town*. It is an isolated location in which the American experience can be examined. In this, it could be said to be Utopia, but here I must very carefully define my terminology, because "utopia" has been—especially within analyses of small towns—defined away from its proper meaning. When Poll discusses the small town as an "island community," he invokes Thomas More by way of Frederic Jameson:

> Jameson argues that the transformation of a space into an island is the "act of disjunction/exclusion that founds Utopia as a genre." This "act," he continues, is "the source of everything problematic about it" ("Of Islands" 100). The borders that separate a utopia from the outside become epistemological and ethical borders as well. A utopian community cares primarily about its contained island form and not with social relations beyond its borders.[19]

The problem here is that—with all due respect to both Poll and Jameson—this discussion is doubly incorrect. In More's work, Utopia is *not* unconcerned with social relations beyond its borders, though it is certainly primarily interested in its own well-being. More's Utopia engages in large-scale trade with its neighbors and makes use of their mercenaries for its own defense. Moreover, the Utopians sometimes wage war on behalf of friendly neighbors.[20] Thus, More informs the reader that—though Utopia makes no treaties with other nations—it has frequently "liberated many of [its neighbors] from tyranny" and so assists them in the governance of their own lands.[21] The island community—though certainly *primarily* concerned with internal relations—does not exist as a self-contained entity in the way that Poll (by way of Jameson) argues that it does.

In the second place, contrary to the popular understanding of "utopia," More's Utopia functions more as a model in the scientific sense—as an experimental space in which ideas and ideologies can be tested. More indicates as much at the conclusion of the book, when the narrator confesses that many of the practices of Utopia struck him as "absurd," though "there are very many features that in our own societies I would wish rather than expect to see."[22] Utopia is presented as a mixed bag and, though More does not give the reader explicit guidance for how to sort out the absurd from the admirable, he does implicitly make such distinctions. The concluding sentences of *Utopia* are the key to the entire book; More is offering a model, in the sense outlined above, and challenging the reader to exercise judgment and determine what aspects of Utopia, if any, are worthy of emulation.

What is being tested in midcentury small-town fiction is precisely the question of whether community is possible or desirable. Robert Nisbet, in the preface to the second edition of his book *The Quest for Community*, considers "alienation" to be a preoccupying force in American thought; he is concerned with "the state of mind that can find a social order remote, incomprehensible, or fraudulent."[23] According to Nisbet, "[a] concern with cultural disorganization underlies almost every major philosophy of history of our time."[24] What is needed, for Nisbet, is a recovered sense of community. As I will show in this study, writers who dealt with the small town were at once hopeful and distrusting of the possibility of community in America. They were hopeful because community offers an escape from the dreadful alienation and fear and loneliness that characterizes modern Western culture. They were distrusting because gaining community may be attended by a loss of individuality. Fredric Jameson argues that post-war small towns were no longer subject to the "pain and sting of absence from the center," primarily because technology made access so much easier.[25] In contrast, my analysis of midcentury small-town literature suggests that it is centrally concerned with that "pain and sting" precisely because the "center" from which individuals in the small town are absent is not the Big City and High Culture. Carol Kennicott in *Main Street* does not miss the City, whatever she thinks—she misses a fundamental connection to herself, to her neighbors, and to reality. This alienation is the basic fact of existence in modernity, inside the small town or out of it. Writers following World War II turned to the small town as both the hope for resolving the gap and as the smallest possible representation of it. As a result of this ambivalence, when redemption occurs—which it almost invariably does—the resolution is undercut or complicated by a recognition of its own fragility. Transcendence is no easy thing, nor yet is it certain to last.

It should by now be evident that, though I am indebted to multiple theoretical viewpoints, my own reading is not categorizable as one thing or another. All disciplines provide valuable tools for analyzing the cultural work of literary artifacts, but they are hobbled by their commitment to exposing those artifacts as facades for some underlying principle. In the case of Poll's Marxist approach to small towns, he argues (rightly) that the small town as a cultural imagination often serves to mystify or disguise American imperialism. He is, however, forced to grapple again and again with texts that actively work against that mystification. This fact suggests that the small town's function in the American imagination is far more complicated and less easily categorizable than such a hermeneutic of suspicion would allow. My own discussion, while taking Marxist critiques into account—along with other theoretical perspectives—will attempt to approach each work with the assumption that the small town in literature is as diverse and complex as America itself. I look here for general trends, not concrete formulations. The small town is a model for America, but the word "model" must be redefined. The American small town, in the works under consideration here, serves a similar function to that of Utopia in More's work: it presents a space in which American ideals can be examined and critiqued in a relatively controlled environment. It also presents a way by which these tensions can be (hopefully) transcended.

My logic of arrangement takes literally Poll's suggestion that the small town functions as a kind of concrete imaginary in the American consciousness. If it is concrete, it can be traversed in a way analogous to psychogeography. In his essay "Introduction to the Critique of Urban Geography," Guy Debord describes the method that he calls psychogeography:

> The production of psychogeographic maps, or even the introduction of alterations such as more or less arbitrarily transposing maps of two different regions, can contribute to clarifying certain wanderings that express not subordination to randomness but complete *insubordination* to habitual influences (influences generally categorized as tourism that popular drug as repugnant as sports or buying on credit).[26]

In the following study, I will take Debord's methodology and apply it to the concrete imaginary small town. In this, I must acknowledge my debt to blogger Elizabeth Sandifer, who for several years examined the BBC TV show

Doctor Who through a lens that she calls "psychochronography," the practice of taking "a specific object and trace[ing] its development through time, looking, as the psychogeographers do, at history, lived experience, and the odd connections that spring up."[27] The idea here, in both Sandifer and Debord, is to de-familiarize familiar objects by approaching them from unexpected or unanticipated angles. The urban space is rigorously planned and designed to funnel individuals from one place to another—to make them part of a collective. The business of psychogeography is to break these dominant narratives and undermine the planned order to allow revolutionary potential to emerge from them (transcendence). This breaking and undermining is precisely my method of reading here.

In the chapters that follow, I will be treating the small town in American literature as if it were a concrete space that can be traversed at will. This book is organized around a series of landmarks, and its structure is a movement between these landmarks. My discussion meanders, taking to heart Tristram Shandy's injunction that "[d]igressions, incontestably, are the sunshine, the life, the soul of reading."[28] The implications for this structure are several. Just as my method of composition was a sort of meandering ramble through the concrete-imaginary small town, so too this study is designed in such a way as to allow the reader to also meander as he or she sees fit. All roads lead ultimately to the same end. This method of organization means that there are multiple potential audiences for this study. The book itself is (like the American small town) both limited and expansive. It is limited in that small towns and their representation in literature is a topic that will be of interest to a few scholars of American mythology. On the other hand, as I will outline below, each chapter opens out to confront broader issues that were (and are) important to American culture. Readers curious about questions of gender, sexuality, and race will find the chapter on the outskirts of interest; students of the religious history of the United States will see that I see small-town fiction as taking a particular theological turn in the chapter on the church. My approach may loosely be considered interdisciplinary; I have in preparing this volume consulted works of psychology, history, and sociology in addition to the primary texts. In this way, this book (much like the literary small towns it studies) attempts to contain within itself as many possible variations of human endeavor as is possible within its limited space.

Moreover, this book will be of interest to people interested in American mythology and particularly in the ways in which the twenty-first century is shaped, molded, by its predecessor. Though my study is periodized, I manifest a grand disregard for temporal ordering; I will move backwards, forwards, and sideways in time as suits my discussion of any given landmark. Like the *flâneur*, I will allow the past and the present (and, perhaps, the future) to collapse onto each other, to interpenetrate and inform each other. *Peyton Place* retroactively has its influence on *Kings Row*, which in turn looks forward to *Calamity Town*. I hasten to add, however, that this disregard for temporal order does not mean that there is *absolutely* no logic to my mode of discussion. In the first place, each landmark visited in this dissertation has a bearing on a different aspect of small town life: the train station has direct bearing on how the small town is imagined from the outside; Main Street has to do with its economic life, the Church with religion, and so on throughout the town. Thus, any seeming digression is ultimately (like Laurence Sterne's narrative style) progressive; each location interacts with and builds upon all of the others.

Readers interested in genre fiction and middlebrow culture will find much to interest them here. Certainly, not all the books I discuss here are critically neglected; *Wise Blood, Strange Fruit, Intruder in the Dust,* and *Peyton Place* have received their share of critical evaluation in the past few years. *Peyton Place*, in particular, has experienced a critical reevaluation as "women's writing" has become an object of critical study. These texts are well known and remain in print. However, I have not confined myself to canonical works. The novels of Ellery Queen, while formerly of central importance to the American tradition of the detective story, have received little critical evaluation outside of Francis Nevins' *The Art of Detection*, though recently the Ellery Queen persona has been examined in the collection *The Centrality of Crime Fiction in American Literary Culture*. My own study marks (to my knowledge) the first concerted effort to fit Queen into a larger discourse about nostalgia and national identity, a move that should be of interest to students of detective fiction. Similarly, Henry Bellamann is often discussed in terms of his contributions to twentieth century music criticism,[29] but his novel *Kings Row* has been the subject of few critical studies (despite being the source-material for a movie that would catapult Ronald Reagan into A-list stardom). Certainly, few critics have remarked on the novel's queer elements, which I do in my chapter on the outskirts. And though James Gould Cozzens underwent something of a critical revival during the 1970s, he has—so far that I've been able to determine—fallen completely off the critical radar, which is only just and fair.

These books are all examples of what might be considered middlebrow fiction. Middlebrow fiction is often dismissed in criticism as a merely bourgeois form, parasitic in the way it feeds upon so-called high culture. But, as Tom Perrin argues in his book *The Aesthetics of Middlebrow Fiction*, "so-called middlebrow literature of the mid–twentieth-century United States possessed a sophisticated and, in important regards, coherent aesthetics."[30] The critic must pay attention to the actual midcentury small-town fictions rather than trying to force them to fit a theoretical framework. The vision of the small town presented to the middlebrow reader (constructed as average, well-educated—though these are not unproblematic) can tell critics the unspoken assumptions regarding small towns and, behind them, America itself. And the assumptions are manifestly not that the small town offers an escape from the alienation of modern life. If anything, small towns crystallize that alienation. *Kings Row* is not a safe space to which readers can escape and ignore the realities of modernity; on the contrary, the communities of Kings Row, Peyton Place, and Green Town in Bradbury's *Dandelion Wine* are spaces in which transgression and loneliness are the norm. All characters in the small town are isolated. Everyone is alienated. These works also share the fall-redemption structural form outlined above—that is, they present an already-fallen Eden, with the protagonist as an Adam-figure who must transcend or attempt to transcend the alienation that comes with the fallen state.

The years 1940–1960 involved a substantial literary re-consideration of the role of the small town in the American imagination. The traditional critical approach to village literature sees a retrenchment following the Revolt from the Village. During the 1930s, according to Orvell, authors backed away from critiquing the small town in favor of singing its praises—a reasonable approach, perhaps, to the stress of the Great Depression, a time when people needed and craved some sort of space free of economic uncertainty.[31] In standard critical accounts, World War II and the Eisenhower years deepened this reluctance to criticize the small town, and by the 1960s the small town had become a fantasy-space where "ideal" America resided. I have already indicated that I consider this reading to be incomplete. My research indicates that representations of the small town invariably focus on the seedy and the alienating aspects of village life, rather than the supposedly pastoral or idyllic. Indeed, whenever a pastoral environment is evoked—as in Queen's Wrightsville novels, Bellamann's *Kings Row* and its sequel, or Bradbury's *Dandelion Wine*—it is only to deflate the idea that there is anything perfect about the small town. Though my analysis does not extend beyond 1960, it is my hope that—by examining a relatively small slice of American small-town literature—I can demonstrate that the small town is a much more complicated and polyvocal symbol than conventional criticism would suggest.

My analysis—though it does not pretend to absolute knowledge—does offer a stable model for analyzing small-town fiction of the period. Though I examine several novels and story collections, my discussion should not be thought of as exhaustive. Several novels, for reasons of space or time, have been excluded from discussion. Thus, I have neglected books such as Morton Thompson's *Not as a Stranger*, a 1954 bestseller which chronicles the life of a small-town doctor. Similarly, Thomas Ward's 1949 novel *Stranger in the Land*—a novel chronicling the experiences of a gay small-town man—receives no attention. A broader reading of forgotten novels such as these would probably give more texture to this study, but would also expand it outside the limits of a single book. For similar reasons, I have elected not to discuss novels such as James Jones' *Some Came Running* (1957) and William Faulkner's Snopes trilogy.

Nevertheless, I am convinced that the interpretive framework I provide in this book can easily be generalized to other small-town fiction of the time, both the canonical and the forgotten. My basic assertion is that the small town during the 1940s and 50s is conceived of as a space where alienation is absolute—where every citizen, no matter who they are, is lonely and cut off from themselves, from each other, and from their ground of being. Each small-town novel discussed in this study chronicles an attempt to overcome that loneliness in various ways. My discussion provides a predictive framework for analyzing midcentury small-town fiction. In my own research, I have found that books I initially believed would be outside the framework, such as Ray Bradbury's *Dandelion Wine* (1957), proved upon closer inspection to fit into precisely the same pattern as the other stories discussed. Thus, my analysis reveals the fundamental concern of midcentury small-town fiction, and that concern—contrary to Poll and others—is manifestly not a nostalgic escape from the pressures of modernity, but a robust encounter with them. The nostalgia present is not regression, but redemption; the fiction here moves back into a purportedly-ideal past and discovers within it both good and bad. It then seeks to redeem the time by discovering within this mixed (fallen) past a way forward—the way of transcendence.

The canon of criticism on small town literature is relatively small, and I have made heavy use of it. Ima Honaker Herron's 1939 study *The Small Town in American Literature* remains the definitive treatment of the subject. In that volume, Herron traces the history of village literature from its inception at Jamestown through the Revolt writers. There has since Herron been no broad-ranging treatment of the literature, though Page Smith's *As a City Upon a Hill* (1966) goes a long way in expanding Herron's study. Besides these two works, I am deeply indebted to Ryan Poll's *Main Street and Empire* as well as Miles Orvell's recent study *The Death and Life of Main Street* and Francis Francaviglia's *Main Street Revisited*. These books provide critical components for my analysis of small towns.

Although I have designed this book to permit perusing at any pace and in any direction, I will conclude this introduction with a brief summary of each chapter. My first chapter will discuss the history of the small town in American imagination—particularly involving the train station. The train station is often the first thing seen by visitors to small towns, and as such provides an opportunity to discuss the ways in which small towns are imagined in the literature. Richard Francaviglia argues that "in the early part of the twentieth century, the small town as exemplified by Main Street was not held in especially high regard[....] We have always been, and perhaps ought to be, ambivalent about small towns."[32] I will argue that the Edenic imagery used to discuss the small town incarnates this ambivalence. While identifying the small town with Eden seems to indicate that it is an idyllic community, my own reading suggests that identifying the small town with Eden necessitates its fallen state, since Eden, as a concept, has no meaning unless a fall takes place. As a result, the protagonists of small-town fiction are universally alienated—a term I will use interchangeably with "lonely." These protagonists are either literal outsiders, coming from the city or another town (as Rip Smith does in *Magic Town*), or they are spiritual outsiders. In either case, they are lonely. This loneliness, and the attempt to escape it, will provide a central thematic node for my discussion of small towns in midcentury American literature. Within this lonely world, shot through with nostalgia, the protagonist attempts to make a wholly-realized existence for him- or herself, to transcend loneliness and reconnect with Edenic innocence. My primary texts for this chapter will be two novels by Ellery Queen, *Calamity Town* (1942) and *Double, Double* (1949), both of which take place in the mythical town of Wrightsville, as well as Cornell Woolrich's *I Married a Dead Man* (1948) and Toshio Mori's *Yokohama, California* (1949).

The small town, as Eden, must have its Adam. And, since the state of Adamic innocency is most closely identified with childhood, chapter two is set in the schoolhouse, where children are formed and molded into young adults. Childhood is a site for the crisis of individuation—the startling realization that the child is at once *not alone*—there are other persons—and terrifyingly isolated. My primary texts will be Ross Lockridge, Jr.'s *Raintree County* (1948), Ray Bradbury's *Dandelion Wine*, William March's *The Bad Seed* (1954), and William Saroyan's *The Human Comedy* (1943). Each of these works (only two are novels) examine childhood in the small-town environment, and each suggests that this childhood—far from being simply idyllic—is riven with crises and tensions. Childhood may well be an unfallen position, but it is also one in which the demand to become an individual—to fall from prelapsarian innocence—is impossible to ignore. If the child attempts to ignore it, as Rhoda Penmark does in *The Bad Seed*, they will lapse into psychopathology. Finally, I suggest that the primary concern of midcentury small-town writers is in imagining ways in which children can overcome, or transcend, this early crisis in order to become fully-functioning (adult) members of society.

Before reaching that point, however, children must pass through the teen years, a newly-created stage of development in which children transform into adults. Chapter three will discuss the life of those teens who mythically gather at the local malt shop. As other studies have indicated in detail, the idea of the *teenager* is one of fairly recent origin, but it is also one that (today) is closely linked to the imagined small town through movies like *American*

Graffiti and television shows like *Happy Days*. In these visual worlds, teenagers hang out at the local diner or malt shop, much as Archie and his pals do in the *Archie* comics. The teenager is associated with growth and rebellion, particularly after movies like *Rebel Without a Cause* made such rebellion chic. However, in small-town literature this rebellion is tempered. What, these authors ask, is the rebellion *for*? And the answer is—culture. My texts for this chapter are Henry Bellamann's *Kings Row* (1940), its sequel *Parris Mitchell of Kings Row* (1948), Grace Metalious' *Peyton Place* (1956) and its sequel *Return to Peyton Place* (1959), and Ross Lockridge's *Raintree County*. These books, as small-town *Bildungsromane*, feature a protagonist who leaves their town only to return to it. This return is not, however, a reintegration into the community, which Franco Moretti argues is central to the *Bildungsroman*. These protagonists leave the town because they find it culturally dead; they return to it with their newly-acquired culture, hoping to change it. Thus, the alienation of the small-town teen is transcended through the absorption of something from outside the town.

Chapter four concentrates on two locations, the one a continuation of the other: main street and the town square. As Ryan Poll points out, the economic life of the small town is a central part of its mythology, and so my fourth chapter will discuss the businesses on Main Street. According to Poll, the small town is historically conceived of as a world outside of the concerns of the market, while the city is framed as "a capitalist space of sin."[33] In fact, the literature of 1940s and '50s does not bear out Poll's assertion. The way in which capitalist exchange is treated in small towns may be seen in the literature's treatment of marketplaces. My primary text here will be *Yokohama, California*, which is (among other things) deeply concerned with the tension between the marketplace and the community. I will demonstrate that even the idealized small town alienates its citizens through the workings of capitalism. Similarly, the town is not cut off from history; the town square serves, instead, as a transtemporal space in which the past intrudes upon the present and the outside world makes itself known within the community. In discussing the town square—an extension of Main Street—I will focus on Ellery Queen's *Calamity Town*. Once again, because the small town is imagined as an Eden that has already fallen, the protagonists within it are alienated from themselves and the world around them. One of the mechanisms of this alienation is the marketplace.

The first four chapters of this study lay out the conditions of small-town life and argue that inhabitants of the community are all alienated. They exist within a fallen Eden. The remainder of this book will look at various ways in which small-town narratives attempt to transcend this alienation. Chapter five will examine the movie theater, a central facet of American culture. Cinema provides a sense of false transcendence. It is here, more than anywhere else, that the idealized/idyllic small town seems to most resemble a comforting fantasy. Though possible points of interest are legion, I will focus here on three adaptations of novels discussed elsewhere in this study: *Kings Row* (1942), *Peyton Place*, and *Raintree County* (both 1957). I will demonstrate that each of these films, in the process of adaptation, strips the source material of its social-critical power and instead turns the narrative into a means of reinforcing heterosexual, patriarchal norms. Thus, *Kings Row* not only removes the novel's only gay character (perhaps inevitably so), but enforces a happy ending in which Drake McHugh, disabled by a malevolent surgeon, overcomes his disability through sheer force of masculine will. Similarly, Norman Page—Grace Metalious' implicitly gay character in *Peyton Place*—is heterosexualized through his experiences in World War II, becoming a fitting mate for Allison. And in *Raintree County*, the titular Raintree—a symbol in the novel of impossible yearning—becomes the avatar of safe, happy, and pure heterosexual marriage. Thus, though I argue elsewhere that midcentury small-town fiction presents a far more complex vision of the small town than many critics suggest, it is certainly true that in the migration to the screen these novels often become safe, tame, and unthreatening.

Religion is a topic not covered at all in Poll's account and only initially glanced at in the study offered by Page Smith. Chapter six will examine the church in greater detail. In my discussion of the church, I will argue that religion in midcentury small-town fiction can only be truly expressed through heresy. Midcentury theology provides the interpretive key for understanding small-town fiction of this period. During this time, theologians attempted to articulate religious beliefs in a way that would account for the horrors of World War II and the sense of alienation that set in during the years following. Small-town fiction follows suit, in both the work of seemingly non-religious writers such as Henry Bellamann and religious authors such as Flannery O'Connor. My texts for this chapter will be Bellamann's *Kings Row*, Ellery Queen's *Ten Days' Wonder* (1948), Lillian Smith's *Strange Fruit* (1944), O'Connor's *Wise Blood* (1952), and Lockridge's *Raintree County*. What emerges is ultimately the destruction of traditional forms of religion and an attempt to touch the transcendent through various acts of irreligion—this irreligion being, in the fiction, the truest form of religion itself.

If the church constitutes the metaphysical or theological heart of the small town, the courthouse is the seat of justice, and so constitutes the seventh landmark in my discussion of the small town. The courthouse has been closely identified with the small town since the early forms of small-town fiction. Law exists to restore a lost Eden, and midcentury small-town fiction grapples with the uncertainty of such a project. I will not in this chapter confine myself to literally legal crimes; instead, I will discuss crimes against community mores. My texts for this chapter will be James Gould Cozzens' *The*

Just and the Unjust (1942), William Faulkner's *Intruder in the Dust* (1948), and three novels that I have already discussed extensively: *Kings Row*, *Peyton Place*, and *Raintree County*. The law represents an attempt to regain Eden by creating cohesion within the society, but its result is to alienate members of that society. The only way out, the only way to escape the law and get at its ultimate end—Eden regained—is to break it. Lawbreaking is thus seen as the truest form of law-keeping within small-town novels of the period, for only by breaking the hard shell of the law can protagonists reach its essence.

My eighth chapter will turn its attention to the outskirts, the home of the outcast. Outcasts may be either spiritually alienated or physically set aside by their geographic location in the small town. Spiritual outsiders include ethnic and sexual minorities, while physical outsiders are typically racially or economically disadvantaged. In the end, this chapter will demonstrate that the small town is constituted by these very divisions—that is to say, the small town could not exist if such divisions did not also exist. Ultimately, the small town is an anti-community made up of lonely, alienated people. My texts for this chapter will include *Strange Fruit*, *Intruder in the Dust*, *Peyton Place* and Metalious' follow-up *The Tight White Collar* (1960), *Kings Row* and Katherine Bellamann's sequel *Parris Mitchell of Kings Row*. Again, a tentative transcendence is suggested; by giving Jamie Wakefield, the gay resident of Kings Row, a happily queer ending, Katherine Bellamann suggests that it is possible to find some sort of peace even within a society that is recognizably oppressive.

The final chapter discusses the ways in which small-town people attempt to escape this fundamental alienation in the graveyard. This chapter will examine *Intruder in the Dust*, Robert Bloch's *Psycho* (1959), Jack Finney's *The Body Snatchers* (1955), and (not unexpectedly) Lockridge's *Raintree County*. Small-town fiction recognizes that the divisions between people persist after death. In small towns, people often find themselves overcome by the spirits of the dead—Norman Bates has his mother, for instance. In each case, the individual transcends only by yielding to a force beyond themselves. Therefore, the small town attempts to unite in other ways, manifesting ultimately in the mindless mob of pod people in *The Body Snatchers*. The cost of overcoming alienation is often worse than the alienation itself. Ross Lockridge's *Raintree County* offers a second solution: a Whitmanesque melding of all with nature and final dissolution in the Cosmic All—a move implicit in the pastoral, Edenic imagery discussed in chapter one of this study.

The conclusion will be a brief epilogue discussing redemptive nostalgia in the literature of the period. The uses of redemptive nostalgia have been little-studied, particularly as relates to such middlebrow symbols as the small town. Academics and social thinkers are, understandably, leery of allowing any significance to attach itself to a longing to return to the 1950s model of society. However, by dismissing nostalgia, academics do both themselves and their society a disservice. It should be possible to honor certain aspects of the cultural imagination without falling into the trap of paralysis or recidivism. What is needed, now more than ever, is an approach that will allow scholars to see with open eyes and open hearts both the evil *and the good* that is latent in the American myth. American small-town fiction offers a lens by which to examine how authors in the years following World War II grappled with promise as well as with peril. This study is one attempt to reimagine an America that is not perfect, but perfectible. The concrete-imaginary small town need not function simply—as Ryan Poll says it does—as a means of blinding America to its own sins. It could also—it does, in all of the books I am examining here—reveal the utter alienation that can permeate American society and offer the possibility of redemption.

One

Columbus on the Platform
The Train Station

It is late 1940. A man stands on a train platform. Observers could be forgiven for taking no notice, for it is difficult to form a clear picture of him, even when stared at directly. He is tall and he has silver eyes. He might be wearing *pince-nez*, though at this stage in his career it is unlikely. Even his identity is unstable, for he is the creation of two cousins working under an assumed name—a name he shares and under which he, himself, writes mystery stories. He is Mr. Ellery Queen and the novel is *Calamity Town* (1942). For convenience, when referring to the authors I will use the singular name "Queen" and when referring to the protagonist I will use the name "Ellery." The town is Wrightsville, U.S.A. This novel marks a fundamental shift in the narrative of Ellery Queen. Previously—going as far back as *The Roman Hat Mystery* (1929)—the Ellery Queen novels (pseudonymously written by cousins Frederic Dannay and Manfred B. Lee) have been largely concerned with a rigorously formalist detective fiction and have taken as their settings the city of New York. In *Calamity Town*, the authors shift their attention briefly to the small town and attempt a character-rich portrait of "real" America. As with other authors of midcentury small-town literature, Queen shows nostalgia for the small town. However, the portrait of Wrightsville does not seek escape, except insofar as that escape could potentially lead to restoration. This approach will be consistent in most midcentury small-town literature, as the following chapters will demonstrate.

Ellery first glimpses Wrightsville from the train station. Trains, thus, are of particular interest when considering the small town in American fiction. They function in two ways: first, they bring the traveler to the village, emphasizing its isolation from the rest of the world. Secondly, however, they connect the community to the rest of the world—in fact, they create the community in a vital sense. This chapter considers what protagonists see from the train station. As I will demonstrate, the small town is constructed as an Eden, but Eden is always definitionally fallen; it is impossible to think of Eden without a fall. The small-town narrative is, thus, one of disillusionment rather than fantasy.

Calamity Town is a detective story, but one in which the murder does not occur until late in the game. Ellery Queen arrives in Wrightsville under an assumed identity, planning to write a book. He takes lodgings with the first family of the town, the Wright family, and quickly finds himself embroiled in their private drama. The oldest daughter is named Nora, and her estranged fiancé, Jim Haight, returns unexpectedly and rekindles a romance with her. They are soon joined by Jim's sister. However, Nora begins receiving mysterious letters indicating that Jim is about to kill her. Eventually, at a party, Jim's sister drinks a poisoned cocktail presumably meant for Nora. Suspicion immediately falls on Jim. The novel details both the criminal investigation and the resulting trial as well as the reaction of the town of Wrightsville itself. Wrightsville turns against its First Family, organizing into mobs to harass Jim and the rest of the Wrights. Ellery, meanwhile, romances Pat, another daughter of the family, though (of course) generic conventions doom this romance from the onset. The novel ends when Ellery returns to Wrightsville and reveals the truth to Pat and her fiancé Carter: that Nora herself had discovered letters written by Jim concerning his actual wife, the woman who pretended to be his sister, and—in a fit of despair and rage—concocted the whole plot to punish both Jim and his wife. At this point, both Nora and Jim are dead, so there is no real reason to reveal the truth. The novel ends with the three characters agreeing to keep silent on the matter.

As the summary above suggests, *Calamity Town* is part of a long line of detective stories that takes place in a small or isolated community. The fact that it takes place in an American small town, however, suggests that the novel is also after bigger game. The first chapter of *Calamity Town* is titled "Mr. Queen Discovers America," foregrounding the argument of the novel as a whole: that Ellery Queen, heretofore an urban character concerned with urban matters, is finally coming face-to-face with "real" America. This "real" America is initially presented through a series of quaint signifiers glimpsed from the platform of the train station. Once he has been in Wrightsville for a while, Ellery realizes that the town is no more idyllic than his native New York City. The image of the small town is thus ironized; Wrightsville may be "real" America, but it is also the repository for the most depraved impulses of the human heart. *Calamity Town*—as with most small-town novels of the period—is fundamentally a novel of disillusionment. But before one can be *dis*illusioned, one must be illusioned; before the fantasy can be exposed, it must first manifest *as fantasy*. Because the fantasy of the small town is fundamentally an outsider's perspective (recall Jimmy Stewart's character in

Magic Town, who holds illusions about Grandview that the locals do not), the train station provides an ideal setting from which to set about this study's psychogeographical ramble around the concrete-imaginary small town. Ellery's entry-point to both the narrative and the setting is a train station:

> Ellery Queen stood knee-deep in luggage on the Wrightsville station platform and thought: this makes me an admiral. Admiral Columbus.
> The station was a squatting affair of black-red brick. On a rusty handtruck under the eaves two small boys in torn blue overalls swung their dirty legs and chewed gum in unison, staring at him without expression.
> The gravel about the station was peppered with horse droppings. Cramped two-story frame houses and little stoop shouldered shops with a cracker barrel look huddled to one side of the tracks—the city side, for up the steep street paved with square cobbles Mr. Queen could see taller structures beyond the fat behind of a retreating bus.[1]

Ellery's impression of Wrightsville is based on this initial prospect, when he thinks "this makes me an admiral. Admiral Columbus." The language of discovery, of being "Admiral Columbus," suggests that Ellery thinks he is discovering an untouched paradise. Columbus is—or was—associated with the discovery and exploration of mysterious new lands. Symbolically, Ellery is here encountering the "real" America, as opposed to his usual cosmopolitan stomping-grounds in New York City. This real America is the American small town. The sights which confront Ellery immediately as he disembarks from the train—the station itself, the handtruck, the two small boys who stare at the detective "without expression"—are all stereotypical, or perhaps archetypal, signifiers of the small town. Even here, however, there is a heavy layer of irony; the evocation of Columbus is made by the *character* Ellery Queen rather than the author. The authorial voice ironically attaches a "Mr." to Ellery's name in the chapter title, emphasizing by way of this formality a certain distance between Ellery and the reader. Queen's style is ironic, and even the most heartfelt descriptions have a trace of coolness. Here and elsewhere, the prose is at once detached and affectionate; "for up the street paved with square cobbles Mr. Queen could see taller structures beyond the fat behind of a retreating bus" combines relative formality ("for up the street"; "Mr. Queen") with racy slang ("fat behind of a retreating bus"). The "smithy with a neon sign" also hints at ironic detachment, evoking as it does both Longfellow's village blacksmith and the world of modernity.

Wrightsville is a point of convergence, "where the Wrightsville station flings the twentieth century into the astonished face of the land." This sense of the small town being a midway point between civilization and the wild is common in fiction of the period, leading to the conviction that the town is out of time, out of step with modernity. If Ellery labels himself Columbus, it is because he has discovered a pre–Columbian paradise. But the irony present in the narration should put readers on guard; Ellery is himself an innocent—

he does not understand the depths of evil lurking in this small town. He will learn, however, that even the most pristine town can harbor murder and mob violence. The narrative of *Calamity Town* is one of initiation. Through his dealings with the Wright family, Ellery will discover that "there is much cruelty [...] in the Wrightsvilles of this world."[2] But he also discovers an element of hope; the structure of *Calamity Town* is circular, charted closely onto the pattern of the year. This pattern of fall and redemption is central the midcentury small-town narrative.

I have opened with *Calamity Town* because this novel clearly lays out the coordinates of midcentury small-town fiction. The novel's initial location—the train station—points to the ways in which the small town is at once set off from and tied to the nation around it. The irony in the opening description is consistent with other midcentury small-town writing. Throughout the fiction of the 1940s and '50s, small towns are discovered by Columbus-like outsiders and seem at first to be a paradise. The language of the garden reoccurs throughout small-town literature. *Calamity Town* is not explicit in this regard, but Queen mines it in a later Wrightsville novel, *Double, Double* (1949). Similarly, *Raintree County* (1948), by Ross Lockridge, Jr., is in part an attempt to rediscover the pre–Columbian paradise within the small town. Grace Metalious and Henry Bellamann see the small town as a garden which conceals at its core a fundamental rottenness. In recounting the experiences of pre–War Japanese-Americans, Toshio Mori sees the small town as a garden-spot through which America can be redeemed after World War II. The small town, thus, is seen as at once set off from and coextensive with nature. There is a rhetorical slipperiness at work here, and authors often move between seeing the small town as part of its natural surroundings and portraying it as a blight upon them. In spite of this ambiguity, the underlying rhetoric is often that of return. The language most often used in these narratives is the language of discovery, of movement Westward (and, therefore, Eastward) toward humanity's primordial home. Thus, though they are often clothed in generic (Queen), Gothic (Bellamann, Metalious), or realistic (Mori) garb, small-town narratives of the midcentury enact a mythic quest for wholeness and redemption in a world gone wrong. That is to say, they enact the Edenic myth.

The myth of the Garden of Eden is at the heart of the Columbian narrative. At the beginning of *Calamity Town*, Ellery speaks of himself as Columbus. His identification with the explorer suggests that he is "discovering" America; he is in a tradition of lonely wanderers stretching back to Marco Polo. He also fits comfortably within the broader tradition of small-town writing. Anthony Chanell Hilfer points out in *The Revolt from the Village* that Revolt novels usually have "a narrator or spokesman who speaks from outside the village perspective."[3] Outsiders have always been important to regionalist writing in general and small-town fiction in particular; through them, the author refracts or reflects the small town. Tom Lutz has argued that this viewpoint is important to what he considers the essential cosmopolitanism of regionalist writing. By framing the small town from the perspective of an outsider, regionalist writers "give these texts their cosmopolitan flavor, since the competing cultural views voiced by visitors and visitees mirror and contend with one another."[4] This visitor-role is one perfectly suited to Ellery Queen. Because Ellery is a detective, his isolation is already a given. Detectives are invariably alienated from their society. Ellery has already enacted the role of disinterested outsider in New York; his journey to Wrightsville doubles that status by making him *both* the detective *and* a stranger to the small town in which the murder occurs. The benefits of having an outsider-protagonist, from a generic standpoint, are clear. The small town is home to its own circles of social and political turmoil, circles best seen from the outside. *Calamity Town* charts the slow discovery of these circles. As a result, Queen's vision of small-town America is no mere paradise, in spite of Ellery's Columbian visions. In the very first sentences of his novel, Queen undercuts the pastoral romance and asserts an ironic view of the small town. Ellery's outsider perspective allows Queen to have his cake and eat it too: he romanticizes the small town but he does so ironically, recognizing that it fails to live up to the pressures put upon it to be an ideal or representative version of America. Insofar as Wrightsville is an Eden, it is already a fallen one.

The Columbian language of small-town fiction leads directly to Edenic/millenarian iconography. Indeed, the one is inseparable from the other. Columbus saw the New World as a garden, "very green, flat and fertile"[5] and claims that "the singing of small birds is so sweet that no one could ever wish to leave this place."[6] On the occasion of his third voyage, Columbus claimed to have discovered Paradise—that is to say, the Garden of Eden:

> I believe that the earthly Paradise lies here, which no one can enter except by God's leave. [...] I do not hold that the earthly Paradise has the form of a rugged mountain, as it is shown in pictures, but that it lies at the summit of what I have described as the stalk of a pear, and that by gradually approaching it one begins, while still at a great distance, to climb towards it.[7]

Drawing on this Columbian/Edenic imagery, visitors to the small town treat it as heaven on earth, a "Miracle Town," in which the hardy traveler—Mr. Smith in *Magic Town*, Ellery Queen in *Calamity Town*, Johnny Shawnessy in *Raintree County*—can discover a respite from the materialistic world of modernity. Sexuality plays into this Edenic imagery as well. Columbus sees Paradise as sitting atop a world shaped like a woman's nipple,[8] an image of fertility, both sexual and maternal (depending on one's attitude toward the nipple itself). Similarly, these writers often see the American Paradise as both deeply sexual and profoundly fecund, as offering nourishment to her children.

The small town is repeatedly envisioned as a Columbian space because America is often seen as such. After Columbus claimed to have discovered Paradise in America, the image of the New World as Eden became cemented in the popular and literary mind. Walt Whitman, in his monumental effort to sing America to itself, spends the entirety of "Children of Adam" reveling in this Edenic imagery. Like Columbus, he ties Paradise to the Far East, a point that becomes essential in both *Raintree County* (discussed later) and Toshio Mori's *Yokohama, California*. The poem "Facing West from California's Shores" offers this vision—which will come to characterize the small-town interaction with Eden—in particularly direct form:

> Facing west, from California's shores,
> Inquiring, tireless, seeking what is yet unfound,
> I, a child, very old, over waves, towards the house of maternity,
>   the land of migrations, look afar,
> Look off the shores of my Western Sea—the circle almost circled;
> For, starting westward from Hindustan, from the vales of Kashmere,
> From Asia—from the north—from the God, the sage, and the hero,
> From the south—from the flowery peninsulas, and the spice islands;
> Long having wander'd since—round the earth having wander'd,
> Now I face home again—very pleas'd and joyous;
> (But where is what I started for, so long ago?
> And why is it yet unfound?)[9]

Whitman is not writing specifically about American villages, but he demonstrates precisely the symbolic coordinates that will later dominate small-town fiction. Whitman charts the course of humanity from its point of origins, around the world (and through the centuries) and finally to the brink of the Pacific—realizing now that the only destination left is Eden. And yet the poem ends with uncertainty: "But where is what I started for, so long ago?/ And why is it yet unfound?" This is the problem facing Whitman—the fact that the thing sought (and what *did* humans seek when they left their infant home?) remains stubbornly elusive. The quest has only produced a cycle, a circle. Circles are particularly important for small-town fiction. Ellery Queen characterizes the square of Wrightsville as round, suggesting that the town itself possesses a property of circulation.[10] Small-town novels almost universally employ the language of escape and return: either the city-dweller escapes to the small town, as Ellery Queen does, or the town-dweller escapes to the city.

In either case, there is a dark undercurrent to imagining the small town as Eden, for Eden, by its nature, requires a fall. The Edenic nature of the small town does not resolve alienation. Alienation is central to its identity because Eden is a manifestation of loneliness. The small town is connected to the nation and the world by bonds of technology, but the very fact that it is connected means that it is also disconnected. Indeed, its very connection depends on its disconnection (its identity as a separate sort of thing). The metaphor of this separation is Eden. One cannot escape into a prelapsarian state because the lapse is an internal reality; the condition of alienation is inescapable, and this is the fundamental insight of midcentury small-town fiction. What is needed is not escape but redemption. Redemption is something altogether different from escape; it is the resolution of anxieties in a progressive, rather than regressive, direction. When midcentury authors cast the small town in an Edenic light, it is in order to suggest that the tensions essentially manifested in the small town can be—*must be*—transcended, moved through and resolved in a way that can bring about a new order.

Midcentury small-town fiction finds the potential, but not always the actuality, of redemption within the small town. In Ellery Queen's *Double Double* (1949), a Wrightsville girl named Rima comes to Ellery for help investigating the murder of her father. Ellery's first impression of her is as a sort of unformed innocent. He thinks of her as "a nymph who lives in the heart of a tree. And then he remember[s] who 'Rima' was. Rima was a child-woman, the bird-girl of the Venezuelan jungle, in a book he had not read for twenty years."[11] Rima (in *Double, Double*) is the daughter of the town drunk, and her name is a reference to William Henry Hudson's 1904 romance *Green Mansions*, which is an account of a peaceful lost tribe in the Amazon, the location of Columbus' earthly Paradise. Wrightsville becomes for Queen a re-inscription of that earthly Paradise. Rima (in *Double, Double*) is an avatar of pastoral innocence, whose "playmates have been birds and small animals, and [… and whose] playground had been the natural world in which Wrightsville squats."[12] Later, her connection to the natural world is reinforced when she charms a bird that has accidentally gotten into the town doctor's study.[13] Rima's connection to the natural world comes at a price, since she also represents the class disparities that have been present in Wrightsville from the very beginning; Ellery observes that she is initially clad in "a house dress of the cheapest cotton, black coarse stockings, flat heeled and papery looking white 'store' shoes, a shrieking bonnet."[14] That is, she comes from the Low Village, on the outskirts of Wrightsville. She could not be so mythically pastoral if she did not live under conditions of poverty, and this is the central paradox—it is, indeed, the core of the Eden-myth itself.

This mythically pastoral girl comes to Ellery because her father has been murdered. Accordingly, Ellery accompanies her to Wrightsville now nine years after his initial visit in *Calamity Town*. In typically ironic fashion, Queen claims that nothing in Wrightsville has changed before proceeding to enumerate several changes including the introduction of more neon signs, the construction of new hotels, and the disappearance of horse droppings from the street in front of the station.[15] In fact, Wrightsville has changed dramatically since its initial introduction to the world of Ellery Queen. Nevertheless, in the figure of Rima, the town maintains something of its Edenic innocence. At the same time, Rima is the ultimate sign that this innocence is about to be destroyed. Thus, the presence of death in the idyll can do more than simply set up a contradiction of murder; the corpse in the bucolic village is a striking reminder to readers that even in a so-called paradise there is death.

Eden, thus, becomes a controlling metaphor for midcentury small-town fiction. Throughout American literature, the small town is an essentially pastoral space, and as such it is subject to the same tensions outlined by Leo Marx in his study *The Machine in the Garden*. According to Marx, American literature exemplifies "the theme of withdrawal from society into an idealized landscape."[16] This withdrawal is not uncomplicated; instead, "these works manage to qualify, or call into question, or bring irony to bear against the illusion of peace and harmony in a green pasture."[17] For Marx, "it is industrialization, represented by images of machine technology, that provides the counterforce in the American archetype of the pastoral design."[18] The slippery boundary between the small town and the natural world makes it possible to extend Marx's discussion to midcentury small-town literature. The fact that Ellery first encounters Wrightsville from a train station platform is instructive here; it is only by the mechanism of the train that the small-town pastoral is accessible at all. Thus, the small-town garden is ironized by the presence of the train. A similar point is made by R.W.B. Lewis in *The American Adam*, when he argues that the primal man is ironized by necessity, since "fiction [...] dramatizes the interplay of compelling opposites."[19] Daniel G. Hoffman locates this contrast within the paradox of American national origins when he says that "[t]he conflicts [...] between Nature and Civilization, between a prelapsarian Eden and the spoliation of Paradise [...] have been among the most fertile sources of tension in our national experience and our literature."[20] In the American Pastoral tradition, these symbolic coordinates are—as per the title of Leo Marx's study—the machine and the garden. But the very idea of a garden is itself a tension, since every garden (perhaps especially the primal Garden of Eden) is by necessity artificial, as Robert Harbison argues in his book *Eccentric Spaces*. Harbison says that "in spite of its special properties a garden is just another image of art."[21] As such, he says, "[g]ardens are built on the idea of contrast: one thing superimposed on another thing, art on wilderness."[22] The very thing that *seems* natural is actually planted there. And so it is with the American small town; though these communities give the impression of being organic, united by bonds of blood and community, they are in fact artificial. modernity creates them; they are no refuge from it. Ellery's conviction that Wrightsville is a midway point between civilization and nature demonstrates this fact. This ambiguity contributes to the darkness of small-town literature. The "inchoate sense of doom" that Leo

Marx locates in Hawthorne's village fiction[23] permeates small-town literature, particularly after World War II. To enter the small town is to become aware of the fact that this garden is doomed to destruction.

Destruction looms over midcentury small-town fiction. In Cornell Woolrich's *I Married a Dead Man* (1948), the setting is the town of Caulfield. As with many small-town narratives, the novel opens with a description of nature—in this case, of nighttime and the scent of "heliotrope and jasmine, honeysuckle and clover."[24] Caulfield is a garden, a place in which there is "the stillness of perfect peace and security."[25] This opening paragraph positions the small town as a refuge, but it immediately undercuts that suggestion when the narrator says that all of this is true, "[b]ut not for us."[26] The first person narration does not extend through the entirety of the novel, though the speaker is eventually revealed to be the novel's protagonist, Helen Georgesson. The first chapter introduces her properly. Helen is pregnant and abandoned. Her dissolute husband has left her nothing except railroad tickets to San Francisco. On the train ride to California, she becomes friendly with a young married couple, the Hazzards, who are traveling to the man's hometown where his parents will meet his pregnant wife Patrice for the first time. There is a railway accident in which the couple is killed. After the accident, Helen is mistaken for the young wife and decides to adopt her persona. The novel charts Helen-Patrice's attempts to maintain this charade. She gradually becomes comfortable in the small town and in her new family; however, her happiness cannot last. Her estranged husband finds her and blackmails her into secretly re-marrying him under her assumed name of Patrice. Helen-Patrice resolves to kill him, but when she gets to his apartment with a loaded gun she discovers that he is already dead. While there, she is discovered by her brother-in-law and he helps her conceal the crime that she did not commit by taking the body to a railway junction and dumping it into a passing railcar. Later that same night, Helen-Patrice's mother-in-law suffers a fatal heart attack and dies, but not before claiming to have murdered the blackmailer. However, the protagonists later learn that this confession is false, throwing Helen-Patrice and her new husband into the hell described in the opening section of the novel. If she didn't commit the murder, they reason, he must have; and if he did not commit the murder, then she must have.

In Caulfield, Helen-Patrice finds temporary refuge from the world of modernity, typified in the cities of New York and San Francisco. There, she finds peace and communion—an Edenic space which she accesses by train. Again, this initial illusion is thoroughly a part of small-town mythology. Seen from the outside, small towns seem to offer a refreshing escape. After all, visitors to Disneyland (and, indeed, to many Disney-branded theme parks) are first confronted with "Main Street U.S.A." as they disembark from a train. Francaviglia quotes Christopher Finch's words on Disney's "plan [which] called for a railroad defining the perimeter of the park, with its main street situated right at the entrance."[27] The train, thus, forms a connection between the outside world of modernity and the insular world of the small town, typically thought of as a respite from the pressures of modernity: corporate capitalism, urban anonymity, the Bomb. But escape is more dangerous than it is refreshing, and small-town fiction is devoted to demolishing the myth of retreat. In the 1960 *Twilight Zone* episode "A Stop at Willoughby," the protagonist witnesses an idyllic small town from the windows of his train-car, but when he attempts to disembark he is killed. Miles Orvell points out that this episode dramatizes the phantasmic element of small-town mythology in the post-war world. The train may take the protagonist to Willoughby, but it also transports him to his doom.[28] The search for an untouched paradise is ultimately fatal, if not physically as in "Willoughby," then spiritually—as it is in *I Married a Dead Man*.

Trains, thus, act in precisely the opposite way to that suggested by Ryan Poll, who observes concerning the frontispiece map of Winesburg that "the railroad is not a part of an interstate, capitalist network; instead, it becomes naturalized and enfolded within the small town's autonomous, contained, circular imagery."[29] The railroad—and, particularly, the train station—exists as an ever-present reminder of the outside world. Poll's reading of the map is incorrect within the world of Winesburg itself—a world interpenetrated with the outside (as with the lodging-house in "Mother") and, ultimately, escapable by that train. Similarly, in speaking of Bill Bryson's 1989 book *The Lost Continent*, Ryan Poll claims that "[s]mall towns are described as spaces outside of modernity, spaces where 'human values' are championed over the capitalist logic of 'progress.'"[30] Certainly, the city-based protagonists of many small-town fictions seem to envision the small town as a space cut off from "progress," but their discovery is that such is not the case; in fact, they often work to prevent progress from occurring in the small town, as is the case with Jimmy Stewart's character in *Magic Town*. The visiting protagonist discovers what he or she expects to find and is then disillusioned by it.

Precisely because of its half-foreign nature, the train station is the best place for an outsider to first encounter the town. The boundary line between the small town and modernity is a railroad station. The train itself is a symbol of civilization; as such, it represents both the expansion of the American imperial project and the limits of the frontier mentality. In Ross Lockridge, Jr.'s, *Raintree County* (1948), the train is explicitly identified with "the future."[31] It is the engine by which modernity is visited upon the small town. Characters within small-town fiction—in contrast to the books they inhabit—tend to mistake the small town for a kind of untouched Eden. This symbolism is particularly present in *Calamity Town*; if Ellery is Columbus, then the train is his *Santa Maria*, the vessel which carries him to the New World. Insofar as the small town is conceived of as being in some way separate from modernity, the train station and the train itself are, at first glance, not a true part of the town—they are, after all, foreign bodies inserted into the community. However, Ima Honaker Herron observes in her 1939 study *The Small Town in American Literature* that "small town" is a more recent term for what was historically called "the village,"[32] and the relative infancy of the coinage might suggest that there is something inherently modern about the small town itself. Ryan Poll argues that "modernity proves the condition of possibility for the dominant small town," and that its image becomes definitive precisely because of the triumph of capitalist ideology.[33] Certainly, Sherwood Anderson used the small town to analyze the tensions of modernity—his depiction of Winesburg is implicitly a depiction of an America that has wholly fallen in line with capitalism, as symbolized by the Puritan work ethic. As Ryan Poll observes, "Anderson presents Winesburg as a relational space within a capitalist modernity" signified by the railroad.[34] Moreover, many small towns only exist because of the train—that is, their very existence is dependent upon the condition of modernity, rather than being antithetical to it.[35] The train is a striking reminder of the existence of modernity and of the dependence of the small town upon modernity.

It is on this train that the fatalist theme of *I Married a Dead Man* receives its first airing. Helen contemplates two possibilities for human existence; either each human creates themselves or "you could not have stopped anyplace else but this even if you had wanted to."[36] William Brevda connects this fatalism to the broader trends in Existentialist thought. He argues that "this question applies to the making of genre fiction itself. It is noir. Even when there is choice, a character must always make the wrong choice. The character of the genre is fate."[37] Helen-Patrice cannot make a choice because of the sort of story she is in. Human lives are like trains—circumscribed, bound to a single track. Throughout the novel, Helen-Patrice attempts to create her own narrative, to take on a new name, a new identity. But at every turn she will find herself cut off, forced to the end that is made inevitable by the novel's prologue: a despairing marriage in Caulfield. *I Married a Dead Man* demonstrates the extent to which disillusionment is the core of the small-town novel. Certainly, the book bears the mark of Woolrich's own philosophical obsessions. The most extensive critical study of Woolrich's work is Francis Nevins' *First You Dream and Then You Die*. In that study, Nevins identifies *I Married a Dead Man* as a distillation of Woolrich's metaphysical worldview, a worldview in which a senseless universe destroys the characters through the force of its own illogic.[38] *I Married a Dead Man* is "Woolrich's last major novel, the culmination of almost fifteen years of white-hot creativity."[39] In Woolrich's world, "reason doesn't work, we are abandoned to the powers of darkness."[40] Other critics have connected Woolrich's style with the concerns of Existentialism.

In his article "Is There Any Up or Down Left? Noir and Existentialism," William Brevda argues that "from the suburban Angst of Woolrich's *I Married a Dead Man*, to the urban Angst of Woolrich's *Deadline at Dawn*, uncanniness pursues being in the world of noir."[41] Similarly, in *Beyond the Gray Flannel Suit*, David Castronovo observes that "[h]uman beings exist against a social backdrop that wants no part of them."[42] *I Married a Dead Man* is an exploration of hopelessness and despair as striking as anything produced by the French Existentialists, but it derives its particular thrust from its small-town setting.

Within *I Married a Dead Man*, the train functions as at once a promise of escape—indeed, it is the birth canal to a new life—and as the mechanism by which that escape is foreclosed. It is on a train that Helen first meets the young couple whose lives she will usurp. Indeed, it is the actuality or the existence of the train that causes the couple to meet her; because the train is so crowded, she is incapable of finding a seat. Her difficulty is compounded by the fact that the train will not be making any stops. If someone were to surrender their seat to her, they face the prospect of standing "for hundreds and hundreds of miles."[43] This enforced lack of concern for the needs of a pregnant woman involves precisely the lack of kindness that put her on the train in the first place. Her husband in New York (that most modern of American cities) abandoned her and sent her across the country on the train, a kind of encapsulated modernity. The result of the growth and prevalence of machine, of modernity, is a lack of human empathy—a lack which causes Helen to suffer immeasurably.

This same train brings Helen into a new life. When Patrice—the real Patrice—sees Helen sitting on top of her luggage, she prompts her husband to give up his seat and the two women become friends—close in the way that people on trains become close, Woolrich says, since "[f]riendship blooms quickly in the hothouse atmosphere of travel."[44] It blooms quickly and it dies just as quickly, blooming precisely because it will die quickly. The women grow close and visit the toilet together, where Patrice allows Helen to wear her engagement ring. While the women are in the bathroom, the train crashes and Patrice is killed. Helen goes into labor but is otherwise unharmed. When she emerges to consciousness she slowly begins to realize that she has been mistaken for Patrice. Thus, in that train crash, two new lives are born, that of her baby and that of Helen-Patrice. Kenneth Payne argues that the action of being pried from the ruins of the train constitutes a symbolic c-section.[45] The train thus becomes a symbol of mutability and rejuvenation—and of death. Helen-Patrice at first struggles against the misidentification of herself with the dead girl, even as she is put on a train to Caulfield—a less crowded train, but one whose wheels seem to warn her to "[s]top while you can, you still can go back."[46] She does not go back.

In Caulfield, Helen-Patrice discovers a home for the first time in her life.[47] She soon finds herself comfortably inhabiting the role of Patrice. Her time in the town is not without stress; she is constantly on the verge of betraying herself. Payne sees the novel as an examination of the battle between dreaming and reality within the "world of small-town bourgeois affluence."[48] Caulfield is "problematic, an unsettling arena of potential disruption, self-betrayal, and entrapment."[49] However, Helen-Patrice manages to maintain her fragile balance until her husband returns. This husband's return should not be read as an encroachment from outside the town, a corruption that follows her from the city. Woolrich makes it clear that this toxic relationship is only one version of a deeper rot. Helen's relationship with her husband is mirrored in her relationship with her brother-in-law—and, eventually, lover—Bill. Bill may be kind, after his fashion, but he is no less predatory. The husband forces her to (re)marry him, to be sure, but so does Bill.

The blackmailer and the lover are mirrors of each other. After the blackmailer has been killed, Bill helps Helen-Patrice conceal the crime—first by manufacturing a card game that would cast suspicion on to the dead husband's former accomplices, and then by taking the corpse to a nearby turnpike beneath an embankment. Unlike the train that brought Helen-Patrice to Caulfield, this train is "a slow freight."[50] Bill drops the corpse into an empty carriage, where it lands with "a sick, hollow thud."[51] The body is carried out of town by the train. While the train in the beginning of the novel—the passenger train, the symbol of modernity—seems to promise new life, this freight train promises only death.

These trains bookend the narrative, and as such provide the two poles between which small-town fiction vacillates. The small-town narrative is one of disillusionment, and the shift in focus here reflects that disillusionment. Bill warns Helen-Patrice that telling her mother-in-law the truth would kill her and the girl observes that "somebody used that argument before."[52] The "somebody" here is her husband, who emphasizes the older woman's poor health as one way of blackmailing Helen-Patrice.[53] Both men corner Helen and force her to assume an identity. After the blackmailer has been murdered and his body dumped on an outgoing train, Helen decides that she must tell Bill the truth (a truth which he has, anyway, already guessed). She begins to speak—and then he stops her. He usurps her confession and then refuses to allow her to continue, saying that he has always known. The significance of this act is not lost on Helen-Patrice. She declares that "[e]ven the one last chance to redeem myself, you've taken away from me."[54] The moment at which she had a chance to finally take ownership of her situation is now lost and becomes an opportunity for Bill to narrate *his* experience. He declares that Helen *as Helen* does not exist, that Helen "only came into existence, as my eyes first took her in, as my love first started in to start."[55] He pulls her to himself, kisses her, and declares, "You are Patrice. You'll always be Patrice. You'll *only* be Patrice. I give you that name."[56] Helen-Patrice cannot narrate her own life because the men around her insist on narrating it to her.

This controlling masculinity is not an aberration. It is a constant, inside the small town or out of it. Bill is not alien to the small town. He is not an example of something that Helen-Patrice brings to town in the same way she brings her blackmailing husband. Bill already existed in the town. He is part of the town and so represents it to Patrice and, therefore, to the audience. The sense of being trapped with which the novel begins and ends is, thus, not simply a matter of entrapment-by-guilt; it is, in a large part, created by the life of the small town itself. This tension is found throughout small-town fiction more broadly considered and is particularly present in midcentury small-town fiction. The small town seems at first divorced from modernity and the existential turmoil associated with it, but—over and over—it is revealed to be no less oppressive than the world from which it seems to offer escape.

Eden is fallen—must be if it is to remain Eden—but that fact does not preclude an element of hope. Within that very fallenness are the seeds of a new beginning. Toshio Mori's collection *Yokohama, California* (1949) suggests with Queen and Woolrich that small-town life is deeply alienating, but Mori argues that this alienation need not be the end of the story. *Yokohama* is a collection of short stories—more properly, vignettes—detailing the lives of Japanese-Americans in the 1930s and '40s. If Queen demonstrates disillusionment and Woolrich claims that fallenness is intrinsic to the small-town Eden, Mori suggests that redemption is also a central reality. The small town (and America itself) is fallen, but it can be redeemed. As a Japanese-American writer of the 1940s, it is no accident that Mori is particularly concerned with racial alienation. David Palumbo-Liu observes that Mori's "protagonists [...] all are attached to the idea of the social,"[57] but this is so precisely because they are cut off from the *actuality* of the social—they are marginalized people. Tsunoda, the titular "Seventh Street Philosopher," longs for "an identity attached to social being and institutional recognition."[58] At the end of the story, Tsunoda comes close but does not find himself fully embedded in the community around him. Palumbo-Liu observes that this crisis is directly tied into the history of racism and discrimination that Japanese-Americans experienced, not only from the internment during World War II, but also in the years leading up to them.[59] And he is correct in this assertion; *Yokohama, California* is, from its very title, grounded in the material-historical experiences of Japanese-American persons.

Mori illustrates with the fundamental loneliness found in *all* fictions of the small town. Mori draws upon his model Sherwood Anderson, who filtered Winesburg through the consciousness of the young outsider George Willard.

But there is a difference here, as David R. Mayer points out, in that the grotesqueness of Mori's characters is rooted in "the unnamed racist society and the increasing number of state laws that hedged in opportunities for the Japanese in California in the first four decades of the twentieth century."[60] Loneliness is a constitutive element of Mori's characters. It is true that Mori often speaks in the first-person plural, as if he were narrating the thoughts of an entire community, just as Faulkner does in "A Rose for Emily," but in stories such as "Toshio Mori" the author makes it clear that his narrator is distinct from those around him. The protagonist in this story is not Toshio Mori but Teruo, who at the end becomes "aware that no one knew him as he knew himself."[61] This Teruo will later appear in "Say It with Flowers," which I will discuss in a later chapter. Teruo/Toshio Mori is in the community but not of it. Indeed, the very act of writing about his community involves, as Malve von Hassell observes, "looking at life with the eyes of another."[62] Mayer argues that "[t]his loneliness exists apart from a feeling that may be caused by racism, prejudice, frustration, or alienation"—it is, in fact, a central feature of existence.[63] There is, of course, no reason why it cannot be two things; the isolation that comes from racial injustice and the isolation that comes from being an embodied being-in-the-world may well be said to feed off each other. Existing, then, in a state of double-isolation, Mori's characters nevertheless are thoroughly typical of small-town fiction of this period.

If Columbus locates Eden in a quasi-mythical Asia, Mori transfers Asia to the Eden of the New World. The story "Slant-Eyed Americans" explicitly identifies the local community with a garden. The title of this story is as bold as the title of the collection it inhabits. If *Yokohama, California*, as a title, argues that these Japanese-Americans are just as typical as the citizens of Winesburg, Ohio, it does so by relying on the reader's knowledge of a prior work. "Slant-Eyed Americans" makes the same argument directly, by appropriating racist characterizations of Japanese and Japanese-American persons and arguing that these people, these citizens of Yokohama, are *Americans*. The title does not deny difference, but it insists on a fundamental unity undergirding that difference. The story itself opens with one of only two direct references to World War II in the collection: "It was Sunday noon, December 7."[64] Pearl Harbor has been attacked; the community is in shock. At first, one character wonders if the attack was "part of a play," evoking Orson Welles' infamous 1938 *War of the Worlds* broadcast, and so placing these Japanese-American residents in the same pop-cultural milieu as white Americans.[65] The immediate connection to Pearl Harbor is deliberate, as is the characterization of the Japanese attackers as inscrutable, alien beings. But this inscrutability, this alienness, is undermined by the fact that the people listening to the radio are themselves Japanese-American. They have connections in Hiroshima, as seen in the story "The End of the Line."[66] Many of them are first-generation

Japanese-Americans. As a result of the attack on Pearl Harbor, however, these *Issei*, first-generation people, not themselves citizens, become "enemy aliens."[67] The attack on Pearl Harbor comes from outside the community, but the racist backlash that will result in the displacement of Japanese-Americans (including Mori himself) is the result of elements existing within the American consciousness already. The citizens of Yokohama are forced to grapple with what it means to be American in an America that is at war with the land of their nativity and which will shortly be rounding them up and imprisoning them.

Their response—unlike the despair of Woolrich—is to re-create in America the already-lost and never-existing Eden. Flowers are an important metaphor for Mori, and so it is no surprise that he depicts Yokohama's shock in the flower market, where "the growers were present but the buyers were scarce."[68] Don Haley, a white businessman, says that "flowers and war don't go together" and determines to put his money into vegetable seeds.[69] He decides, that is, to abandon the flower-trade in favor of a trade fitted to wartime. Mori's Japanese characters are not so mercantile. In the face of World War II, one character imagines the work of gardening as redemptive:

> "Yes, if the gardens are ruined [by Japanese bombs] I'll rebuild them," he said. "I'll take charge of every garden in the city. All the gardens in America for that matter. I'll rebuild them as fast as the enemies wreck them. We'll have nature on our side and you cannot crush nature."[70]

This is the decision of Mori's Japanese-American characters. Some of them, like the narrator's brother, become soldiers. Others go "about [their] daily task, picking and bunching the flowers for Christmas."[71] Both jobs are important. If America is a garden, it is one that has been defiled—by the war in this case—and one which must be restored at the cost of hard work. Again, the small town is identified with nature while remaining the product of human labor. That is to say, it is a garden, an example of nature under control. Mori presents a picture of America as a system of garden-spots, communities dedicated to human (and plant) flourishing. That is, he presents the reader with an Eden in the past (the already-lost community of Yokohama) and in the future (the prospect of rebuilding these collapsed gardens). Tellingly, the mechanism for rebuilding here is the Japanese-American community. The truest vision of America is in its racial minorities, and they will be responsible for restoring it.

Thus, at the beginning of this ramble about the American literary small town, the basic coordinates are set. Small towns are typically imagined in the literature as a kind of Edenic space, with protagonists often seeking to escape from the pressures of modernity and into the idyllic small town. The literature of small towns is a literature of disillusionment. Ellery Queen realizes that Wrightsville is in fact a *Calamity Town*; Helen-Patrice finds Caulfield no less a prison than New York. In this way, writers in the years from 1940 to 1960 carry forward the sort of skepticism manifested by Anderson and Lewis toward the small town. For some of them, however, there is a hope that the lost Eden could be used in a kind of redemptive work. For Mori, the Edenic imagery charts directly onto the contemporary situation. Edenic imagery provides a way forward from the anxieties and traumas of the mid–twentieth century.

Two

"The Crisis of Individuation"
The Schoolhouse

Fiction presents the small town as an Edenic space, and the protagonist is its Adam. Adam—the first man, the childhood of the race—is himself often identified with pre-fallen innocence and innocence is generally linked with childhood. To lose innocence is, thus, to leave the state of childhood and enter the (reportedly) more complicated world of adulthood. As locations of the primal American myth, small towns have been closely identified with childhood. And, since the small town is Eden, these childhood narratives are reenactments of a primal fall. Indeed, childhood—like Eden, like Adamic innocency—only has meaning in its inevitable destruction. The goal of these childhood narratives is not to insist on a permanent state of being, but rather to work toward embracing impermanence. Authors rarely prize childhood *qua* childhood; they are much more interested in it once it has passed. Although the middle of the twentieth century, under the influence of thinkers like Freud and Dewey, steps away from an unproblematic identification of children with untouched innocence, this symbolism of growing into adulthood as a kind of fall continues. Most often, this maturation is characterized by an awareness of one's own individuality and—therefore—the inevitability of death. These two are in fact inseparable, since to be divided from the organic unity of the world is to enter the arena of time and flux. Certainly, some authors attempt to portray a return to that organic unity; in Ross Lockridge, Jr.'s *Raintree County*, death is central but is transcended through a mystical union with all living things. Within the context of midcentury small-town fiction, this transcendence is not a simple escape; it provides an engine for critiquing or engaging with the modern world. Thus, the slippery boundary between the small town and nature allows fiction of this period to engage in the same movement described by Jennifer Ladino in *Reclaiming Nostalgia*. Ladino argues that "[a]s a broad, affective narrative with the potential to unite disparate groups of people, nostalgia acts as midwife to various kinds of newborn stories."[1] Narratives of small-town childhood, however, suggest that simple return is impossible. The problem for the protagonists of these novels—and, implicitly, for the reader—is how to transcend mortality. Ray Bradbury suggests in *Dandelion Wine* that transcendence is attained through human connection. In *The Bad Seed*, William March presents a child protagonist who refuses this connection (and its necessary correlative, the acceptance of separation) and instead opts for obscene continuance when she becomes inhabited by the "bad blood" of her murderous grandmother. William Saroyan's *The Human Comedy*—in step with then-contemporary thoughts about childhood—prizes education or development as the ideal way to overcome fundamental loneliness. Since the small town is identified with America, for Saroyan this process also means a struggle to become fully American, part of a diverse and harmonious whole. The fall, which must be experienced by all children in order to gain adulthood, becomes fortunate. The child-protagonist escapes the fundamental existential loneliness at the heart of the human condition, if only in part. Transience and tentativeness characterize this shift.

These are accounts of education. Small-town fiction is often concerned with the development or education of children as they pass from prelapsarian innocence into adulthood. This development is physical and emotional, but it is also fundamentally intellectual, and the schoolhouse is where these young minds are shaped. Moreover, the schoolhouse setting permits authors to quickly sketch characters and their social relationships using an eye that has already been long on the scene: that of the schoolteacher. The protagonist of *Kings Row*, Parris Mitchell, is introduced in the first chapter through the eyes of his schoolteacher, Miss Sally Venable. Venable is an extremely minor character in the novel, but Bellamann uses her perspective to introduce all the major characters: Parris Mitchell, his best friend Drake McHugh, Jamie Wakefield, Cassandra Tower, and Randy Monaghan. Miss Venable's reflections on these children predict their fates: Parris, "her pet," is "different in every way" from his peers, having on him a mark of foreign blood as well as a mark of destiny.[2] Drake's future womanizing, Jamie's homosexuality, and even Cassandra's tragic future as a victim of murder-incest (her "[o]dd eyes"[3] are ultimately revealed to be the result of mental disturbance brought on by her father's abuse) are presented as the reflections of this schoolteacher on her students. Grace Metalious, in *Peyton Place*, makes a similar move. Both *Kings Row* and *Peyton Place* begin at a school because each novel is an account of the development of its young protagonist from childhood to adulthood. Both novels, that is, are concerned with *education*.

The problem of how to create citizens occupied writers of this period. During the middle part of the twentieth century, childhood was in the process of becoming standardized, as Steven Mintz observes in *Huck's Raft: A History of American Childhood*. The 1920s saw an increased interest in scientific control of childhood,[4] and by World War II schools were expected to both run along scientific lines and instill patriotism in their students.[5] In this century, children were seen neither as sinners nor as angels but as adults in training. Small-town fiction analyzes this problem from what might be thought of as an existential perspective; the coming-to-awareness of death is united to the increasing demand that children develop into good citizens.

These small-town children function as Adamic types. To be an American Adam is, fundamentally, to be lonely. The protagonists of such novels as *Peyton Place*, *Raintree County*, and *Kings Row* are alike in their Edenic childhoods and in their near-complete isolation from the people around them. The recurrence of Adam places these novels in a tradition of American literature stretching back to at least the nineteenth century, though the symbolism can be traced as far back as Columbus (and, back of him, Marco Polo). In *The American Adam*, R.W.B. Lewis argues that Adam is a central metaphorical construct for the entire American tradition in literature. Lewis' project, appearing as it did in 1955, is as much political as it is literary, since "this image had about it always an air of adventurousness, a sense of promise and possibility—of a sort no longer very evident in our national expression."[6] Lewis' observations about the centrality of Adam are, thus, arising from the very society that gave birth to the small-town fiction I discuss here. Since America was the New World, an earthly Paradise, it demanded a new protagonist—a new Adam.[7] According to Lewis, this typology appears in the works of all the major nineteenth century authors and philosophers, including Thoreau and Whitman. The perspective is different from author to author, but all are united in seeing the American as a new Adam. Loneliness—both social and existential—is an important component of this imagery. Adam symbolizes a number of things—innocence, potential—but at the core of his character is that he is *alone*. This fundamental loneliness, in the Biblical story, predates the fall; the creation of Eve, the first woman, is predicated on God's realization that "[i]t is not good that the man should be alone."[8] By Lewis' account, this loneliness is central to the American Adam. Even the most hopeful of the writers he discusses, Whitman—who combines the freshness of Adam with the creative vitality of God, making him a kind of self-created Adam—is aware of this central aloneness. Lewis says that Whitman "was lonely, incomparably lonely," and as such "introduced what more and more appears to be the central theme of American literature, in so far as a unique theme may be claimed for it: the theme of loneliness."[9] To be an American Adam in an American Garden of Eden is to be lonely.

What the critic expressed in criticism, novelists of the small town expressed in fiction. The most explicit use of the Adamic theme comes in

Two • "The Crisis of Individuation" 45

that most Edenic of small-town novels, *Raintree County*. This novel, roughly, recounts a span of nineteenth century America through the reminiscences of a schoolteacher named John Wickliff Shawnessy. Over the course of a day's walk around town—and over a thousand pages—Shawnessy recalls the events of his life: his blissful childhood, his early infatuation with a girl named Nell, his marriage to the mad Susanna and her subsequent suicide—all events implicitly and explicitly tied to the growth of America through the Civil War and to the turn of the century. The events recounted are often dark and terrible, and the outlook for America seems bleak, but Ross Lockridge, Jr., finds hope within nature itself. If there is no escape from alienation, there is at any rate a symbol of transcendence. In *Raintree County*, the crystallizing symbol is the Raintree for which the county is named. The Raintree itself is a quasi-mythological tree that might have been transplanted from Asia; the mention of Asia evokes the original inhabitants of Raintree County who first named the Shawmucky River, inhabitants that Lockridge insists migrated from Asia.[10] Here, again, the Columbian imagery discussed in chapter one of this study returns—the Tree of Life Columbus speaks of and hopes to find in China is symbolically identical to Lockridge's Raintree. The Raintree's origins are found in the legend of an itinerant preacher, a kind of Johnny Appleseed, "carrying with him the seed of an oriental tree never before planted in America," who plants the seed in the earth of the county and prophesies that the tree "will blossom in the western earth. The tree of life will drop its golden fruit in the new earthly Paradise."[11] The tree, however, like the Tree of Life in the Biblical Garden, is lost and returns to the narrative through the philanthropist Robert Owen, who founds a town and plants a "tree, bearing the scientific name of Koelreutera paniculata, [which] had been called the Golden Raintree in its native China."[12] The Asian-Edenic Raintree becomes Lockridge's central symbol within the novel.

This mention of China is no mere orientalist exoticism. For Lockridge, Asia functions as a primal location for Raintree County and for America itself. The first Americans were travelling nomads come from Asia, the legendary home of the Garden of Eden. And Eden now abides in America. Accordingly, Raintree County takes on the characteristics of Eden. In the Biblical account, there are two trees in the Garden: The Tree of Life and the Tree of the Knowledge of Good and Evil. The former brings eternal life while the latter induces a fall, since Adam and Eve become "as gods, knowing good and evil."[13] Lockridge blends the two trees, but they are already symbolically united in the Eden myth itself by the simple fact that both are in the midst of the Garden and that one cannot be spoken of without invoking the other. Again, here is the paradox of the Eden myth: that it can only exist if its opposite also exists. Prelapsarian innocence demands a lapse. The Tree of Life depends on the Tree of the Knowledge of Good and Evil for its very existence—indeed, for its very intelligibility. This paradox runs through every symbol associated with Eden, including Adam. Eden is impossible without a fall, which means that the protagonist must inevitably be fallen as well. In this, small-town protagonists enact the same double-existence embodied by the train station and the community itself. They explore the world and discover Eden within themselves, and so discover within themselves their own alienation.

These protagonists who are born to the town still position themselves—and are positioned by their authors—as outsiders, alienated from the town around them. John Wickliff Shawnessy is in many respects a powerful figure in his community—a respected schoolteacher (the educated becoming the educator)—but he is most clearly defined by his outsider-relationship to the county around him. This alienated status is apparent from the very beginning of the novel. Shawnessy is introduced through a bizarre dream he has of a naked woman in the local post office asking him the riddle the Sphinx asked Oedipus: "What creature is it that in the morning of its life—."[14] This riddle will haunt the novel, for the narrative of *Raintree County* is the story of a man's life. The novel, which follows Shawnessy's perambulations around town for over a thousand pages, is at pains to paint the schoolteacher as substantially different from those around him, even from his more successful childhood friend and rival Garwood Jones and his old mentor "the Perfessor," both of whom serve as a kind of Greek chorus to the schoolteacher's reflections. Shawnessy is a failed poet; the flashbacks that intersperse his travels around the home of his youth are shot through with memories of an idyllic, pastoral childhood. His youth is Edenic, taking place "on the banks of the Shawmucky [where] the naked American boy, seventeen years old, read in the pages of the greatest poet of all time [Shakespeare]."[15] Nakedness has its own double-association with innocence and experience and is tied in its own way to the Edenic myth; Adam and Eve "were both naked [...] and were not ashamed."[16] Nudity is, thus, tied to both the infantile existence of the first parents and to the paradox of innocent sexuality.

If Raintree County is Eden, then John Wickliff Shawnessy is its Adam. Like Adam, Johnny is naked and unashamed; like Adam, he sees his childhood love also naked and unashamed. This girl is Nell, and she becomes for him "nothing if not Raintree County."[17] Lockridge pushes the Edenic metaphor about as far as it will go, but this metaphor is filtered through the consciousness of Shawnessy himself, a poetic back-reading of his childhood. It is for this reason that Leslie Fiedler, in *Love and Death in the American Novel*, dismissively labels Shawnessy a *"poet maudit"* of the sort also written about by Thomas Wolfe.[18] Fiedler has no use for such figures, considering them fit only for "the high school department, on the shelf of masturbatory dreams."[19] Nevertheless, within small-town fiction, the self-absorbed alienation of the protagonist serves an important structural function that transcends the psychologizing of Fiedler. By focusing so much of the novel through the perspective of a *poet maudit* remembering his childhood, Lockridge allows the small town to occupy a space removed from the reader, abstracted. His protagonist is not a stranger to the town in a physical sense, but he is nevertheless a stranger.

These authors connect the loneliness of the small town with the loneliness of the grave. Loneliness is inevitably the result of maturation and lurks around every corner for the child-protagonist. Similarly, death is not only the end-point of the small-town dwellers but the miasma in which they circulate. Death is isolation and is innate in every member of the small-town community. Ray Bradbury's *Dandelion Wine* (1957) is, on the surface, a collection of bucolic reminiscences of small-town life. Much about Bradbury's portrayal of Green Town, the book's location, is nostalgic—the author's obvious affection for the easy pace of life, the antiquated technology, and the play of adolescent children, all conspire to suggest that Bradbury is romanticizing a lost past. However, closer analysis reveals that Bradbury views death and alienation, rather than simply sunshine and laughter, as the central truth of small-town life. Protagonist Douglas Spaulding initially exerts over his town a tremendous (one might be tempted to say authorial) control. However, he soon makes the startling discovery that he is alive—a discovery which Bradbury presents as at once the glory and the tragedy of growing up. Douglas' fall is initially less catastrophic than some of the other encounters in this study. The crisis of individuation is rendered in positive, even ecstatic terms. Douglas ventures with his father and brother into the woods searching for grapes. The father instructs the boys to "[l]ook for bees."[20] Bees are significant; they are "no more, no less, said Father, the world humming under its breath."[21] Bees represent a fundamental unity, existing as they do in a mass. Bees mirror society as well as nature—an organic unity among individuals that can also be thought of as typical of the childhood experience. Indeed, the opening section of the book shows Douglas enacting a form of authorship over the town, eliding any distinctions between him and the townsfolk. On this trip into the woods, Douglas encounters a break within that unity. After a tussle with his brother, Douglas realizes that he is "*really* alive! I never knew it before, or if I did I don't remember!"[22] He has experienced differentiation from the world around him and from other people.

In the garden of the world, Douglas discovers his separation from those around him. This discovery is central to his role as a small-town Adam. Adam is as impossible without a fall as Eden is. He is definitionally alone. Loneliness is another word for estrangement, and this estrangement is the necessary position of the American Adam; there is no point at which Adam is not fallen; even in his prelapsarian state, the fact of the fall is a given. As with Eden, the thought of a prelapsarian Adam necessitates the concept of a *lapsed* Adam. In fact, the primal father is only important (in the Western Christian tradition) insofar as he is thrown out of Eden. For American authors, this image of the fall is central; R.W.B. Lewis points out that "the literal use of the story of Adam and the fall of Man—as a model for narrative—occurred in the final works of American novelists, works in which they sought to summarize the whole of their experience of America."[23] Though some American authors—Whitman, Emerson, Thoreau—would have denied the reality of the fall, others, such as Henry James, Sr., considered the fall to be the fundamental reality of human existence, since "[g]rowing up required the individuating crisis which in Genesis is dramatized by the fall of Adam: the fatal, necessary quickening within the unconscious chunk of innocence of the awareness of self."[24] An "individuating crisis" is precisely the mechanism by which humans become aware of themselves as themselves. Ray Bradbury takes seriously the inevitability of such a crisis, as well as the fact that—once the crisis is initiated—it can never be rolled back. Though initially joyous, Douglas Spaulding's fall into life comes with the tremendous consequence of alienating him from the world around him. He is now separated and can never be reunited.

Structurally, *Dandelion Wine* demonstrates Bradbury's interest in this crisis of individuation. The book divides roughly in half. The first half covers Douglas' growing understanding of himself as alive; the second half deals with the radical estrangement brought on by this realization and by the corollary realization that if he is alive he must die. Death is inseparable from loneliness. The clearest illustration of Douglas' loneliness is, however, not explicitly linked with death but with social alienation. In the section dealing with John Huff,[25] Bradbury at once introduces and takes away the most important person in Douglas' life, outside of his family. John Huff is "the only god living in the whole of Green Town Illinois."[26] Douglas worships John Huff. Huff is a central part of Bradbury's own understanding of childhood. With his dark hair and mature demeanor, the boy is recognizable as a predecessor to the enigmatic Jim Nightshade in *Something Wicked This Way Comes* (1962). Bradbury's long-delayed sequel to *Dandelion Wine*, a novel called *Farewell Summer* (2006) is dedicated to John Huff, who nevertheless does not appear in the book. Huff occupies a spectral position within Bradbury's small-town cosmology, a position defined by loss (just as the chief fear of William Halloway in *Something Wicked* is that Jim will abandon him). Huff haunts the narrative, the ghost of a lost childhood friend.

Indeed, it could be said that John Huff—like Adam, like Eden itself—is important primarily in his absence. He is only introduced properly—and in his role as Douglas' idol—in the very story that pulls him away from Green Town. One day, abruptly, John announces that his family is leaving Green Town—leaving, in fact, that very afternoon.[27] Douglas is devastated, and over the course of the story, while the two boys and their friends go about town, he attempts to postpone John's departure in various ways. He tries to fill in all the conversations they will never have[28] and sneakily sets his watch back an hour.[29] None of these tricks work. John himself is also anxious; though Bradbury does not give the boy's thoughts directly, at one point John demands that Doug "remember me, promise you'll remember my face and everything."[30] The climax of the story involves the boys playing statues—a kind of early version of red-light, green-light—and Doug commands the boys to freeze. He goes up to John and says, "John, now, [...] don't you move so much an eyelash. I absolutely command you to stay here and not move at all for the next three hours!"[31] Doug is attempting here to stop the flow of time, to stop change, and preserve his own immortality in his relationship with John Huff. But he has already fallen into life. Now that he realizes that he—and everyone around him—is alive, he cannot stop the inevitable separation. John at last breaks ranks and declares himself to be "it." He commands the boys to freeze and then "Douglas felt John walking around him even as he had walked around John a moment ago. He felt John sock him on the arm once not too hard. 'So long,' he said."[32] John Huff, wiser than Douglas, preserves a single moment and vanishes forever. As he leaves, "[f]ar away, a train whistle [sounds]."[33] The train that brings the stranger also carries off the friend. Douglas learns here that, after that initial ecstasy of being alive, he must reconcile himself to the fact that to be alive is to be alone and, ultimately, to face alone the long loneliness of the grave. The traditions of childhood wither and fall away. Old people and family members die and dear friends leave, possibly never to return. The story of John Huff is possibly the most heart-wrenching tale in Bradbury's collection and it expresses the alienation that midcentury small-town writers saw as being fundamental to the small town more clearly than any of the nostalgic reminiscences of the book's first half. When Douglas eventually determines people are unreliable, since they may leave or die, the story of John Huff is grouped with other reasons.[34] Death and separation are thus linked. The fall into life, which occupies the first half of the collection, is a fall into death as well. One sign of that death is the inevitable separation from friends. The central theme of the last half of *Dandelion Wine* is the fact that everything must end, and the end of all things is death itself.

For midcentury small-town fiction, individuation is the birth of loneliness. These writers hold the awareness that a child does not exist in a primal unity with all things but is instead separate from the world in ways that even he (or she) cannot fully grasp. Ben Lazare Mijuskovic frames the phenomenon in terms of Freud's reality principle before declaring that "narcissistic loneliness is a universal and necessary structure in all human consciousness."[35] Eden exists only as an ideal location from which the American Adam has been cast. But key to all these visions is the fundamental understanding that the paradise these authors seek is not only lost—it is fundamentally impossible. It is impossible because Eden is not a physical location; it is a symbol for the tragic isolation of the human. For twentieth-century philosophers and theologians, the problem of human identity became increasingly important. Alienation was seen as core of that identity. Reinhold Niebuhr, in his 1941 study *The Nature and Destiny of Man*, argued that "[t]he essence of man is his freedom. Sin is committed in that freedom [and] can only be understood as a self-contradiction, made possible by the fact of his freedom but not following necessarily from it."[36] Niebuhr held that the world of modernity, in abandoning the Christian concept of sin, set itself up for the perils of the twentieth century. Particularly, by ignoring the paradox of human wrongdoing, moderns "lost [...] individuality immediately after establishing it by the destruction of the medieval solidarities."[37] What was needed—according to Niebuhr—were "religious presuppositions which can do justice to the immediate involvement of human individuality in all the organic forms and social tensions of history, while yet appreciating its ultimate transcendence."[38] Other writers agreed with Niebuhr in essence if not in details. As Mark Buechsel argues in *Sacred Land*, much of the work of what Buechsel calls the Midwestern Modernists was concerned with regaining organic involvement, thus achieving some form of transcendence. Unlike Niebuhr, these Midwestern authors put the blame for modern alienation on Protestantism itself, echoing the work of critics like Weber.[39] The Regionalists, too, were concerned with precisely this question; their quest was to redeem America from "the acids of modernity."[40] Though Niebuhr expressed himself in a particularly theological way, his interest in human alienation was very much in line with the rest of the intellectual work of the twentieth century. The work of midcentury small-town fiction is concerned with alienation, with disillusionment and fallenness, and with the potential for redemption that might still adhere to the small town.

This desire may be called nostalgia, but it should not be confused with sentimentality. Sentimentality dulls the senses and covers over the impossibility of the past. Nostalgia, as practiced by these authors, does the opposite: it sharpens the senses and confirms that the past is indeed impossibly distant. Like the dream of Eden, nostalgia is predicated always on the fact that the thing itself is forever lost, and this recognition is key to Bradbury's narrative. The unfallen world partakes of the same paradox as all such states. Like Eden, it only has meaning once it is gone. Nostalgia in Bradbury is always accompanied with an awareness that in exchange for the lost past something else has been gained—an awareness of life itself, an appreciation for the relationships formed even though these relationships are short-lived. About midway through *Dandelion Wine*, Bradbury's interests shift from celebrating the life of the village to mourning the passing, not necessarily of the village itself, but of the people in it. The exact narrative pivot occurs with the account of the final ride of the town trolley, which will soon be replaced by a bus. The bus is more efficient and (as a result) less Romantic. Clearly there is an irony here; the trolley is itself a creation of the modern industrialized world, and Bradbury obviously fetishizes it *as a machine*. But this machine, too, presumably replaced older modes of transportation, just as its replacement will eventually be replaced when the time comes. What is important here is not the thing itself—not the transportation itself—but Doug's awareness that the world is changing, that it does not exist in a static form.

The true center of *Dandelion Wine*, thus, is an ever-present awareness of the transience of life. Death is most centrally personified by the Lonely One, a serial killer who haunts the margins of the narrative as well as a marginal space within the town—a ravine running through the village's center. This ravine is a gulf, a yawning gap in the center of the seemingly-placid community, suggesting that division and alienation are not antithetical to the small town. Rather, they constitute it. And within this ravine lurks the Lonely One. Just as the ravine is central to Green Town's physical identity, so the Lonely One is central to its psychic identity. The killer's name—*The Lonely One*—ties him to Doug Spaulding and his brother; he is the incarnation of what they dread, an entity so cut off from kin and town that he can only make human contact through brutal murder. The boys' first realization of loneliness comes in the shadow of the Lonely One, when Tom, Douglas' brother, goes with his mother to find Douglas. Their search takes them to the ravine where, hearing no answer from Douglas, Tom finds himself suddenly afraid, which leads to the realization that "all men were like this: that each person was to himself one alone. One oneness, a unit in a society, but always afraid."[41] If the conflict between the one and the many is a political concern going back to Tocqueville, Bradbury here unites it to a fundamentally existential crisis. This loneliness touches even Mother, who cannot "look anywhere, in this very instant, save into her heart, and there she would find nothing but uncontrollable repugnance and a will to fear."[42] The boy and his mother stand side by side, but they are psychically worlds apart, separated by the very alienation that constitutes the human mind. Tom's realization comes early in the collection and then subsides quickly when Douglas returns, but this hint of darker themes will become overpowering as the collection progresses.

Death and loneliness are the theme of the second half of the book. In a vignette directly dealing with the Lonely One, previously published in 1950 as "The Whole Town's Sleeping" and dramatized on the radio series *Suspense*, Bradbury follows three women as they go about town. The Lonely One has killed again; two of the women find the body. Later that evening, one of them—Lavinia—decides to walk home alone through the ravine where the body was found, the same ravine where Tom first feels the existential loneliness of humanity. On her way home, Lavinia becomes terrified; the ravine seems to shut out the world until "[o]nly the ravine existed and lived, black and huge, about her."[43] She seems to see a man waiting for her up ahead.[44] Panicked, Lavinia runs to her house and locks herself in. Her tension eases; she starts to rationalize her fears. And then "[b]ehind her in the living room, someone cleared his throat."[45] The Lonely One has killed again. Or, at least, that is how the original version of the story ends. This conclusion gives the Lonely One an almost supernatural power to move through walls and insert himself into any situation. He is more than a killer; he is a kind of principle of darkness, finding his victims, not in the ravine, but in the comfort of their own houses. Death comes to everyone, and when it does they will inevitably be alone. In the context of *Dandelion Wine*, Bradbury reveals in the following section that Lavinia defends herself and kills the Lonely One—though the boys, who have granted the Lonely One a kind of mythic power, very quickly reject the idea since the stranger does not look like they expected him to.[46] The fact that Bradbury recontextualizes the story in the larger shape of *Dandelion Wine* might suggest that he has undercut the story's power: in the small town, nothing bad can happen. But such a reading does Bradbury a disservice. Within *Dandelion Wine* bad things *do* happen, and frequently; the murders of the other women are not removed by the successful destruction of the Lonely One. He is, in his own way, the incarnation of the loneliness to which all the town's citizens are doomed: a lonely life and, finally, a lonely death.

For Bradbury, any attempt to escape death ends in failure. Many of the stories in *Dandelion Wine* end in death—Colonel Freeleigh, great-grandmother, Helen Loomis. For Douglas Spaulding, the discovery of death follows the discovery of life, and the realization of mortality leads Douglas to conclude that "any time they want to they can, no matter how you kick or scream, they just put a big hand over you and you're still."[47] As a result of this realization, Douglas becomes obsessed with attempting to forestall or prevent his own mortality. The old circus display, Mme Tarot, who sits "in her glass coffin, night after night,"[48] seems to offer Douglas a chance to escape death. He plots to rescue her from her imprisonment and force her to grant him eternal life. As a symbol of immortality, however, Mme. Tarot is particularly unsatisfactory; though Douglas insists that she is alive, she is simply a carnival attraction encased in her "glass coffin." Even the narrative of immortality that Douglas constructs for her is unsatisfactory; he claims that "a long time ago someone got jealous or hated her and poured wax over her and kept her prisoner forever."[49] Any life Mme. Tarot lives is a kind of suspended death, and the price of her continuance is isolation. Douglas' plan is to free her from this prison and so gain from her the ability to "live forever, or next thing to it."[50] But, removed from her coffin, the witch is silent and can offer Douglas only the same portent she has previously given: a blank white card which the boy must fill with his own meaning.[51] This, for Bradbury, is the true way of transcendence—not the forestalling of death but its embrace as an essential part of life. The path forward is uncertain and ambiguous. *Dandelion Wine* ends with a return to the celebration of life, but this return is tempered by the recognition that, as Grandfather observes, summer "was over before it began."[52] Douglas puts the town to bed and ends the summer.

In *Dandelion Wine*, the attempt to escape alienation and death is futile; in William March's *The Bad Seed* (1954), such an effort is fatal. *The Bad Seed* is unique among the books I discuss here in that March, based on his notes, intended the novel to take place in a "fairly large city."[53] Nevertheless, reviewers such as Alistair Cooke still read the book as a small-town novel.[54] *The Bad Seed*, thus, takes part in the small-town fictional discourse surrounding childhood. It is, in some ways, the obverse of Bradbury, demonstrating the real dangers faced by children during this age of anxiety. When characters fail to incorporate ambiguity into their lives, they lapse into psychosis. In the Bradbury novel, the young protagonists confront loneliness and separation and successfully incorporate it into their psyches. In contrast, the child-protagonist of *The Bad Seed* seeks to escape the loneliness of mortality by way of posthumous possession. *The Bad Seed* tells the story of Rhoda Penmark, an eight-year-old girl whose suspicious perfection conceals a sociopathic mind. The story is told from her mother's point of view as she gradually realizes that Rhoda, the grandchild of a famous serial killer, is murdering people. Over the course of the novel, Rhoda commits two murders—that of a schoolmate who won a medal she wants, and that of a groundskeeper who discovers her secret. In addition, Rhoda has committed at least one other murder in the past and is contemplating a fourth. The mother determines to end the homicidal rampage by killing Rhoda. At its base, *The Bad Seed* is about a child who fails to (or chooses not to) incorporate into herself the ambiguity that Douglas Spaulding encounters in *Dandelion Wine*. Douglas moves through the crisis of individuation over the course of a summer; Rhoda rejects this individuation and embraces sociopathology instead.

Childhood is lonely in part because it is subject to more demands than adults often recognize. Rhoda, with her loving mother and perfect life, may not seem to be a candidate for loneliness, but the role of the child is one bound up in culturally symbolic, and isolating, fields. Children are expected to act in certain ways, to fill certain (often contradictory) types. Thus, for instance, they must operate within the paired roles of hellion and angel. Rhoda challenges the demands placed upon her in an ironic and paradoxical way. She does not refuse to fill them; rather, she fills them too well. There is about her a sense of being too perfect that unnerves both her mother and her schoolteacher. Early in the novel, Mrs. Penmark reflects that "there was a strangely mature quality in the child's character which [her parents] found disturbing."[55] Rhoda's psychosis manifests itself, not in the fact that she cannot copy society's strictures but in the fact that she mimics them too well, "as though sensing for the first time some factor of body or spirit separated her from those around her, [she] tried to conceal the difference by aping the values of others."[56] The recognition that she is "separated [...] from those around her" is, in the end, not very different from Douglas Spaulding's realization that he is "*really* alive."[57] But Rhoda, rather than working through the tension of separation, works instead towards a state of bland perfection—precisely the impossible perfection that is expected of children.

Perfection is obscene, which is why Rhoda's mother fears it; to be perfect is to exist in stasis, without change, in an prelapsarian state. It is a fundamentally impossible mode of existence. It is, one might say, a manifestation of the death-drive. Rhoda's perfection becomes a warning that ancestral misdeeds are being revisited in the present. As Chuck Jackson observes in "Little, Violent, White: *The Bad Seed*, and the Matter of Children," heredity is a theme that obsessed certain writers during the period of the novel's publication. He observes that in "the first half of the twentieth century, American novelists experimenting with the Southern gothic embedded eugenic ideology into their fiction to flesh out an aberrant character."[58] Jackson points out that William March was himself a Southerner, and his novel bears traces of its Gothic ancestry. In Southern literature, examples of bad blood are easy to spot—Jackson points to Benjy Compson in William Faulkner's *The Sound and the Fury* (1929) as an obvious example—but Rhoda is different since "Rhoda Penmark's evil *cannot* be read on her body."[59] That is, she bears no deformity to set her apart. For Jackson, Rhoda's crimes signify a "failure of whiteness."[60] But Jackson misreads Rhoda's perfection. Rhoda is threatening because her evil *can* be read upon her body—her very perfection is the sign of an obscene core. She is outwardly perfect because she is inwardly perverse.

Rhoda's behavior is a response to a forced choice. Children are expected to be hellions and they are commanded to choose not to be so. In his book *Violence*, Slavoj Žižek observes that all social exchanges function around just such a false choice—that is, the individual is presented with the command "freely to embrace and make [...] our own choice [of] what is, in any case, imposed on us."[61] Children are expected to at one and the same time be little devils—rowdy and dirty—and perfect angels. There is no escaping this choice if the child wishes to survive in adult society and not be branded a deviant. Since the full force of society compels the child to make the choice, the choice is not freely made. Rhoda, outside the bounds of society, freely chooses to be bound by that society's strictures not only in a nominal way but in an essential way: she becomes the angel. This choice is the mechanism of her agency in the novel, of her power over the adults around her. It is also the source of the terror that confronts her mother. Nothing is as fearful as a child who fulfills its roles to perfection, since such perfection is a denial of process, of growth. Its static condition carries with it the stench of death. As Chuck Jackson observes, this exposure also lays bare the falseness of the original vision. He argues that "*The Bad Seed*, both film and novel, deconstructs 'cuteness' and exposes it as a performance aesthetic, one that depends on a specific race, class, and gender combination."[62] In *The Bad Seed*, performance is the way Rhoda attains agency.

Rhoda's psychopathy is a response to loneliness. Loneliness and death are, as Bradbury demonstrates, a matched set. The Lonely One in *Dandelion Wine* is defined—in his very name—by isolation. Rhoda rejects the crisis of individuation and seeks to abolish all distinction between her own desires and the world around her. She expresses this rejection within herself by embodying or incarnating her murderous grandmother. Rhoda's psychopathy is, thus, a form of continuance, a return of the repressed dead, and so finds its mirror in other small-town fiction of the period. Jackson rightly observes that *The Bad Seed* is at pains to underline the interior origin of Rhoda's evil; she is not possessed by demons, but motivated by her own bad blood.[63] She is possessed by the evil grandmother's tainted genetics. I may note, in passing, that Rhoda is not unique in this. In *Psycho* the dead Mrs. Bates is exhumed by her son Norman—also her murderer—while "she" takes over Norman's consciousness. William Faulkner's "A Rose for Emily" demonstrates a similar movement, with Miss Emily attempting to keep the body of her controlling father and then successfully retaining the body of her murdered lover. In each of these cases, the individual is subsumed by a demonic superego, the voice of social and familial order. The psychopath and the sociopath both represent a fear of where the loss of connection may lead. To be cut off from others is ultimately to open oneself to the indwelling of the unholy spirit.

The failure of the adults around Rhoda to diagnose her psychopathy is a failure of education (it is no accident that her first crime in the novel is the murder of a classmate). The desire to protect children and to help them become healthy adults is one that literature of this period emphasizes. Children *must* be socialized in such a way that they overcome the crisis of individuation and live in society as functional adults. Rhoda Penmark represents a psychopathic response to the problem of loneliness and change. Other authors of the period suggest ways in which children can be socialized *away* from such a destructive response. During World War II, the schoolhouse represented a training ground for the production of citizens. Citizenship is part of the period's attempt to deal with the crisis of individuation, for the political and the existential coexist one atop the other. Nowhere is this more clearly seen than in Williams Saroyan's *The Human Comedy*. *The Human*

Comedy is a gentle work, open to charges of nostalgia and sentimentality. Unlike most of the novels or collections discussed in this study, *The Human Comedy* is set during the time it was composed—at the height of World War II. Saroyan is interested in the condition of coming of age and reaching adulthood—leaving childhood—under the shadow of World War II. Thus, Saroyan most clearly of all the books discussed here indicates the ways in which the small-town Eden is conceptualized as a necessarily falling. He further demonstrates the ways in which midcentury small-town writers recognize the necessity of some sort of fortunate fall.

The Human Comedy tells the story of two boys in the small town of Ithaca, California. Their names are Homer and Ulysses. Through the eyes of these two boys—one a young teenager and the other a child—Saroyan narrates a year in the life of the community. As with his obvious inspiration Balzac, Saroyan wants to paint a tapestry of life in an advanced society—in his case, America during World War II. In so doing, Saroyan emphasizes the polyvocal nature of America—that it is not monocultural but vibrantly diverse—and the necessity of raising children who can function within that society rather than reject it in a quest for monotonous perfection. *The Human Comedy* examines the lives of several citizens of Ithaca in thirty-nine short vignettes. The book could hardly be said to have a plot; like *Dandelion Wine*, this novel is interested in preserving small slivers of life as seen in the small town. Thus, Saroyan introduces his readers to the goodhearted Spangler, the alcoholic William Grogan, the school teacher Ms. Hicks, and several other briefly-sketched but vibrant characters. In the process, Saroyan makes an argument for diversity and common-feeling as the means of escaping existential alienation.

In this novel, the war is central to the crisis of individuation. The protagonist is young Homer Macauley, whose brother is fighting abroad. Homer is introduced at his job at the telegraph company and his first action is to take a message to a woman named Mrs. Sandoval. Mrs. Sandoval is Mexican, in keeping with Saroyan's multicultural theme. The message is from the War Department informing her that her son has been killed in the war. The experience is world-shaking for the fourteen-year-old boy:

> Now, suddenly, she began to make strange soft breathing sounds, holding herself in, as if weeping were a disgrace. Homer wanted to get up and run but knew he would stay. He even thought he might stay the rest of his life. [...] He got to his feet as if by standing he meant to begin correcting what could not be corrected and then he knew the foolishness of this intention and became more awkward than ever. In his heart he was saying over and over again. "What can I do? What the hell can *I* do? I'm only the messenger."[64]

Homer is here confronted with the existential fact of death in the face of total war. And, just as an awareness of life causes Douglas in *Dandelion*

Wine to enter the inevitable flow of time, so for Homer "everything else had started and he knew there would be no stopping them."⁶⁵ Change has entered Homer's perspective; he has left the world of childhood in which everything seems eternal. This shift in viewpoint is a fall. The specter of death serves as Homer's introduction into the world of adulthood. Later, Homer's mother makes this point explicit. Homer tells her that "I'm lonely and I don't know what I'm lonely *for.*"⁶⁶ Loneliness is, as I have demonstrated, the fundamental condition of the small-town children in these novels, and here it is linked to an awareness of mortality. His mother says that the boy has entered the world of adulthood. She argues that "the world has always been full of that loneliness. If a message comes to me as to the Mexican woman tonight, I can't tell you what I shall do."⁶⁷ Her words prove prophetic, since the novel concludes with her receiving precisely such a message. Homer has left the static world of childhood and been inserted into the world of change and malleability and, ultimately, death. For William Saroyan, the mechanism that causes this fall from grace is World War II. But, again, the existential and the political are inextricably intertwined. They are inseparable; humans, as political animals (where "political" means "having to do with the *polis,*" or city) feel existentially the force of world events. Existential fears of death are in part what drives humans—and therefore the development of history. History alienates humans and drives them to seek a place of belonging. For Saroyan, it is Ithaca which, like the native shore that drew Odysseus home from the sea, issues a call to its children to return. But world-historical events—no less shattering events than total war and mass bloodshed—make this Ithaca, this Eden, a problematic destination. It is a world made up of lonely people, a world of alienated (*fallen*) people. As the mother observes here, the world has always been full of lonely people and what is important for Saroyan is that this loneliness (and, back of it, the death that creates it) is transcended. But, because the process of maturity is a process of realizing that one is alone, transcendence is by no means guaranteed. For Saroyan, alienation is a fundamental truth about growing up—to grow up is to fall.

Having fallen, all that is left is to reach out to other fallen people. Since *The Human Comedy* is a novel set during the war, death is always in the background of the characters' minds and forms the basis of the young protagonists' maturation. There are, by Saroyan's account, two responses to the fact of the existential crisis brought on by total war. The first is to become an alcoholic and ultimately die of that alcoholism, as the telegraph operator Mr. Granger does. However, Saroyan's political commitments (so deeply tied to his existential commitments) suggest another way of transcendence. The means of escaping or transcending death is suggested when Ulysses sees an elderly black man on a passing train. The man is singing a song about going home and as he passes he waves at the boy and shouts that he is "[g]oing home."⁶⁸

In the context of the novel, the idea of home is powerful; multiple characters experience alienation from their home. One character for whom home becomes an important touchpoint is a young man who attempts to rob the post office. Spangler, the head of the office, attempts to dissuade him, but the thief responds that morality has lost its meaning under the conditions of war, since "[e]verybody's killing everybody."[69] Saroyan presents the danger facing the homefront: that individuals, trapped in their existential shells, will turn against each other and dismantle the very thing that the war is (presumably) being fought to defend. Spangler's response is another example of Saroyan's domestic prescription. He gives the boy money and urges him to return home to his mother, saying that the young man's "mother's waiting for you. This money is a gift from me to her."[70] This idea of home is central because the problem that preoccupies Saroyan is the measure of relief home can offer in a time of stress.

In this case, home can provide comfort and safety in a world gone wrong. Spangler answers the young man, who wonders "if the only man in the world I have ever known who has been decent to another man just to be decent—just for itself—was *truly* so."[71] Spangler's actions confirm the essential goodness Saroyan sees at the heart of Ithaca (of America). This goodness—this homeliness—is the only hope for getting through the trauma of the war and providing healing afterward. The book concludes with the oldest brother, Marcus—who has been in the army throughout the novel and only intermittently seen—dead, killed overseas. His friend Tobey comes to Ithaca and is welcomed into the Macauley family. He becomes, in a way, a replacement for the dead Marcus. His arrival corresponds with the family learning that Marcus has died. His "return" home is parallel to the man on the train's boast that he is "going back where [he] belong[s]."[72] The idea of belonging to a certain place—a home—is one which powerfully motivates Saroyan. However, this home is distinct from the blood-and-soil vision held by the Nazis. For Saroyan, the idea of belonging means an embrace and transcendence of loneliness, not its obliteration.

Saroyan's treatment of education mirrors his cultural moment. He reflects contemporary conceptions of the nature and purpose of education. For Saroyan, the schoolhouse is of central importance. Young people must be educated so that they can reject the totalizing demands of perfection and embrace instead the tentative joys that can be found even in loneliness—loneliness being, as in Bradbury, a kind of fortunate fall, the cost one pays for living. *The Human Comedy* is fundamentally concerned with articulating a vision of American society during a time of crisis—that is, during World War II. During the war, schools—those laboratories of childhood—as well as the emerging youth culture became centrally interested in fashioning children and young adults into citizens of a democracy. As Grace Palladino observes in her book *Teenagers*, "high school educators were using their classrooms to 'teach for tolerance.'"[73] Based on Saroyan's narrative, the same can be said of lower levels of education. Though Homer's mother argues that "[s]chools are only to keep children off the streets, but [that] sooner or later they've got to go out into the streets,"[74] Saroyan suggests that this very act of sequestering children serves to better prepare them for the world beyond the school-house doors. Miss Hicks, the schoolteacher, argues to her students that, in the middle of a World War, the study of ancient history is essential in order to develop a broad base of knowledge.[75] She tells Homer that "[i]n a democratic state every man is the equal of every other man up to the point of exception."[76] And this equality, importantly, includes ethnic equality. When Homer disobeys Coach Byfield by running in a school race, the boy's fellow student Joe Terranova defends his friend, prompting the coach to yell that he should "keep [his] dirty little wop mouth shut."[77] The force of this slur prompts Joe to attack the older man, resulting in the principal rushing in to break up the fight.

Here the teacher takes it upon herself to educate both boy and man in civic responsibility. When the principal demands an explanation, Miss Hicks calmly explains that Coach Byfield needs to apologize to Joe. When Joe objects that he doesn't need an apology, Miss Hicks explains that the coach needs "the privilege of once again trying to be an American."[78] The principal agrees, saying that "the only foreigners here are those who forget that this *is* America."[79] Saroyan is arguing that the essence of America is its multicultural nature, something he reinforces later in this same passage when he emphasizes the polynational nature of the schoolchildren. America (in contrast to the homogeneous culture celebrated by the Nazis) is defined by the principle of *e pluribus unum*; out of the many races and creeds, one thing exists, a thing that is loosely and ambiguously defined as "America." For Saroyan, this multiculturalism is not accidental to what it means to be "American" but essential—that is to say, it is not the sort of thing that can be subtracted from America and still leave national identity intact. Rather, an acceptance and even celebration of multiculturalism is the core of the American way of life.

The polyvocal nature of the American experience is central to *The Human Comedy*. This celebration is no mere lip-service. Saroyan is fully aware of the existential tensions facing immigrant persons in the United States, as his account of the Armenian grocer Mr. Ara demonstrates. Mr. Ara is painfully conscious of the fact that he and his family are "probably seven thousand miles from what had for centuries been their home in the world."[80] Saroyan carefully observes the ambiguity of the grocer's position. Though he admits that this detachment from his homeland has made him lonely, Mr. Ara speculates that he would possibly have been just as lonely in Armenia. This observation is important, particularly in a time when blood-and-soil ideology was sweeping Europe. What Mr. Ara and the other inhabitants of Ithaca need is not a homeland but a *home*, a place defined by acceptance and congenial affection. In the face of Nazi aggression, the danger facing the citizens of Ithaca (and, therefore, of America) is that they will lose the home they have so carefully created. If people on the homefront turn against each other, tearing themselves apart along ethnic lines, the essence of America will be lost. To "be American,"[81] the characters must choose to put aside differences and become a unified front. Thus, for Saroyan, the existential and the political are deeply intertwined with each other; most of these characters would be lonely anyway, but the reality of the war emphasizes the need to escape that loneliness in the face of a larger threat.

Saroyan makes clear what other authors of the period—Bradbury, March, and so on—leave implicit: that the process of maturation, the process of becoming lonely, is not only inevitable but can (perhaps) be navigated through education. Bradbury recognizes that this education is essential— why else would Douglas Spaulding write out his experiences?—and March demonstrates, *via negativa*, what the lack of such an education can do. Saroyan, writing in the white heat of World War II, expresses hope that children can be socialized in such a way that they overcome their existential and political alienation and enter into a healthy relationship with the world around them. But this growth requires education and development, which during this period was being increasingly associated with a new domain—the category of "the teenager." This new classification changed what the shift into adulthood looked like. The expectation eventually was that rebellion—not cohesion—is the key goal of young adult life. During the 1950s, many teen-oriented texts, such as the film *Rebel Without a Cause*, suggested that rebellion is a virtue, or at least an inevitability, in itself. Small-town fiction does not take this perspective. As I will demonstrate in the next chapter, rebellion in the literature of the period has a *telos*—it is going somewhere. The question, then, is where this rebellion is ultimately heading.

Three

The Small-Town *Bildungsroman*
The Malt Shop

Perhaps the most striking and ubiquitous symbol of small-town innocence is the malt shop. The 1950s have been associated in popular consciousness with teenage innocence and maturation, a connection solidified in George Lucas' *American Graffiti* (1973) and the TV series *Happy Days* (1974–1984). In the 1970s, these nostalgic invocations of small-town innocence occurred under the shadow of the Cold War and anxieties regarding youth culture. Midcentury small-town fiction anticipates this concern with youth culture. One of the earliest examples of the new model of teenager was Archie Andrews, who first appeared in a 1941 issue of *Pep* comics. There is an idyllic aspect to the world of the Archie Comics. Archie and his two girlfriends Betty and Veronica, together with his sometime-nemesis Reggie and his best friend Jughead Jones, are less characters than they are types commonly associated with young people at midcentury. They also represent an Edenic, prelapsarian existence; nothing bad ever happens in Archie's small town of Riverdale—or, at least, nothing permanently damaging. Archie may pratfall, but his injuries never last for more than one story. The gang's most frequent hangout—outside of their school—is Pop Tate's malt shop. The malt shop is a space in which teenagers can explore their own desires in a safe environment that is unstructured (unlike the school) but public (unlike, say, the back seat of their cars). Over the years, this location came to be identified strongly with small-town teendom.

None of the novels discussed here have a malt shop, but all of them deal—to one extent or another—with teenage characters. The introduction of Archie and his friends coincides with the invention of the idea of the teenager. Grace Palladino describes how the term teenager emerged in 1941. As Palladino observes, "teenagers were tied to the new high school world of dating, driving, music, and enjoyment […] they were a commercial cross between authentic high school students and adult projections."[1] Archie and the gang, designed to appeal to teenagers, nevertheless represent this doubling. Archie is concerned with dating (alternately Betty and Veronica) and often finds himself struggling with recognizably teenage problems. At the same time, his continual youthfulness and unchanging social relationships say more about how adults viewed teenagers. Archie lives in a continual state of innocence. The invention of the teenager as a distinct social set allowed Americans to thematize maturation in a way that had not been done before. In the years of teenage rebellion, young persons were expected to shake off their parents' influence and strike out on their own. The teenage years are, thus, a period of exploration and discovery. That is to say, they are the raw material of *Bildungsromane*.

The *Bildungsroman*, as Franco Moretti notes, arises at a time of tension and uncertainty. Tom Perrin argues that midcentury middlebrow writers used the *Bildungsroman* "to refunction a traditional aesthetic paradigm in order to meet the demands of modernity in their own way."[2] Midcentury small-town narratives dramatize the tension between alienation and a desire to transcend that loneliness. Characters often move from the town to its outskirts—and, ultimately, to the city—in an attempt to escape isolation. Nature, which often bleeds into the small town, calls to characters and seems to offer an opportunity to be more fully human. The first chapter of *Kings Row* includes an account of the Catholic priest Father Donovan visiting the countryside around the town and reading St. Francis. In *Peyton Place*, the protagonist, Allison MacKenzie, has a similar sort of experience. Indeed, both novels open with a description of nature: *Kings Row* with a spring day on which "the vast sky seemed vaster than ever"[3] and *Peyton Place* with a description of a feminized Indian summer, "[r]ipe, hotly passionate, but fickle."[4] These two books follow Columbus' sexualized vision of the world as well as his faith in the Edenic fecundity of America. The small town is set within and itself is a garden of Eden. As such, sex is never far away, and it has both a hopeful and a menacing aspect. For Allison MacKenzie, the pastoral surroundings of the town of Peyton Place offer an escape, a retreat. She visits the hidden groves around the town and is disillusioned when Selena Cross tells her that these locations are used as make-out spots for the young people of the town.[5] In spite of its seeming detachment, nature offers no immediate escape from isolation.

Thus, disillusionment forms the core of the small-town narrative. But this disillusionment does not force characters to accept their isolation. They fight it in a very particular way: they return to the small town and attempt to reconcile with it. Reconciliation is not acceptance. When Allison MacKenzie ultimately returns to Peyton Place and finds it within herself not only to endure the town but to love it, she is not giving up her critique of the town.[6]

Johnny Shawnessy leaves to fight in the Civil War and in the process becomes not only Adam but Christ by "dying" and resurrecting.[7] This death-and-resurrection pushes Shawnessy to continue his life-work of writing an Epic of America, which he anticipates will be published in 1948—not coincidentally the same year that *Raintree County* itself was published.[8] For Shawnessy, the myth of Raintree County is a myth for the future. For Lockridge, the narrative of the past speaks to the present. In both cases—that of Allison MacKenzie and that of John Shawnessy—the return is not about assimilating to the society. It is, rather, about changing the society by bringing to bear tools acquired during their absence from the small town.

The *Bildungsroman* is a genre particularly suited to periods of intense social change. Franco Moretti's influential study *The Way of the World* provides a helpful analysis of the *Bildungsroman* in its classic form. According to Moretti, the *Bildungsroman* arose at a crucial point in European history when, abruptly and seemingly without warning, "Europe plunges into modernity, but without possessing a *culture* of modernity."[9] The *Bildungsroman* exists as a way in which Europeans can think about modernity and the place of the person within modernity. The problem, as Moretti sees it, is how young persons can be integrated into a society. He argues that the *Bildungsroman* "dictates, and re-enacts as we read it, a relationship with the social totality permeated with that 'intimate and sweet well-being,' with that serene and trustful feeling-at-home that Schiller mentioned to Goethe during the composition of *Wilhelm Meister*."[10] Of course, by Moretti's own account, the *Bildungsroman* is a highly changeable form, one whose pure incarnation died "when the new psychology started to dismantle the unified image of the individual."[11] That is to say, the *Bildungsroman* is for Moretti a form which is confined temporally within a limited span of years and geographically within Europe.

The idea of the *Bildungsroman*, however, transcends the limits placed by Moretti. In America, the genre seems to have assumed a particularized form. Ryan Poll suggests that the American *Bildungsroman* differs from the European in that the protagonist escapes society rather than integrates with it. Thus, Huckleberry Finn lights out for the territories and George Willard escapes Winesburg for the big city. The American ideological stance, by Poll's analysis, is one that at least pretends to reject systems of authority. Of course, from a Marxist analysis (or even a simple psychological one) these stories demonstrate how American imagination conceals from itself the grounds of its own ideology. That is to say, it is precisely in the act of pretending not to prize social integration that social integration is set up as the highest priority—a kind of invisible command that must be obeyed precisely because it is invisible. The American *Bildungsroman*, by this reading, allows middlebrow readers to engage in ersatz rebellion while ultimately succumbing to social demands.

The middlebrow *Bildungsroman* accepts the idea of integrating into society, but it also suggests that society needs to change. Typically, critics are dismissive of middlebrow fiction, arguing that it has no independent aesthetics of its own. In contrast, Tom Perrin's book *Middlebrow Aesthetics* argues that the middlebrow was actively involved in creating its own aesthetics in competition with Modernism. Perrin suggests that part of this aesthetic formation was the re-creation of the *Bildungsroman*. Perrin says, "in the United States such novels contributed, with a sophistication that has gone largely unrecognized, to the period's widespread public debate over the meaning and purpose of aesthetic experience."[12] Perrin argues that, though the pressures of postwar uncertainty forced authors to employ more ambiguity in their resolutions, nevertheless "a modified version of the *Bildungsroman* could continue to play its traditional role of enabling the reader, through her enjoyment of its formal orderliness, to adapt herself to the order of the social world."[13] For Perrin, then, middlebrow *Bildungsromane* are tools for critiquing the radical nonconformity implied in Modernist aesthetics.[14] Maturation is associated with the abandonment of Modernist aesthetics, as in *Peyton Place* when Allison leaves New York to assimilate with the town of Peyton Place.[15] Perrin's analysis of Middlebrow Aesthetics is incisive and provides a helpful counterpoint to Ryan Poll; nevertheless, in some senses Perrin oversimplifies the journey of the typical middlebrow *Bildungsroman*. Within midcentury small-town fiction, there is in fact a healthy awareness that the small town represents an oppressive and inescapable presence in the lives of its protagonists. Similarly, the movement Poll identifies—the escape from society—is neither so simple nor so clear-cut as Poll asserts. The society—the culture— that these questing protagonists seek to escape is recognized on all sides to be ultimately inescapable. Thus, midcentury small-town fiction is based on the idea of cycle, of flux, and of recurrence. The protagonist leaves the small town, not to escape culture but to acquire it and, having acquired it, to bring it back to the cultural wasteland that is their small town. In consequence, the return is not (as Perrin asserts) simply a matter of abandoning Modernist aesthetics and joining the social world; it is, rather, a decision to return in order to change the social world.

I do not mean to speak here of "cultural capital" nor of the common critical assertion that middleclass readers were seeking the gains that come with such cultural capital. As Perrin observes, readers of middlebrow novels were more interested in self-improvement than cultural capital.[16] "Culture" here means a collection of tools that allows persons in a society to interact with and understand the grounds of their own humanity. This definition is admittedly not exhaustive and is open to critique on all sides, but it is one which fits the literature produced during the years of World War II and following. Insofar as postwar prosperity gave America a certain amount of overweening pride, it also induced a great deal of anxiety about the place of the individual within the postwar climate. In studies such as *The Lonely Crowd*, postwar America is portrayed as hostile to the individual. This awareness intensifies anxieties that can be traced all the way back to the Revolt from the Village. If Gopher Prairie is a cultural wasteland, the worlds of *Kings Row* and *Peyton Place* are positively malevolent in their hatred of anyone who might be considered different. A key contrast is the way culture is used by the protagonists of these stories. Carol Kennecott, for various reasons, cannot bring culture to Gopher Prairie. The town is too resistant, for one thing; for another, Carol herself is not so cultured as she thinks. In midcentury small-town fiction, while the town is even more hostile, the protagonist tends to be more self-aware and properly embedded in the culture he or she seeks out. Parris Mitchell doesn't *think* he knows music; he *does* know music. Allison *is* a writer. This fact changes everything. For when the protagonist returns to the small town, it is not to become part of the machine; it is, rather, to reform it, to *humanize* it. The work of making small towns more humane is the work of small-town literature.

Young people were particularly influenced by the inhumanity of World War II. As Grace Palladino observes in her book *Teenagers*, "the harsh realities of world war made serious new demands on teenage youth, demands that turned carefree sixteen-year-olds into valuable citizens overnight."[17] Young people threw themselves into the war effort, and in response institutions such as schools were reformulated to make education itself a patriotic act.[18] Just as in *The Human Comedy* the school becomes a laboratory for democracy, so experts in education and childhood development worked to be sure "that the next generation would not be handicapped by the kind of social prejudice that had trapped their parents and given rise to the Nazis."[19] Following the war, "economic prosperity was quickly translated into personal freedom."[20] Now that teenagers had ready money, they presented a new market for business groups, who played on the sense of teenage alienation in order to expand their profits. And as teen identity developed, adult attitudes turned sour and these newly-prosperous teens began to chafe against social conventions.

This development coincides with the rise of the hipster. Hipsterdom is broadly outside the purview of this study, but its concurrent development suggests some of the pressures facing midcentury writers and the teens they create. Norman Mailer, in his essay "The White Negro," argues that the rise of the hipster is tied to the recognition that death is an ever-present reality in the world of twentieth century modernity.[21] The advent of the atomic bomb means that death may come quickly; the advent of the death camps means that state apparatus can reduce humans to mere statistics. The advent of postwar conformity, meanwhile, means that the individual has little recourse within the mechanism of the state apparatus. For Mailer, all of these elements together lead the hipster to seek a life of hedonistic satisfaction. Protagonists of small-town fiction—though they often do engage in innocent hedonism, as in *Raintree County*—do not follow the hipster in this regard, though the world their authors are reacting to is the same. Rather than running from or rejecting this world, small-town *Bildungsromane* typically suggest that it is possible to make the world more humane. These authors believe that it is possible to break out of the eternal cycle, or at least to modify it by making it more humane. The quest for humanity, then, is particularly pressing in the years during and following World War II.

The teenager exists in a paradoxical state of changeless flux. The teen years are years of change and growth, but once that growth has occurred the individual ceases to be a teenager. When the teenager is portrayed in small-town fiction, this paradox becomes doubly acute; for not only is the *teenager* in an eternally changing-unchanging state, but so is the small town (if it changes, it will cease to be what it is). Early representations of teenage life were designed to guide young people to properly assimilate to the adult world. The Andy Hardy films present their young protagonist as "a vital member of a very democratic family."[22] While offscreen reality suggests that teenagers during this period were far from compliant, the cultural artifacts were focused on emphasizing a harmonious development into a contributing member of society.[23] Taken from this point of view, the world of Riverdale in the *Archie* comics exists at a curious midpoint between the narratives of childhood discussed in the previous chapter and the narratives of teenage life discussed here. Archie is changeless, and so is his home town. In his study *Twelve-Cent Archie*, Bart Beaty observes that "each and every story is set in the eternal present."[24] Riverdale is a small town frozen in time, which "could be any place."[25] There is no development. Similarly, Archie is exceptionally static, "a young man to whom things happen."[26] And this is a paradox, since to be a teenager is by definition to be changing; the idea of perpetual teendom is an impossibility, for the teenage years are precisely those times in which children struggle and eventually win the struggle toward becoming men and women who are fit to live in society. This is their journey.

Rebellion and revolution are core concepts in the cluster of symbols that make up the "teenager." These concepts are also central to the small-town narrative, but with a difference; in these accounts, "revolution" means less sudden social change and more something akin to the turning of a wheel. Small-town fiction posits escape and return as necessary both to maturation and to the continued reformation of the community. In this chapter, I will analyze passages from five novels that chart the process of development in the context of the small town. These novels are *Kings Row* and its sequel *Parris Mitchell of Kings Row*, *Peyton Place* and its sequel *Return to Peyton Place*, and *Raintree County*. These novels show a similar pattern: the young protagonist, an outcast in their hometown, leaves that hometown in order to acquire culture and then returns with the power to transform the small town and re-narrativize it in such a way as to make it more human and more humane. The development of the teenager is tied to a cycle, a sort of eternal recurrence or circular motion that will be recognizable to readers of small-town literature. As early as the Revolt from the Village, this theme is present: George Willard must ultimately leave the small town of Winesburg, though he carries Winesburg with him. Similarly, Parris Mitchell must leave Kings Row and return to it in order to bring the fruits of his development back to the small town. Indeed, the novel in which Parris exists is structurally curious because its protagonist is absent from a good portion of the book—in Vienna, studying psychiatry. In *Raintree County*, Shawnessy leaves his hometown during the Civil War, "dies" and then returns to be a kind of poetic Messiah. And in *Peyton Place* and *Return to Peyton Place*, Allison must leave and reenact her mother's affair in order to become her own woman.

These writers see rebellion as a natural response to an inhumane world. If childhood is about coming to terms with death, teenage life is about coming to terms with inhumanity. These novels of development are tied to travel, tied to escape and return—an eternal cycle—and are tied to education in the arts (music, poetry). There is ultimately a quest for the human and for the humane. Here midcentury small-town novels differ from other popular representations of small-town teens. Archie Andrews is barely human; he and his confederates are sexless icons in a small town that perfectly encapsulates the idea of the small town as an ideological construct, unchanging and unchangeable. But Archie is not the only representation of a small-town teen in literature. The *Bildungsromane* of the 1940s and 50s demonstrate a struggle to become humane and to bring that humanity back to an inhuman society. For the small town is inhumane and becomes increasingly so over the course of the decade. Once the teenager is seen as a discrete block—and especially once *Rebel Without a Cause* raises the rebel to the status of celebrity—society is seen as an oppressive force. This force must be resisted in some way. Often, resistance manifests itself as in interest in sex, but sex here is a stand-in for interest in humanity and human experience. What small-town protagonists want—what they need—is culture.

Culture becomes a way of dealing with existential anxieties. It brings together the mental, intellectual demands of philosophy with the sensuous demands of art. Henry Bellamann's *Kings Row* (1940) is particularly concerned with the cultural development of its protagonist, Parris Mitchell. *Kings Row* is a novel about Parris' life from childhood to early adulthood, but it is also a scathing indictment of small-town hypocrisy. Over the course of the novel, Parris discovers sex (first with Renée, the daughter of a groundskeeper, and then with Cassandra Tower, his mentor's daughter) and comes to grips with death—first when his beloved grandmother dies and finally, at the climax, when he euthanizes his best friend Drake McHugh. The novel contains much melodramatic material—Drake loses his legs to a malevolent surgeon, Cassandra is murdered by her father—and Parris stands as witness to all of it. Parris Mitchell combines the intellectual and the sensual. Parris is a psychiatrist (an intellectual) but he is also musical (an artist). Indeed, his earliest traumas are tied to music. In the first book of the novel, Parris befriends Tom Carr and his mentally challenged wife Lucy. Parris often visits them and plays the piano for Lucy. Though the piano is out of tune, Parris plays to please Lucy, who cannot appreciate music rightly played, but who can recognize even the mangled beauties of Bach. Toward the end of this storyline, Lucy Carr attends a parade and, overcome with excitement, falls mortally ill. As Lucy dies, Tom begs Parris to play the out-of-tune piano and Parris obliges:

> The afternoon light faded, and the still spring twilight came on gradually. Still Parris played on and on. He thought Lucy must be falling asleep. He could scarcely hear her. The insane witches' music that came from the piano was beginning to make his head ache. He dropped his chin on his chest and played more softly. The sounds were ghastlier than ever—like the chattering of ghouls and devils.[27]

This scene is unexpected in its darkness, in its wildness. The image of a fourteen-year-old boy playing an untuned piano while a mentally retarded woman dies strikes the imagination more forcefully than anything Bellamann has yet presented in the novel. In its intensity, it is a key scene. *Kings Row* is structured around a series of deaths; each section in the novel ends with a death. These deaths push Parris further along in his *Bildung*. In this case, the death of Lucy Carr is an example of Parris maturing by facing death up-close for the first time. Tellingly, this death is associated with music, which is in Bellamann's cosmology a sign of culture.

For Bellamann, music is a way of accessing emotion, of feeling one's own humanity. Parris' deepest conversations, outside those with the Catholic priest, are with Herr Berdorff, a German minister who teaches him how to play the piano. Bellamann was himself involved in the music world, so this association is hardly surprising. Once, when Berdorff plays "a familiar little folk song," Parris finds himself unexpectedly moved, since "the music suggested and brought back to him so many details of the past five years."[28] Music, as a product of culture, has the power to evoke emotions in a way that few other things in *Kings Row* can. Again, this sensual pleasure is linked to the intellectual, since Parris is also a psychiatrist—what might be thought of as a poet of the human mind. His role once he returns to Kings Row, particularly in the sequel, *Parris Mitchell of Kings Row*, is to be a healer, to be an author, and to be a narrator—that is to say, to restore full humanity to the people around him. The last third of *Kings Row*, indeed, involves Parris returning dignity to his best friend Drake McHugh after Drake has had his legs removed by a malevolent surgeon. As Parris expresses it in a letter to Randy, before he returns to Kings Row, "[Drake's] psychic injuries strike at his pride, his self-respect, his independence and self-reliance. We shall have to save all of these if we are to save Drake."[29] What Parris sees is that Drake must have his own story narrated back to him.

This maturation comes at a heavy price, however, for Parris is doomed to always be an outsider, to be fundamentally alienated. Because Parris Mitchell is raised by his Francophone grandmother, he finds himself at odds with the town around him. When he is introduced, it is through the observation of his teacher, who thinks "[h]e looks foreign."[30] Later, his grandmother observes that "Parris is halfway a foreigner—at least, most people think so"[31] and—small towns being what they are—the fact that most people think so converts the proposition into a reality. Topographically, too, Parris occupies foreign ground. His grandmother's house, where Parris grows up, is a spot of alienness in the town, "of foreign fashion, laid out [on] elaborate grounds, and planted [with] extensive vineyards."[32] A portion of this land is, tellingly, given over to a nursery; Parris grows up in a garden. Within this home, his conversation with his grandmother is a mixture of English and French. His status as an orphan underlines his essential estrangement from the "normal" order of society. The suggestion that he should alleviate his boredom by playing with his friends is met with silence, since "he felt like an outsider when he saw other boys, and he saw that they felt the same way [that he was an outsider]. All except Drake McHugh, who was always the same, and—and Jamie Wakefield."[33] These two friends serve, not to make Parris less lonely, but to emphasize his fundamental estrangement.

To be lonely is not, it is clear from *Kings Row*, the same as being alone. Parris is not entirely friendless; Drake is his best friend, as Bellamann repeatedly points out, but he is the opposite of Parris: an over-sexed, rowdy boy who exemplifies all the masculine qualities Parris seems to lack. Jamie, on the other hand, is different; the dash before his name in the above quote suggests worlds of possible meaning, a hesitation in Parris' affection for the other boy. Parris meditates that "[h]e liked Jamie. Yes; he was sure about that. But why was he always a little embarrassed about it?"[34] He is embarrassed, as it develops, because Jamie is gay. The dash stands to suggest that Parris cannot, for whatever reason, be as close to Jamie as he would perhaps like. The problem for Parris is not that he has no friends, but that these friends are closed off from him in key ways. He cannot interact with Drake on the crass, vulgar level that Drake embodies; nor can he (or *dare* he) interact with Jamie on the sexual and emotional level that *he* demands. The two boys represent unrealized potentials within Parris himself, and navigating those potentials becomes a dominant theme of the novel.

Education does not integrate Parris into the town; it drives him further from it. As part of his education, Parris leaves Kings Row and, after being absent for much of the novel, returns with a doctorate in psychology. Parris returns to Kings Row and attempts to create a positive order around himself, in spite of the fact that the town's death-dealing touches those closest to him. Rather than representing a homecoming, however, Parris' experiences have made Kings Row more alienating than ever before, and this alienation is directly tied to his self-sufficiency, since "[h]e had to travel too often by the uncertain light of his own unsteady self."[35] Here again is the loneliness of Whitman: if the American Adam must be at once creator and created, he is inevitably cut off from himself as well as everyone around him. Parris' colleague Dr. Nolan observes that Parris "had not really made friends. No one knew him very well, and no one made any special effort to know him."[36] Randy, a childhood classmate who marries Drake, is more incisive in her evaluation. She thinks that "Parris was lonelier than he himself knew. You can't live forever with just ideas."[37] But ideas are all Parris has. His childhood lover Renée is taken from him; he is forced to euthanize his grandmother and then watch as his friend and mentor Dr. Tower reveals his own secret shame of incest by killing both his daughter and himself. Left with two friends in the world, he is pulled from Jamie by that young man's own internal struggle and then forced to watch while Drake—crippled as the result of a needless amputation—struggles through despair. Parris is, fundamentally, alone, and so ideas are what keep him going. Having lost Eden, Parris is forced to create an Eden of the mind.

The development in these protagonists is not about (as it is in Moretti) finding a fixed place in society. Nor is it about entirely rejecting the world, as Poll would have it. These characters gain a more complete humanity and then return to the small town in order to transform the inhumane condition of the world. This move is less obviously rebellious than James Dean, but it is revolutionary nonetheless. What sets these narratives of development apart from the developing narrative of the "teen" is a question of *teloi*—of ends. Rebellion in narratives of the 1950s is often undirected. The rebels *Without a Cause* are defined by their lack of an object, as the title itself argues. The marketing of teen rebellion means it cannot be teleological—it cannot be rebellion *for* anything. It can only be a rebellion *against* something—the parents, the school, the authorities, the Man. Moreover, during World War II thousands of young people actually did die for a cause. The resulting distrust of ideology—together with, as Norman Mailer observes, the realization that death could come quickly through the atom bomb, slowly through the mechanisms of the death camp or, most slowly of all, through conformity—leads to a profound anxiety on the part of young people (and anxiety within the portrayals of young people). Rebellion thus becomes a constant movement—and, since this rebellion has no *telos*, but is rebellion for the sake of rebellion, marketers can continually sell product.

Though the protagonists of small-town novels rebel, their rebellion looks distinctly non-rebellious. The small-town novel differs from traditional American youth fiction in its insistence on return. The American protagonist (male) is a perpetual adolescent, is defined by either the rejection of culture or else a cynical adoption of it for other ends (as is the case with Jay Gatsby). Culture is not generally in American literature considered to be The Good. Culture is *a good*, a product, to be rejected or leveraged. However, since the Revolt from the Village, at least, the representation of the small town's relationship with culture is much more fraught. In *Main Street*, Carol Kennicott tries and fails to bring culture to Gopher Prairie. If small towns model America, the insinuation for Lewis and his followers is that America itself is a cultural wasteland. The rebellion of teenage characters in small-town fiction is not directionless rebellion, but a lashing out against cultural vacuity and repression. They are not rebels without a cause but rebels whose cause is to shake off their blinders and become engaged in a search for a culture to give life meaning. Thus, as with the Modernist writers—and as, later, with the Beats—these young protagonists are looking for a way to humanize in the inhumane world of modernity.

And the world of *Kings Row* is inhuman in ways that Parris cannot at first even grasp. Part of his initiation is a recognition of the darkness of the town, and that darkness takes the form of discovering that a mentor is an incestuous rapist. By this time, Parris has already made strides toward finding his place in adult society. His grandmother, having learned that she is soon to die, calls Major Skeffington (her lawyer) and Dr. Gordon (himself, unknown to anyone in the town, a sadistic killer). The grandmother is determined to send Parris abroad to study medicine, but she and the two men decide that first the boy must be mentored so that he is able to progress in his researches in Vienna. Notably, Parris has no say in any of his grandmother's plans. Indeed, Bellamann observes that "Parris was dismayed when he heard that he was to go to Aberdeen College."[38] At Dr. Gordon's suggestion, Parris is apprenticed to Dr. Tower, a widower who lives in solitude with his daughter Cassandra. Dr. Tower represents a paradox for both Parris and his author. On the one hand, the intellectual life of Dr. Tower is seen as a portal into a more humane way of existing. Parris' time at the college is unhappy, but his time with Dr. Tower gives the young man "hours of excitement and revelation."[39] Dr. Tower presents Parris with a role model: a man who is "quietly and intensely alive" in a way that Parris has not seen elsewhere.[40] Because of this quiet liveliness, Parris associates Dr. Tower's speech with poetry.[41] What Parris has discovered—and this in a book written before the language of teenager-dom had become prevalent—is precisely that middle position that defines the reality of teen existence:

> Parris could not sleep that night. He was more deeply excited than he had ever been in his life. For the first time there were intimations of authentic communication between his world—which had been until this very day the world of childhood—and the adult world which had always moved a little mysteriously either to the side or above him.[42]

Put in other terms, terms more proper to the *Bildungsroman*, Parris feels that he is on the cusp of being integrated into adult society.

The society into which Parris is being integrated is evil. Dr. Gordon, who first sends Parris to Dr. Tower, is a malevolent fiend who tortures patients for pleasure. Dr. Tower, meanwhile, is exposed as an incestuous rapist when he kills his own daughter, Cassandra, in a murder-suicide, having learned that Parris has been conducting an affair with her. Dr. Tower thus becomes a figure of dark enlightenment. It is through him and his family that Parris is conducted into the adult world of sex; one stormy night, Parris kisses Cassandra and then she turns out the lamp and pushes him onto the couch.[43] Bellamann's description is one that evokes light and shadow, describing the flashes of lightning by which Parris sees her disrobe and then stand in front of him "slender and white."[44] Eventually, he discovers that Cassandra is a nymphomaniac. She craves sex to an extent that terrifies the boy. But Bellamann insists that she is not simply deranged; her father, Dr. Tower, is largely to blame for her condition—he has been raping her since she was a small girl. Dr. Tower represents a fully intellectual approach to life, divorced from what might be called the spiritual. His incest is the result of overweening pride—he thinks he is beyond morality and so can do whatever he wants.[45] This position is very attractive to Parris, but he ultimately must reject it if he is to become a fully functioning human being. Parris' struggle to integrate his awareness of his mentor's failure is a large part of his decision to leave and become a psychiatrist—he wants to understand the dark recesses of the human mind. And so, just as Cassandra initiates him into the mysteries of adult sex and adult depravity, Dr. Tower ultimately introduces him to the world of humanity. This is, again, a kind of fall.

Education is no proof against barbarity. *Kings Row* is concerned with the thin line between civilization and depravity, and the novel's sequel, *Parris Mitchell of Kings Row* (1948), returns to this anxiety. *Parris Mitchell*, begun by Henry Bellamann before his death as the second volume of a trilogy and finished by his wife Katherine, charts the further adventures of Parris and the surviving characters from the first novel. It is in all respects an inferior production. Parris is largely marginalized in the novel that bears his name, with more interest given to the incestuous pederast Fulmer Green and the tragic Drew Roddy. At one point in the novel a freshman at the local Aberdeen College is severely beaten by a number of upperclassmen. Parris—as a local celebrity and a graduate of the college—is asked to say a few words. His comments betray a deep anxiety about the ability of education to provide moral uplift. He observes that the students at the college "came to be educated—cultured, even—and to advance a step on the road that leads from savagery, through contemporary civilization, to some as yet unguessed but probably beneficent end."[46] However, Parris recognizes that education alone is not enough to lift humans from the position of savages. Particularly in the years following World War II—with the revelations regarding the Nazi death camps and the total collapse of faith in human progress—his comments are telling:

> The college graduate who has had three years of practice in the A.B.C. of the process will be well-prepared to lead a masked mob. *And* he won't mind if the victim is rather bloodied after 40 lashes on the bare back. He won't mind if the victim happens to be a woman. His sensibilities will be heard by a few screams. There is only a difference in *degree*, not in *kind*, in the impulse that moves a mob to a pogrom, or a cracker guard of the chain gang to a brutal nocturnal beating of a helpless convict, and the youthful blood-lusting impulse that sends a sophomore gang down the freshman corridor.[47]

Thus, Parris cautions against believing that education is, in itself, any proof against savagery. Dr. Tower was educated, and yet he raped and murdered his daughter. The students at Aberdeen College are educated, and yet they will beat an innocent freshman without thinking twice about it. The urge to join a group can be stronger than any amount of education; indeed, education (as Parris argues) can be a cloak or covering for brutality. Erich Fromm sees this movement as the condition of modern humanity. There are, he says, two choices for mankind: to "progress to 'positive freedom'" and "to give up his freedom, and to try to overcome his aloneness by eliminating the gap that has arisen between his individual self and the world."[48] In his book *Crowds and Power*, Elias Canetti suggests that the crowd is the only place in which humans can overcome their "fear of being touched."[49] The crowd transcends individuality and it transcends class, as Canetti observes when he says that "[o]nly together can men free themselves from the burdens of distance; and this, precisely, is what happens in a crowd."[50] This unification with others is at once an attractive and a dangerous event. It was particularly so during and following World War II, when war itself seemed to have taken on the aspect of crowd-action.[51] Because war now made its victims *en masse*, individuals paradoxically found themselves more isolated than ever before. Erich Fromm points out that "since [World War II] the possibilities of destruction have increased so tremendously [...] that the threat of war has become a nightmare," leading to a recognition of "individual powerlessness."[52] Total War does not create alienation, but it heightens the anxieties associated with it.

Mobs are, in this context, identified with the threat of fascism. This worry corresponded with the development of what David Riesman refers to as "the other-direction," which he sees as "the dominant mode of insuring conformity."[53] As Nicolaus Mills argues in *The Crowd in American Literature*, crowds are complex and help critics to see "American democracy as a collective process epitomized by men in flux, not merely a body of institutions or a state of mind symbolized by an Adamic figure alone in nature."[54] If the small town is a model of America, then the conditions that give rise to mob violence and fascism must already be latent in America itself. Ryan Poll argues that Shirley Jackson's 1948 story "The Lottery" posits that "the small town should be recognized as a fascist form."[55] The small town is fascist because of the way in which communal belonging supersedes individual freedom:

> [W]hat makes the dominant small town a fascist form is its aesthetics of erasing racialized bodies and cultures, and instead producing and projecting an ethnically homogeneous space, culture, and people. In *The Souls of Black Folk* (1903), W.E.B. Du Bois famously predicted that the twentieth century would be defined by the "color line" [...] this color line manifests itself as the border that frames the dominant small town.[56]

Poll misstates the role of the color line in small-town fiction; rather than framing the small town, the color line (as well as the class-line) cuts through it and undermines all fantasies of communal belonging, a point I will address in the chapter on the outskirts. His argument that the small town is a fascist form is, however, well stated. Poll does not go far enough, however; the fascism of the small town is no dark secret at the heart of the myth—it is an important feature of the myth itself. The community promised by the small town functions in the fiction as both a promise and a threat: the promise that individuals might make genuine contact with each other and the threat that such contact might destroy all traces of individuality. Wartime concerns about fascism are not distinct from postwar worries about conformity; in both cases, the concern is rooted in an awareness of increasing existential loneliness and is manifested in literature about the small town. Such a reading puts postwar concerns on a continuum that stretches all the way back to the prewar regionalists.

When these protagonists seem reconciled to the town around them, the authors generally insert ambiguity. *Peyton Place* (1956), like *Kings Row*, is a *Bildungsroman*, one which is essentially concerned with female sexuality and female development. The novel concerns Allison MacKenzie, a young woman with dreams of being a writer, as she slowly becomes aware of the hypocrisy and malice beneath her community's pleasant façade. Like *Kings Row*, *Peyton Place* stages a number of melodramatic incidents—abortion, incest, and murder chief among them—but its focal-point is the development of the protagonist herself. Allison attains self-actualization both through the process of becoming a writer and by having an affair which replicates her mother's own romantic history. The end-point of this development is a newfound love for Peyton Place:

Oh, I love you, she cried silently. I love every part of you. Your beauty and your cruelty, your kindness and ugliness. But now I know you, and you no longer frighten me. Perhaps you will again, tomorrow or the next day, but right now I love you and I am not afraid of you. Today you are just a place.⁵⁷

By Perrin's account, as mentioned above, this reconciliation is a matter of rejecting Modernist aesthetics. However, this moment also suggests that Allison is fully aware of *both* the "beauty and [...] cruelty" of Peyton Place. Allison's moment of love for Peyton Place is earmarked as potentially fleeting. If she is not afraid of the town now, she might be "tomorrow or the next day." This love Allison expresses might be as fleeting as one of the town's Indian Summers. But the fact that it is fleeting does not matter so much as the fact that it exists; Allison has one moment in which she can embrace the town. This embrace is not willfully blind to the town's faults. Since the reader is intended to understand that her novel will be *Peyton Place* itself, it can hardly be said that she intends to conceal the sins of the community. Rather, she will expose and by exposing end them.

To effect this change, Allison must create herself. Unlike Parris Mitchell, Allison has no mentor; insofar as *Peyton Place* is concerned with gender and gender expectations, each woman is isolated and on her own, forced to discover for herself the proper way of being in the world. Allison's social maturation depends upon her relationships with the various men in her life. In the sequel, *Return to Peyton Place* (1959), Allison begins sleeping with a much older married man, the publisher of her novel. Meanwhile, Allison is involved in the process of creating a persona. She thinks that she has "created herself."⁵⁸ Throughout *Return*, Metalious dramatizes Allison's struggle to define herself against the various men in her life. Her friend David, a less-successful writer, earns a rebuke when he attempts to tell Allison how she should see herself.⁵⁹ Meanwhile, her publicist Paul attempts to create a publishing persona for Allison. This persona plays into midcentury expectations of teenagers. Paul tells her that "the United States has glamorous lady authors, and old lady authors, and housewifely lady authors and school-teacherish lady authors. We do not have a scrubbed, clean-looking, young girl author, and you are going to fill this big gap."⁶⁰ In Paul's account, Allison must seem to be a young, naïve girl who has stumbled upon the wickedness in her world rather than a fully developed woman. The narrative of *Return to Peyton Place* is in some ways an account of Allison resisting male attempts to narrate her life to her.

Allison strikes back against male narration by playing the game more perfectly than could ever be expected of her. She develops as a person and as an author-persona. But what is set up by this struggle is not an eventual reconciliation with Peyton Place. Rather, it is an uneasy double-life, an awareness of the evil of the town while at the same time a recognition that Peyton Place is the only location where Allison feels "safe."⁶¹ Ultimately, however,

Allison must find safety in herself. At the conclusion of the novel, after her lover has died in a car crash, Allison is visited by the actress Rita Moore, the closest thing to a female mentor she has, who advises the girl that "when everything else is gone, friends and lovers and husbands, we have got our work."[62] Finally, Allison must define herself *for* herself and find her meaning in her work as a novelist rather than in romantic relationships or location. The community does not finally define her; she defines it. She creates it. This is the true *Bildung* of *Peyton Place*—the coming-into-being of an author who is not only reconciled to her community but is active in bringing it into being. But to create Peyton Place, Allison must return to it. This is the point at which small-town fiction diverges from accounts of teenage rebellion, for small-town fiction is typically cyclical in its construction. This circle is an essential symbol of small-town existence. The process of growing up is a cycle—these young people exit their small town and then return to it. But the cycle is not to be thought of in a determinative way. These narratives are about breaking the cycle of eternal recurrence—like the cycle of violence of the twentieth century. The cycle of violence plays out in *Peyton Place* and in *Kings Row*: young people are victimized and ultimately become victimizers. These protagonists must break the cycle by way of addition—that is, they must break the cycle by changing the world around them. These protagonists break the cycle of banality through culture. What small-town fiction shows, then, is a distrust of revolutionary violence but an ultimate faith in revolution—in the turning of the wheel and of the earth. What these protagonists encounter is a cycle, a wheel of eternal recurrence which must be broken and escaped in order to achieve something like transcendence. However, the protagonist's journey is itself a cycle: they leave the small town, acquire culture, and return to their home in an effort to make that town more humane. This paradox is baked into the underlying mythology of small-town fiction.

The resolution to this paradox lies within the mythic substructure of the small-town narrative—that is to say, within the Eden myth. *Raintree County* provides a helpful way to understand this paradox. Life and sex are already deeply intertwined—as early as Columbus both are applied to America—and sex and sin are particularly connected in American literature (see, for instance, *The Scarlet Letter*). For Lockridge, the search for the Raintree becomes a recurrent theme throughout the novel. The tree's location, hidden in the dank recesses of a swamp, suggests its primal centrality to human existence. At one point, young Johnny Shawnessy goes out into the swamp, following the river (the river is, for Lockridge, another primal symbol, perhaps evoking the four rivers flowing out of Eden). The boat Johnny is rowing sinks and he is forced to head to the shore, while around him "the solid substance of the earth dissolved with life. The creatures of the river swarmed, shrieked, swam, coupled, seeded, bloomed, died, stank around him. He appeared to be in the very source of life, a womblike center."[63] As with other sections of *Raintree County*, Lockridge is hardly subtle about his intentions here. The lake from which all rivers run is called Paradise Lake, and it is on the banks of this lake that Johnny will eventually meet his second wife.[64] Swamps are primordial, fetid places where life exists at its most vegetable and reptilian.

Johnny is initiated into the primal truths of existence. In entering the swamp, Johnny enters the mystery of life itself, and in that encounter he is overcome by the sexuality of everything around him, as Lockridge makes clear when he describes the boy as "half naked, an intruder, his body scratched and itchy, his shirt torn by branches, his pants ripped half off, his hair stiff with seed."[65] The sexual imagery here is blatant. Nature takes on both the traditional female role—associated with water, life, and birth—and the male role. Johnny, in turn, is feminized and receives nature's ejaculatory seed. He is manhandled by Nature. Johnny wants to discover the mysteries of Raintree County, but he can only do so by becoming a sexualized object of the county. At last, he falls into a deep pool (a feminine symbol) where "[a] thick net of roots and lily stems laced his body" and he is nearly dragged to his death.[66] Lockridge combines male and female here, the feminine pond with the phallic roots. This moment is one in which Johnny realizes his own smallness in the face of inscrutable nature. His near-death has a transformative effect; when he emerges from the swamp, Johnny meets Nell, the young woman with whom he is in love, with his rival Garwood Jones. Garwood greets the boy with the exclamation "It's Johnny Appleseed!"[67] The name ties Johnny to the original Raintree planted by an itinerant preacher back in the early days of the county. Garwood is mocking him, but he speaks more truth than he knows. Johnny has symbolically become Adam, the bearer of a new world.

The incident in the swamp shapes Johnny's interactions with nature and therefore with the town-as-garden metaphor outlined above. Johnny encounters his second wife Esther (after having taught her in school) when she becomes a teacher herself and, as part of the Raintree County Teachers Institute, goes on a retreat to Paradise Lake. Esther's full name is Esther Root, evoking the willow root that Johnny used to pull himself out of the swamp.[68] Over the course of this retreat, Esther and Johnny become close and he talks to her about the history of Raintree County and its identity with the earth (and with America itself), using words which are "graven upon her memory with a stylus of flame."[69] One day, looking for Johnny, Esther wanders into the swamp. Her reflections reinforce the Edenic nature of Raintree County, beginning with an incantatory "Come, o, come to Raintree County" and speculating that in this county "grew perhaps the Tree that flowered above the garden in ancient days." This "little transplant from the Asian homeland and heartland of the race" is the "biblical tree" of life.[70] The language here is, as is typical for Lockridge, high-flown and incantatory. The words are a religious/

prophetic call designed to evoke from the reader a sense of the wonder of the land. The invocation of the Edenic Tree of Life is important, since what follows in the novel itself is an induction into knowledge. The two trees in the Garden of Eden—the Tree of Life and the Tree of the Knowledge of Good and Evil—are conflated. Esther very quickly gets lost, in a parallel to Johnny's earlier experiences in the swamp. She feels threatened by the fecundity of the area around her, which shows "endless variety of forms, each form endlessly and savagely repeated."[71] At last, she encounters "the snake, a long lewd fellow."[72] The snake evokes the serpent who tempted Eve in the Garden of Eden. The words "long" and "lewd" combine to give the impression of sexuality; the snake is a phallus planted deep in the heart of the primal mystery and it is part of that primal mystery. Just after encountering the snake, feeling herself finally and totally lost, Esther meets Johnny Shawnessy. Johnny is represented as both being part of this dank, fecund world of the swamp and also a deliverer from it.

The mystery of Eden, the mystery of the maternal body, the mystery of sex—for Lockridge these are tied together. The story Johnny relates to Esther is that of his own initiation, and the language he uses is (again) profoundly and complexly sexual. While he is talking with Esther, Johnny tells her the story of a boy who "swam over here eighteen years ago and found his way into this region and never came out again."[73] During this adventure, the boy sees a mysterious tree; Johnny says that "[o]nly later did he realize that he had seen the Raintree. It was then a slender tree with a rooty base and it dropped its pollen on the boy's naked arms and shoulders and into his ear, for that with the season of its blooming."[74] As in the earlier account, the boy in Johnny's recollection is made into a sexual object by the world around him. Feminine nature feminizes him. Or, more properly, Nature is at once male and female. Certainly, the Raintree is recognizably phallic: slender, with a rooty base, dropping pollen on the boy. He is being impregnated by nature itself (nature itself impregnates itself, being perfectly self-sufficient, like God in the works of some theologians). And this impregnation is what catapults Johnny to a knowledge of the world. Sex is both a kind of fall (a fall into knowledge) and a redemption from the condition of aloneness and estrangement that characterizes the human being.

Again, though, a true return to Edenic innocence is fundamentally impossible. After Johnny tells Esther the story of the boy who lost himself trying to find the Raintree, Esther asks whether the two of them shouldn't go looking for it. Johnny refuses. He says that the physical existence of the tree is less important than what it means. For Shawnessy, "the tree is not the secret, but is itself, like the letters chipped on the stones [around its base], part of the secret only."[75] To see the thing as it exists in reality is to lose it, and in losing it to confirm that it has already been lost. At the same time, the existence of the Raintree as an ideal permits Johnny to extend that ideal to all of nature; like Eden, the sacred is only present by its absence. Eden represents, thus, a symbol of potential—of the possibility of growth and renewal—as well as a tragic sense of fallenness. Eden is always absent. Shawnessy insists that "America [...] is still waiting to be discovered" and when he describes the America awaiting such discovery he lapses into pastoral language.[76] For Shawnessy, "America is an innocent myth that makes us glad and hopeful each time we read it in the book of our own life."[77] Ellery Queen's feeling of having discovered America in the first chapter of *Calamity Town*—and even his explicit comparison of himself to Columbus—aligns itself with Lockridge's identification of the small town as an Edenic space. The difference lies in the nature of the protagonists: Ellery is a city-dweller seeking solace in the small town, while Shawnessy is a spiritually-isolated citizen of the town. In *Raintree County*, in spite of the broader historical claims made by the various characters, the pastoral imagery is resolutely personal. Shawnessy views America as part of his own personal *Bildungsroman*, as a collection of symbols and mythic resonances that make up his life.

In *Raintree County*, Lockridge associates sex with fecundity and with humanity. One early poetic effort by young Johnny is a sonnet for his childhood sweetheart Nell after he sees her swimming naked in the Shawmucky River. When his instructor, Professor Stiles, sees the poem, he wonders, "[s]hall the Shawmucky be another Avon?"[78] Poetry becomes a way of transfiguring the quotidian world of rural America. For Johnny, this transubstantiation is a matter of creating "a new myth, the American myth [...] the story of the hero who regains Paradise."[79] Johnny argues that America is a poetic act of incarnation:

> The early Americans [...] were poets of the open road. They rediscovered the earth. They uncoiled the Mississippi, they unrolled the Great Plains, they upheaved the Rocky Mountains. They brought the miracle of names to an earth that was nameless, even as Adam did when God bade him name the earth and its inhabitants.[80]

The true poem is *enfleshed*, as "the Perfessor" observes. Accordingly, it cannot be found in books (not even in *Raintree County*). Johnny's great poem is his own life.[81] Similarly, as becomes clear later, Lockridge fully believes Whitman's assertion that "[t]he United States themselves are essentially the greatest poem."[82] The true poem of America is America itself, and this recognition drives the climax of the novel.

The cycle of escape-and-return is, thus, boiled down to its mythological essence in *Raintree County*. John Shawnessy is the Adam of Raintree County, but he is also the New Adam—the Christ—incarnating all the mythic substructure of the novel. Lockridge makes this association explicit during the section of the novel dealing with the Civil War. Shawnessy goes to fight and is reported dead. Of course, Johnny himself is unaware of his own "death";

he finds out after the fact, when a man shows him a clipping recounting the event and tells him that "[t]hey had quite a service for you, and everybody's got used to the idea now of you being a *dead* hero."[83] Shawnessy is even memorialized with an empty grave in the graveyard at Danwebster.[84] The death and return of Johnny Shawnessy position him as a Christlike figure who is thus enabled to incarnate America itself:

> America is a memory of a boy who was dead and then came home anyway, hunting for an old court house and a home place in the County. America is the memory of millions of young men who came home and never came home and never could come home. America is the land where no one who goes away for a year can come back home again. America is the land where the telegraph keys are clicking all the time and the trains are changing in the stations. America is the image of human change where the change is changed by experts.[85]

Behind this description are any number of dying-god myths, tales in which the deity suffers a mortal wound and recovers from it, bringing his people through the darkness of winter into the fullness of spring. Johnny is Christ, but he is also Osiris. And, like these dying gods, his purpose is to return from death with something new. Though he returns, the old Shawnessy is "really dead (though it took his successor a little while to become aware of that fact)."[86] Johnny thus stands between the old America killed by the Civil War and the new one represented by Garwood Jones.

As such, it is after his return that Shawnessy begins to formulate his new religion. Johnny is positioned within the narrative not only as an American Adam but as a kind of prophet. He expects to publish the epic of America on which he is working in 1948—not coincidentally the year in which *Raintree County* itself was released.[87] Shawnessy's identity as a poet defines his relationship with Raintree County. The purpose of this poetry is redemption. The redeemed Paradise is not primal but accretive—by bringing into itself all the myths in all the legends of all periods of time that ever existed, it creates a new Paradise on earth. This is for Shawnessy the very heart of poetry—the metaphoric urge.[88] In this sense, all the overwrought prose of Lockridge's novel is an attempt—a strained attempt, and one that is never totally successful—to replicate the cyclical pattern of American history as it barreled through the early twentieth century and into the era of global imperialism.

The malt shop is the domain of the teenager, and it accordingly gives a window into the ways in which teens and young adults were portrayed at the time. None of the novels discussed here feature such a concrete setting, but all of them dramatize the ways in which teenagers were expected to move from childhood into adulthood. The teens in midcentury small-town fiction are in many ways the opposite of that prototypical small-town teen, Archie Andrews. Archie never changes because he is (paradoxically) eternally a teenager. His pratfalls never bruise, never scar. He is the nationally imagined small-town teen. But his innocence, as midcentury small-town writers show, is phantasmic. These authors offer a countervailing version of growing-to-adulthood, of *Bildung*, as one of leaving childhood innocence, of leaving the small town entirely, in order to acquire tools of culture. These tools allow characters to return at last to their place of origin and begin working anew, attempting to cultivate the dilapidating small-town garden and return it to a shadow of its Edenic state. These authors focus on restoring Eden rather than simply escaping to it.

That the small town is a garden ties it both backward to the Garden of Eden and forward to a redemptive millennium. The tradition of utopian communes reaches back through the nineteenth century, through experiments such as Brook Farm and its fictional counterpart Blithedale, all the way to the Puritan settlements and Winthrop's dream of a city on a hill. These small communes were designed to serve a redemptive purpose in the world, and this vision carries over into portrayals of small towns. It is toward this sort of redemptive millenarian vision that the protagonists of small-town *Bildungsromane* move. They leave the town to acquire culture and, having acquired it, they return in order to make their inhuman society humane. It is, perhaps, a fool's errand. It is certainly an idealistic, or even Romantic one. For the essential nature of both the Garden of Eden and the millennial kingdom is that both are *absent*. In either case, the idealization of the small town invariably locates the actual goodness of it in the past or in the future. The condition of Eden only exists once it has been lost, once it no longer exists. Its presence is an absence; to be prelapsarian necessitates a lapse. Similarly, a millennial kingdom is by definition a kingdom that does not yet exist. When writers present the small town as a world inevitably destroyed, sunken in time, they are not offering comforting fictions. Tales of small towns are ironic laments. And yet, with this double-pull—toward the past Garden and the future one—authors of this period evoke from this fallen space an element of hope.

FOUR

No Town Is an Island
Main Street and the Town Square

Throughout the 1940s and '50s, small towns are seen as places in which circular movement binds residents to their place. Inhabitants of the small town live, that is, within an eternal moment which is, nevertheless, *not* eternal but bound fundamentally to historical-material circumstances. Circles are important. A circle by its nature must revolve back onto itself; a circle is fundamentally non-teleological. It is entirely self-sustaining and self-consistent. Thus, the circle is a central image in the American mythology of the small town. Ryan Poll refers to Franco Moretti's scholarship as a way of explaining the American small town in literature. Poll's thesis is that the American small town is ideologically conceived of as an autonomous island, cut off from the rest of the world. Moretti argues that the island is seen as having its boundaries broken down in the process of modernization—the ongoing march of capitalism inevitably forces island communities to open up to the rest the world.[1] Poll suggests that the action of the American small town is precisely the opposite, that "whereas a capitalist modernity renders European villages obsolete, the dominant American village thrives."[2] For Poll, the small town is thought of as self-enfolding and this ideology carries over into American understandings of national politics. In spite of Poll's observations, however, small towns are not cut off from "capitalist modernity," even in an ideological or symbolic sense. Instead, they are deeply implicated in the workings of both the field of commerce and the field of war. The symbolic manifestation of this linkage is the town square. Thomas Wolfe's "The Lost Boy"[3] shows the young, doomed boy perceiving "the union of Forever and of Now" in the town square.[4] The square becomes the center of the vast wheel of time, "the earth's pivot, the granite core of changelessness, the eternal place where all things came and passed, and yet abode forever and would never change."[5] In a story centrally concerned with loss and loneliness, the town square becomes alienating precisely because of its timelessness; the connections to the past and to the outside world reinforce the existential loneliness that is, for Wolfe and other authors of the small town, a fundamental component of human existence. No town is an island community. But that fact does not make the town less lonely.

Wolfe's image of the town square as the hub of a wheel casts light on a curious Queenian observation about the square in Wrightsville, repeated throughout *Calamity Town* as a sort of joke. After looking at the statue of Founder Wright, Ellery "circumnavigated the Square (which was round)."[6] The mention of circumnavigation continues the Columbian imagery initiated in the first paragraph of the novel. Ellery may think that Wrightsville is an autonomous island, cut off from the rest of the world, but it is manifestly not, either in the future (with the oncoming storm of World War II) or in the past. Just as Poll remarks that "[Sherwood] Anderson goes to great lengths to make clear that the titular small town was never a pastoral, and hence never a circular imaginary"[7] so Queen and other midcentury small-town authors explode the myth that the small town was ever anything but complicit in the workings of capitalism. Anderson's observation does not stand in contrast to the dominant (literary) myth of the small town; it is an essential part of that fabulation.

The square's circularity extends beyond the one-line joke in the first chapter of *Calamity Town*; it indicates both the motion of the plot (with old sins returning) and the symbolic framework of the novel. *Calamity Town* is based on a circular pattern: the wheel of time, the wheel of fortune, the cycle of the year. Circularity is also central to *Calamity Town* from an ideological perspective, and that ideological perspective is not simply one maintaining the bourgeois *status quo*. The cycle within *Calamity Town* is not the same as the one identified by Poll in *Our Town* (1938), wherein "the history that unfolds [...] seems to be a cyclical, unchanging pattern that is socially reproduced from generation to generation."[8] What sets *Calamity Town* apart is the fact that Ellery self-consciously acknowledges the fundamental malice of the small town when he says that "[t]here are no secrets or delicacies, and there is much cruelty, in the Wrightsvilles of the world."[9] The fact that the circle revolves again, that the *status quo* is propped up (on the basis of a lie of omission—keeping secret the true story of the Wright murder), fundamentally undercuts the rosy picture of the town presented in the opening paragraphs of the novel.

This understanding of the circularity of small-town life helps to clarify treatments of the small town's most famous icon: Main Street. This central avenue, still used today to indicate small-town, all–American thriftiness and neighborliness in the context of business (kind capitalism, nice capitalism), is a recurring symbol in midcentury small-town fiction. The introductory dream in *Raintree County*, while not featuring a location literally named Main

Street, nevertheless describes the main street of the town as a bustling location. The protagonist, John Wickliff Shawnessy, moves through a "crowd that poured from three directions into the south arm of the cross formed by the County and National roads."[10] Similarly, in *Intruder in the Dust* Faulkner envisions the town as at its busiest on weekends, "when all the other Negroes and most of the whites too from the country came in."[11] In Robert Bloch's *Psycho* (1959), similar imagery applies.[12] Weekends are a time for commerce of a particularly democratic sort: everyone, both outcast and insider, converges on the small town. The divisions between people appear to be shallower. However, as I will show in this chapter, this seeming community carries with it its own loneliness, its own alienation, precisely because commerce and leisure have become deeply intertwined, to the extent that they are the same. The imagined small town seems to already illustrate Marcuse's observation in *One-Dimensional Man* that "leisure" is transformed under industrial capitalism into "free time."[13] Capitalism is, thus, central to the small town's identity, though here (at least) it seems to be presented in a relatively benign way. However, as this chapter will demonstrate, the appearance of gentle capitalism is a façade (like so much else in the town). The actual mechanics of that capitalism remain the same: exploitation and disregard for workers.

The small town is not an island space—it is in fact continuous with national trends, and the authors of small-town fiction are aware of this connection. Poll says the small town is an island in that it is ideologically cut off from capital and from history. I am arguing the opposite. This chapter will examine two locations: Main Street and the town square. One is the continuation of the other. Main Street is the center of economic life, and so I will discuss the ways in which economic exploitation works in the small town: workers are alienated by the mechanics of capitalism. My analysis here complicates most critical evaluations of post–Revolt writing on small-town fiction, which hold that the small town is presented as pure and non-capitalist (or, at least, holding to a kind of gentle capitalism). Ryan Poll, for instance, argues that "the small town is imagined as a microcosm of the nation, and therefore the United States becomes allegorically cast as innocent in relation to capitalism's development."[14] Poll's formulation does not hold up when close attention is brought to bear on small-town fiction itself. Small-town fiction does not present the small town as a location of "soft" capitalism, and it certainly does not work to absolve the United States of capitalism's depredations. Quite the contrary; the alienation of labor is an essential part of the small-town mythos, a part of the cycle in which its characters are trapped. In his 1937 introduction to *Main Street*, Sinclair Lewis says that "the ghetto-like confinement of small towns could be [...] a respectable form of hell."[15] From Lewis and his fellow Revolt writers through the 1950s, the overriding view of the small town is that it is hell, and the marketplace of Main Street is a central aspect of that inferno. I will focus on one primary example: Toshio Mori's *Yokohama, California*. Mori is particularly useful because, insofar as his treatment of commerce is discussed at all, he is often taken to be advocating communal ties over the demands of the marketplace. That is, in his own way, he would seem to be complicit in the argument that America—as typified in the small town—is innocent of capitalism. I will show that, in fact, Mori sees capitalism as deeply imbedded in the community, inseparable from it. The workings of the marketplace alienate Mori's characters, cutting them off from each other and from themselves.

Thus, the small town is not a means of escaping from the world but a means of reflecting upon it. The town square is a continuation of Main Street, but its primary focus is temporal or historical rather than economic. *Calamity Town* moves my discussion to the town square. I will demonstrate that, while Queen seems to follow some of the tropes outlined by Poll, Wrightsville is not some sort of island separate from the rest of the world. The square is a transtemporal space that ties the small town backwards in time and outwards to the world around it with bands of blood and business. The Revolt from the Village did not (as Anthony Channell Hilfer and others suggest) die away in the 1930s. Rather, it continued into the '40s and '50s. Revolt writers lambasted the small town for its closed-mindedness. Their targets were not, however, simply small towns; these communities were closely identified with America as a whole. Sinclair Lewis' novel *Main Street* opens with a prologue claiming that the small town should be read as a type of the nation; the setting is "'Gopher Prairie, Minnesota.' But its Main Street is the continuation of Main Streets everywhere."[16] Thus, writers recognized that the small town functioned in such a way that what could be said of it could be extended to the nation as a whole. By and large, the Revolt writers were merciless toward small towns, though Lewis argued that he was equally unforgiving of big cities.[17] This mercilessness was part of a larger critique of American culture. If H.L. Mencken would later claim that the American South was a cultural wasteland, Lewis was already making the argument that America itself was precisely such a desert.

The central identity of the small town is not found in community but in alienation. The financial dynamics of small-town literature prove as much. Poll and others claim that the ideology of the small town is masked by its emphasis on neighborliness over commerce, of the local over the national or global. Many critics see the small-town narrative developing away from the early critique exemplified by Lewis and his contemporaries. According to this view, the 1930s saw artistic representations of the small-town environment taking a turn toward the positive, with representations of Main Street following suit. The Great Depression takes a large measure of responsibility for this shift. As Miles Orvell observes, "Main Street came to occupy a mythic plane in American culture."[18] According to Orvell's analysis, this move was not simply a matter of elevating small towns—it was a self-conscious attempt on the part of large corporations to give themselves a human face at a time when business was particularly unpopular. Main Street is important for this process, since "the peculiar nature of Main Street was that it was a place for private enterprise that was also a public space."[19] Orvell charts the development of this mythic space through the 1960s, where, in the *Twilight Zone* episode "A Stop at Willoughby," a salesman dreams of escaping from his high-pressure job to a nineteenth century town. The small town, thus, comes to be seen as a place of escape from the encroachment of capitalism, particularly the impersonal capitalism seen in big-city life. Ryan Poll argues that the isolation of small-town economic life from national capitalism is a central part of its mythology. The small town is historically conceived of as a world outside of the concerns of the market, while the city is framed as "a capitalist space of sin."[20] In fact, Poll argues, the small town could not exist without capitalistic forces, though these forces are disguised as "a benevolent form of capitalism" in representations such as *It's a Wonderful Life*.[21] In what follows, I will argue that this disguise—if such it is—remains paper-thin even in the gentlest iterations of the small-town myth.

In fact, small-town fiction of the period is quite cynical about the economic life of the small town. Often, the literature presents a deeply ambiguous portrait of small town capitalism. Nowhere is this more evident than in Toshio Mori's *Yokohama, California*. Mori's collection—originally intended to be published immediately before America entered World War II—presents a vision of America that is unique in the literature of the period. Its title self-evidently refers to *Winesburg, Ohio* and, like that book, Mori's work is a collection of vignettes and visions rather than short stories—daily events in the life of small-town Japanese-Americans. Mori stands apart from Anderson, however, in two key ways. First, Mori's Yokohama seems less oppressive than Anderson's Winesburg (at least, on the surface). Lawson Fusao Inada, in his 1985 introduction to the collection, argues that—as opposed to the radical isolation of Anderson's characters—the people in Mori's book are united by a "community [which] will continue to survive, intact."[22] It could, thus, be argued that Mori follows other authors of small town fiction after the 1930s in valorizing small communities in contrast to big cities (with the added twist that he is valorizing communities made up of racial minorities). As I will demonstrate, such a reading of Mori ignores the ways in which the marketplace isolates his many characters; for now, however, I will leave Inada's proposition as it stands.

The second distinguishing feature, alluded to above, is that Mori's community is entirely made up of Japanese-Americans. The importance of this focus on minority experience cannot be overstated, and has indeed generally been observed by critics dealing with *Yokohama*. Malve von Hassell treats the book as an anthropological study of the Japanese-American community during the time period. The decision to make this small town—modeled on a typical American small town—into a community of first-, second-, and third-generation Japanese-Americans would have been a curiosity before the war; following the war (when the book was actually published) such a move becomes positively revolutionary. Where Anderson's *Winesburg, Ohio* is thought of as a typical American community and is made up largely of people of European decent, Mori presents his reader with *Yokohama, California*, a place whose very *name* locates it as foreign to European ears. The fact that his title rhymes thematically with Anderson's is an argument. For what Mori is saying here is that his small town is no less typically American than a small town made up of Polish, German, or English immigrants. Japanese-Americans, by Mori's implicit claim, are typical of the nation as a whole. In what follows I will treat Mori's work as an expression of universal experiences, in addition to being a representation of the lived experiences of minority persons during the period. That is, I take at its full strength Mori's implicit assertion that Yokohama—like Winesburg, like Gopher Prairie—*is* America.

Mori also adopts Anderson's distrust of the claims of any community to care for its own. This is as it should be; if Mori is situated in a tradition stretching back to the Revolt from the Village, then it should be expected that his portrayal of small-town life should be deeply ambiguous. However, critics do not always recognize Mori's quiet cynicism, as is demonstrated by Inada above. In fact, Mori's characters are just as lonely as any others in small-town fiction. Margaret Bedrosian observes that the inhabitants of Yokohama "are often ruled by a daimon that takes over their lives and makes them express dormant, deep-rooted desires, even at the cost of alienating the community or losing their security."[23] That is, they are ruled by a fixed idea, just as Anderson's grotesques are. The difference is, as David Mayer observes, that Mori's characters are warped by the unspoken specter of racial injustice.[24] However, this loneliness is no less existential than that of Anderson's characters.[25] To divide existential isolation from its political environment is to present a half-realized diagnosis. For Anderson, the inhabitants of Winesburg are made grotesque by the pressures of conformity. For Mori—much of the time, though not always—the citizens of Yokohama are warped by the pressures of racism. The theme of racial oppression is certainly present in Mori's work, and I will discuss it in a later chapter. The racist atmosphere of America enforces loneliness within Mori's characters. Racism is not the only force at work, however; Mori's townsfolk are also warped by the pressures of commerce.

Mori complicates the idea that small towns are envisioned as isolated from the larger capitalist society. Though he is most often discussed vis-à-vis his importance to the foundation of an Asian-American literary canon, and so with an eye toward his themes of race and community, Mori is possibly the most economically concerned writer under consideration in this book. Janice Tanemura recognizes as much when she says that "Mori's interest in middle-ness is the cultural expression of the Japanese economic position as middlemen within a capitalist system that needs intermediaries to deflate the increasingly antagonistic relation between large capitalist corporations and the individual laborer."[26] For Tanemura, Mori is engaged in combating this middle-ness by emphasizing the quotidian.[27] Tanemura reads Mori from a perspective centered on the material-concrete experiences of Japanese-American citizens. If Tanemura is interested in how particular the world of Yokohama is, I am focusing here on the ways in which Mori aligns with other texts—that is, on the extent to which his work is universal in the midst of its particularity. My reading is, thus, not intended to replace or contest but to complement Tanemura.

Mori is possessed of a mild but subversive sense of humor, and this humor sometimes leads critics astray. Inada seems to read Mori as if he is saying precisely the opposite of what he is saying. In "My Mother Stands on Her Head," Mori presents a conflict between communal ties and convenience. In this story, a street vendor is regularly (intentionally or unintentionally) cheating his customers. The reaction of the family at the center of the story is significant; the father recommends that they abandon the street vendor and "buy at the Safeway and save."[28] In this line, Mori demonstrates two factors in the community of Yokohama: first, that the encroachment of department stores has begun driving out smaller businesses (that is, he illustrates the way in which the small town is changing in the face of modernity); and, second, that this encroachment has changed the very language of the residents of Yokohama. "Buy at the Safeway and save" sounds as much like an advertising slogan as it does natural dialogue; it speaks of the ways in which commercial language has entered the daily life of these Japanese-American families. The mother's response—that she has been buying from the peddler for twenty years and so owes him a debt of loyalty—illustrates, then, a tension between modernity (exemplified in the father) and tradition (the mother). Inada's argument, quoted above, is that Mori is praising the authentic community of Yokohama over the arid modernity of the Safeway. For Inada, "thanks to the efforts of both the mother and Ishimoto-san (the street vendor), and the unspoken understanding of the family, the community will continue to survive, intact."[29] Similarly, Malve von Hassell praises the story, saying that it demonstrates that "[t]he sense of community expressed in tolerance toward one another's transgressions [which] overrides individual decisions based on rational recognition of fact."[30] The implication with both critics is that personal ties override the convenience offered by mass retail.

In fact, Mori is subtly mocking the idea that the division between capital and community exists at all. The street vendor is by no means an innocent; the father points out that the peddler "buys his stuff [at the Oakland Free Market] and brings it out here and sells it at profit."[31] That is, he replicates precisely the mechanics of capitalism exemplified by the Safeway, albeit on a smaller scale. The mother's dilemma is not between modern capitalism and traditional communal ties; it is between competing forms of capitalism—the one that appeals to the bottom-line interests of consumers ("Buy at the Safeway and save") and the one that appeals to perceived loyalty between neighbors. Read in this light, the climax to the story is more ironic than critics such as Inada or Hassell admit. Here is the actual scene in question:

> On his next round we watched Ishimoto-san from the house while Mother went out to meet him with the bill. We watched him add several times. Finally he scratched his head. He burst out, "Ho-ho-ho-ho-ho." His sweat-stained derby went up and down with vibration.
> When Mother came in the house she had with her two bean cakes and a big head of cabbage.
> Did you buy those, Mama?" Father demanded.
> "No. He gave these to me," she said somewhat sadly.[32]

This conclusion suggests that Mother's sadness is directly related to the fact that she knows that she is in an impossible situation. Mori relates that the family held out for some time against Ishimoto-san before finally falling back into "the old habit" of buying from the street vendor. And this "old habit" includes—implicitly—the habit of allowing him to periodically cheat them. Community has been maintained, it is true, but the street vendor is the winner here, having defused the situation through his (wholly inadequate) gift of a cabbage and a couple of bean cakes. The choice here is not community or commerce; it is which kind of exploitation the characters would rather live with. Mori is not praising communal ties; he is exposing them. These claims of community are just as predatory as the Safeway, though they use different means of coercion and play on different emotions.

Throughout *Yokohama, California*, whenever a character enters the marketplace he is exploited. This exploitation occurs whether the ties are inorganic—Safeway, Wall Street—or organic—the street vendor, the local flower nurseries. The story "The Finance Over at Doi's" shows a man (Satoru Doi) who is helplessly caught in a game of trying to speculate on the stock market. The narrator visits him often and finds him with copies of various newspapers, including the *Wall Street Journal*. At first, Satoru Doi's investments are purely theoretical. He does not put any money behind his speculations. He excitedly tells the narrator, for instance, that "I would have cleaned up $314,786 if I had played with real money."[33] He shows the narrator that he has been engaging in such speculation since 1933 (the main action of the story takes place in 1937), and that—had he invested actual money—he would now be $300,000 richer.³⁴ For theoretical investments, the investor sees a theoretical return. Doi becomes so obsessed with speculating that he finally saves to buy a single stock.³⁵ However, the stock he buys—in Consolidated Textiles—fails dramatically. Meanwhile, the stocks Doi *didn't* buy (but marked in red as if he *had*) continue to make him theoretical fortunes.³⁶ This irony would have been particularly acute at the tail end of the Great Depression, when Mori was writing his stories. Wall Street mocks its investors, offering phantoms and delivering only dust and despair.

The stock market becomes a repository for desires and hopes that can never be realized. The narrator sees that Doi is doomed and "wondered then and there if there would be anything like a change in his little world or in Satoru Doi which would reconstruct his life of pathetic hope and miserable failures, help him to regain some kind of respect for himself and the dignity that is deserving to the living."³⁷ In seeking fortune, Doi has lost dignity. There are intersecting themes in this passage: first, the stock market—the mechanism of modern capitalism—has crushed Doi. Like the Safeway, Wall Street represents a detached form of commerce that promises high rewards while robbing its victims. The second theme, however, serves to counterbalance this economic critique: Doi is, like the characters in Anderson's *Winesburg*, a grotesque—a man obsessed with a single idea to the point that he is incapable of functioning outside that idea's orbit. He cannot function properly in his community because of his *idée fixe*; nor can he attain his obsessive dreams. By bringing these two themes together, Mori continues the argument made back in *Main Street*: that the small community is typical of America itself. Writing in the midst of the Depression, Mori argues that the very mechanics of capitalism have reduced Americans to lonely, twisted figures. But, tellingly, he does not offer here some sort of fantastic escape into a Great Good Place—there is no indication that Yokohama can do any better by Doi. Yokohama *is* America, and it is no less implicated in the economic injustice of the nation as a whole.

The contrast between community and commerce proposed by Inada is illusory. The organic economic life of the town itself is, if anything, *more* exploitative than the Wall Street speculation that overthrows Doi. In "The Chessmen" Mori examines the gulf between two friends engaged in an employer-employee relationship. The title itself sets up a tension: while the characters in this story are treated as salt-of-the-earth, small-town types, the title positions them as pieces in a game of chess controlled by the market economy. The Hatayama Nursery provides the setting for this story. The nursery is run by Hatayama-san and Nakagawa-san, who are characterized as "[t]he boss and his help."³⁸ These men run the nursery together, only hiring additional hands during the summer. The narrator says that "[t]he Hatayama-

Nakagawa combination worked beautifully. For seven years the two men never quarreled and seldom argued with each other."[39] As with the imagery discussed in the previous chapter, the language here is Edenic. Indeed, this happy homosocial arrangement takes place in a flower nursery—that is to say, in a kind of commercial garden. Though Yokohama is presumably a fully-functioning town with (presumably) a fully-functioning economy, most of the monetary exchanges in the town revolve around the cultivation and selling of flowers.

Flowers are central to Mori's understanding of the small town; one might even say that the image of the flower is rooted in the idea of organic community. Out of twenty-two stories in *Yokohama, California*, five are concerned with flowers. And of those five, three treat flowers as a market commodity. In all of these stories, the market-transaction surrounding flowers alienates the characters involved. In "The Chessmen," the boss and his employee work in perfect harmony with each other and nothing intrudes upon their male camaraderie (even wives—who do exist, but are of negligible importance). Again, for all Mori's well-deserved reputation as a chronicler of the Japanese-American experience, he is here in lock-step with the broader American small-town canon. Mori also locates the garden within the context of small-town capitalism. The Hatayama Nursery is a typical small-town business, centered around the quiet friendship of two men. These men are defined by the conditions of their working relationship: Hatayama is "the boss" and Nakagawa is "his help," but such an association seems to be purely formal—at first. However, their association begins to break apart with the introduction of George Murai, a young man from the city who is taken on as additional help at the Nursery. At first, the young man simply seems eager to please, eager to learn the business of carnation-growing. George even has a kind of familial connection to Nakagawa, having known the latter's son in college.[40] As the business declines, Hatayama decides that he will have to lay off one of his hired hands. Initially, he plans to fire George Murai, but later the aging Nakagawa is let go because he is no longer useful.

Business in the small town is not communal; it is competitive and devastatingly isolating. George Murai provides the key for understanding this story. First, he is "from the city"—that is, he represents the incursion of the city onto the communal life of the small town.[41] He is an outsider. Second, he is young, which points to shifting generational ties—possibly from the fraternity of the old men to something more market-oriented. This second point should not, however, be pushed too far; after all, it is not he who determines that Nakagawa is too old to continue in the nursery. Third, George is lonely and he is made so by the conditions of his employment. He visits the narrator and says, "Over at Hatayama's I don't see any young people. I'll go crazy if I don't see somebody. In Oakland I have lots of friends."[42] This dialogue emphasizes the three aspects of George's personality mentioned above. While the city is conventionally seen as alienating, for George it is the small town that enforces loneliness. That loneliness is directly tied to George's work; his problem is not that Yokohama has no young people (his visits to the narrator prove that); rather, the nursery itself has no young people. George's work has isolated him from his peers and pitted him against his elder in a frantic struggle for dominance. George does not inflict this struggle on the small town—that is to say, his presence as an outsider does not create the conditions at the nursery—but he does suffer from it. For Mori, exploitative labor is baked into the small-town experience. George and Nakagawa—neither, seemingly, aware of the sword hanging over their heads—continue to work, but it is a work defined by "the struggle that knew no friendship."[43] In the narrator's eyes, the men become competitors, and the story portrays them as such, measuring George's youthful energy against Nakagawa's increasing frailness. The field of flowers becomes a field of combat, and the narrator wonders "how they could share the little shack [in which they both sleep] after what was happening on the field."[44] Finally, the struggle becomes too much and Nakagawa injures his back, leading Hatayama to reverse his previous decision and fire his loyal retainer instead of George.[45] In the end, the demands of the marketplace—even in a small town—override the demands of friendship or loyalty.

Business, in Mori's book, depends upon deception. The worker is obliged to destroy any inner communal feelings to succeed. In "Say It with Flowers," a young salesman named Teruo proves to be a failure at his job because he insists on selling the freshest flowers instead of the days-old bouquets on display. The young man's idealism runs counter to the cynical perspective of the small-town marketplace; his coworkers urge him to lie to the customers and reassure them that the flowers are fresh, but Teruo retorts that such a lie is "hard [...] to say when you know it isn't true."[46] Teruo bears a strong resemblance to George Murai in "The Chessmen." Like George, he comes into the business hoping to learn as much as he can about it so that he can "start from the bottom" and build his own career. He is "a glutton for work."[47] Both men develop an aptitude for their chosen careers. The narrator describes Teruo as "a slick sales clerk, but for one thing"—that one thing being that he can never lie to the customer.[48] George slips easily into the work-environment of the nursery, but Teruo cannot function in the flower shop. He finally embarks on a mad act of rebellion, selling all the freshest flowers he can and leaving at the end of the day, never to return. Teruo's soft-heartedness makes him particularly unsuited to conducting business; he could not "be a boss."[49] Margaret Bedrosian argues that "[r]ead in terms of conventional ethics, this story is about an inspired fool; but in the context of Mori's non–Western metaphysics, it is about wisdom breaking through the mundane illusions about profit and success that trap most of us."⁵⁰ Very possibly; however, the story of Teruo is also a story about the demands made by the market upon the individual. Being a boss—a businessman, even in the small-town environment of Yokohama—demands a cut-throat willingness to lie to customers and take advantage of them in ways small enough not to be noticed but large enough to yield a profit. It also demands, as seen in "The Chessmen," a willingness to pit employees against each other and discard the useless, worn out employees even if they have provided many years of loyal service. Teruo's idealism makes him unfitted for such an employment.

Mori does present the possibility that residents of small towns could find fulfillment in work, but work itself must be re-organized around a principle other than earning money. In "The Six Rows of Pompons," a young boy named Tatsuo is given the responsibility to care for a section of the family flower-plot. He is, as boys tend to be, neglectful of the flowers, with the result that "few plants survived out of the six rows."⁵¹ The adults around him want to burn the plot, but Tatsuo's uncle insists that it be left alone because such an action "will kill Tatsuo."⁵² Instead, the uncle sells the flowers and gives the money to Tatsuo. The indifferently undertaken labor, combined with praise for that labor, have a civilizing effect on the boy, though his father argues that Tatsuo "will become a wild animal" within a year.⁵³ The story ends with a comment about Tatsuo's "unfinished work in the world," suggesting that the cultivation of pompons is training for the boy's eventual flowering into adulthood.⁵⁴ Though the worth of his labor is still judged in terms of the market-economy, the work also gives Tatsuo a chance to learn the inner value of his own endeavors. The small town becomes a garden-plot where the tender buds of posterity are carefully prepared in the hope that one day America itself may become a garden-spot.

Within Mori's symbolic economy flowers are intimately tied to the ideas of family and of future generations, which are in turn tied to the marketplace. The work of cultivation is central to Mori's understanding of commerce. Flowers—by their very transient nature—lend themselves to the cycle of constant replacement (as seen in "Say It with Flowers") and boom-and-bust ("The Chessmen") that defines the capitalist mode of production. At the same time, to work in a nursery is to cultivate. Mori's treatment of the marketplace informs his treatment of interpersonal relationships. The story "Three Japanese Mothers" makes this connection clear in a negative way; Tane, one of the titular mothers, rejects the idea that it is the responsibility of parents to prepare the future for their children, arguing that instead parents should "let [the children] worry about the much-used soil and the rotting greenhouses."⁵⁵ Her viewpoint is contrasted with that of Kiku, who describes herself as "a gentle fool sacrificing [herself] for the children."⁵⁶ Within the story itself, Mori clearly comes down on the side of the gentle fool, but his title indicates a reluctance to suggest that Kiku is at all typical; if anything, the two other mothers—who refuse to "coddle" their children[57]—should be read as typical, and Kiku is the self-abnegating exception. Rather than being a nurturing community, the family is seen here as an entity that works on precisely the mechanism of the Hatayama Nursery: use up, wear out, and then discard. Kiku herself, while admirable, is still—in her own eyes—a failure and a fool; if the mother does not use up the soil, then she (the symbolic soil) will be depleted by her children (the flowers).

If the small town is not cut off from modernity in economic matters, neither is it cut off in temporal matters. Main Street leads to the square, which forms another symbolic landmark in the small town. Despite the seeming timelessness of the small town, it is bound tightly both to its own history and to that of the nation surrounding it. The town square, even more than Main Street, can be thought of as giving in monumental form the central identity of the small town. When Ellery Queen encounters Wrightsville in *Calamity Town*, he takes a walk around the town square. In its middle is a horse trough and a statue of the town's namesake. Ellery observes that the statue "had once been a bronze, but he now looked mossy, and the stone trough on which he stood had obviously been unused for years. There were crusty bird droppings on the Founder's Yankee nose."[58] The statue features a plaque commemorating the town's foundation on the site of an abandoned Indian village. In this passage, Queen presents the square as a distillation of Wrightsville's identity. The passage continues and describes the various shops laid out around this central symbol. There is at once something very much alive and slightly morbid about the description offered here. On the one hand, the paragraph ends with an invocation of Willa Cather—and, behind her, Walt Whitman:

> All the past we leave behind,
> We debouch upon a newer mightier world, varied world,
> Fresh and strong the world we seize, world of labor and the march,
> Pioneers! O pioneers![59]

Whitman writes praising the expansionist spirit of the American frontiersman, but Queen offers a subtle but nonetheless powerful corrective to the poet's vision. The past has not been left behind; the statue of Founder Wright rests upon an unused trough—unused, because the advent of the automobile has rendered horse-drawn wagons obsolete.

The automobile, as much as the train, stands in small town fiction as a symbol of modernity. Ryan Poll dates the evocation of the automobile back to Booth Tarkington's *The Magnificent Ambersons*, which he claims "perpetuates the ideology that the small town is the nation's foundational form and ideal community [which] has become a space in the past that must now be remembered."[60] According to Poll, "*The Magnificent Ambersons* posits the automobile as a symbol of foreign modernity."[61] At first blush, Queen seems to replicate this ideology, but closer examination reveals a more complicated vision. Behind all of these signs of a lost or decaying small town lies the specter of genocide: the "abandoned Indian site" ties Wrightsville to the legacy of a vanished people who were forced from their land by white settlers. This double vision puts Queen less in line with Tarkington and more in the camp of the 1920s Regionalists. As Robert Dorman observes in his study *Revolt of the Provinces*, pioneers represented for the Regionalists both a lost way of life connected to the land and the encroachment of modernity at the expense of older, more settled (generally Indian) communities.[62] Queen speaks of both here. The statue of Pioneer Wright seems to tie Wrightsville to its communitarian past, but the fact that Pioneer Wright is the ancestor of the town's banker (and so, the founding father of the capitalist class in the town) suggests that he also represents the fundamental link between commerce and community.

In *Calamity Town*, the commerce of Wrightsville clusters around the square and, having obliquely invoked Whitman, Queen lists—Whitman-fashion—the town's businesses. It is a bucolic town and Ellery "liked everything," though all is manifestly not well; the town's newfound prosperity depends upon the fact that "the woolen mill had taken on extra help—army orders."[63] Trouble is brewing on the horizon. The War is just around the corner, and if Wrightsville is prosperous it is *because* of that War. The square embodies a central negation of small town ideology as articulated by Poll. Wrightsville is not cut off from the outside world; it depends upon that world if it is to continue to prosper. This fact, together with the dung-encrusted statue and the dry stone trough and the dead Indian village—in short, the collision of past and present that occurs in the town square—suggests that things in Wrightsville are not as they seem, that it sits on the edge of a precipice.

The imaginative function of the town square as a tether to the past is more important than its business connections. The central square of Wrightsville becomes a sort of time capsule—or, more properly, a timeless space in which past and future collide in complex and unpredictable ways. The very presence of a town square in the American small town is itself a transtemporal event. Historically, the town square arose in Britain in 1611 and was quickly transferred to America, where it provided a point of continuity with European civilization.[64] The square thus becomes a focal point for small-town identity, one that links it to its village ancestors across the Atlantic, and it is often here that monuments are erected. These monuments unite the past and present in a sort of trans-temporal space.[65] Town squares, as might be expected, appear in most novels of the period from 1940 to 1960, from *The Just and the Unjust* (1942) to *Psycho* (1959). That these locations are homes to historical markers, as with the war memorials in *Psycho*,[66] proves again that the small town is not an island, that it is connected to the outside world in ways that go beyond simple commerce to issues of life and death. Thus, if the train can be conceived of as a negation of the small town's isolation, so too can the square be taken as an internalized symbol of the fact that no small town is an island. The idea of the town square as a transtemporal space helps to connect individuals to the past, in its beauty and its ugliness, but it also alienates the spectator by emphasizing the flow of time.

The Queenian project is also Whitmanian. Ellery begins the novel by evoking Whitman. This quotation is bookended at the conclusion of the novel. The narrative ends with Ellery, Patricia Wright (daughter of the town's First Family, whom Ellery romances), and Carter Bradford (her lover) sitting in a bar discussing the murder while an old drunkard rambles off lines from *Leaves of Grass*:

> "I believe a leaf of grass is no less than the journey-work of the stars,
> And the pismire is equally perfect, and a grain of sand, and the egg of the wren,
> And the tree-toad is a chef-d'oeuvre of the highest,
> And the running blackberry would adorn the parlors of heaven—"
>
> "Siddown, Mr. Anderson," said Gus Olesen gently, "You're rockin' the boat."
> "Whitman," said Mr. Queen, looking around, "And very apt."[67]

The passage is "very apt" because in it Whitman affirms the glories of cycle and the assurance that the world is, in its own way, good. But this observation is undercut by the speaker. "I was a poet," he says, "and l-look at me now," to which Ellery replies, "That's very true indeed."[68] The poet has been ground into dust by the cycle of small-town life, just as Nora Wright, the murderer, was destroyed because she was "sensitive, inhibited, [and] self-conscious."[69] The wheel of fortune turns, and as it turns it grinds exceeding small.

Circularity is central to the small-town narrative. Most small-town novels written during the period surrounding World War II seem to be built on some sort of circular structure. For some of them, the circle is purely generic (thus, *Calamity Town*, as a detective story, necessarily depends upon a circular foundation); for others, however, such a cycle is not necessary to the genre in which they are working. In *Strange Fruit* (1944), Lillian Smith ends with a return to the *status quo*. The revival ends, the lynching is over, and the characters (those who survived) revert to their former states with very little change. Elsewhere, authors insist that the small town is not disconnected from the world outside its borders. The cycle seen in the small town is part of a larger national cycle. *Raintree County* and *Parris Mitchell of Kings Row* (1948) are both self-conscious about setting the small town within national trends. Indeed, most small-town literature considers the influence of the nation upon the town. *Strange Fruit* deals with African American soldiers returning from World War I, and *Yokohama, California* features discussion of Japanese-American internment. Again, the small town is never cut off from the world around it. Both capital and history are part of the small-town fabric.

This chapter has analyzed the workings of business in the small town and shown that, far from mystifying the workings of capitalism, small town fiction during this period portrays business as alienating protagonists. My primary text—precisely because it seems at first mystifying—has been Toshio Mori's *Yokohama, California*. I have demonstrated that, for Mori, business does not fall before communal ties. Instead, communal ties are deeply bound to concerns of business. From there, I have moved to the town square and demonstrated that it shows the deep connections between the small town and the larger world. Main Street and the town square are physically connected, but they are also ideologically connected in that both seem to present the small town as isolated from the rest of the world while in fact demonstrating that the town can never be an island. And, since the larger world is in the grip of modernity, so is the small town. Thus, these seemingly communal spaces ultimately alienate the characters in these narratives. This loneliness—what in theological terms would be called fallenness—is central to the small-town myth. Given such centrality, it is to be expected that authors of this period attempt to find ways to navigate or ameliorate—or, more properly, transcend—the alienation visited upon their characters. The following chapters will examine ways in which small-town narratives attempt to transcend loneliness.

Five

False Transcendence
The Movie Theater

Though this study is concerned with *literary* representations of small towns—that is to say, with small towns as they appear in books—it would be unwise to ignore the world of film. The gulf between the two forms is not so wide as it would appear. Though they are different media, both the majority of the books discussed here and the films covered in this chapter are aimed at a broad audience. I have demonstrated that literary small towns are far from the bucolic escapes that both criticism and the popular imagination suggest. Rather, these communities are deeply implicated in the tensions and anxieties that beset America during the years of World War II and following. Insofar as these spaces are Edenic, they are *fallen* Edens, worlds in which the protagonists and other characters feel deeply the terror of isolation, an isolation that is both existential and political (the political being, in the end, deeply tied to the existential). Characters are isolated as children by the fact of individuation, as teenagers through rebellion, and as adults by the demands of the marketplace. This isolation, this fallenness, must be transcended, and the novels under consideration suggest a number of possible paths toward that transcendence. The following chapters will analyze the modes this transcendence can take. Briefly, there are three possible sites of transcendence: the cinema, the church, and the courthouse, which for the purposes of this study are symbols of conformity, mysticism, or creative lawbreaking. A fourth possibility—the recognition that everyone in the small town is alienated and the embrace of that fact—is represented by the town outskirts, and seems to be the dominant conclusion of midcentury small-town fiction. Most of these proposals are subversive in some way, but in the case of the cinema, representations of the small town hew closely to contemporary critiques of middlebrow culture. Rather than challenging the audience or offering uncertain resolution, films—and, particularly, film adaptations of small town novels—

tidy up the uncertainties present in the original texts in favor of clean, happy endings. The reasons for this shift are varied. Though both the novels and the films are aimed at a broad audience, the consumers of cinema cut a much broader cross-section of class and race. Moreover, the Production Code forced a number of alterations that diminish the subversive power of the source material. Whatever the reason, the difference is stark. While the novels of the period present a deeply compromised small town which must be, tentatively and with no promise of success, moved beyond, movies tend to resort to much easier forms of transcendence.

It is from the movies, rather than from the literature, that the image of the small town as a safe space emerges. As such, it would be well to pause in this ramble around the small town and step into the local cinema. Emmanuel Levy, in his book *Small-Town America in Film*, points out that "small-town films have been a permanent staple of American cinema from its very beginning."[1] This fact is not surprising if the small town is a form of national self-fashioning. Here the mass entertainment of America speaks the nation to itself in the form of the small town. It is here that Ryan Poll's critique is most accurate. Movies attempt to make the small town seem hospitable and friendly. Poll argues that the lesson of *It's a Wonderful Life*, for instance, is that George Bailey must accept his home town rather than chafe against it.[2] This acceptance is eased by the fact that the movie "mystifies Capitalism by imagining two competing forms"—that of George Bailey (good) and that of Potter (bad).[3] By Poll's reading, the audience is still left with a banker, no matter which one they choose to side with; there is no radical suggestion that the institution of banking *itself* is a problem. Cinematic small towns typically work toward an acceptance of the small town as basically good, in contrast to the more conflicted versions offered in the literature.

Indeed, in the process of adapting small-town novels to the screen, the filmmakers typically alter the source material to insert a happy ending. *No Man of Her Own* (1950), starring Barbara Stanwyck and John Lund, an adaptation of Woolrich's *I Married a Dead Man*, ends with the discovery that Helen's blackmailer was *actually* murdered by a gang of gamblers. As a result, the tension between the couple is resolved and they are allowed to start a happy life in the bucolic small-town setting—complete with a non-ironic return to the opening monologue praising the virtues of the town. In the film, then, the anxiety the characters feel is transcended, but it is transcended in a way that is recognizably false—false to the source material, but (more importantly) false to the nature of the film itself. This pattern repeats itself in the three films discussed below. *Kings Row* (1942), *Peyton Place*, and *Raintree County* (both 1957) all make substantial alterations to their source material. Of course, the process of adaptation demands that the source material be changed; I am not suggesting here that every re-configuration of characters or events is some sort of betrayal. Some of these alterations are for convenience; characters and events must be eliminated to save time (this is, after all, the challenge of fitting a novel of four hundred or more pages into a comfortable length for film). Other alterations have to do with evading the censors, and these changes are at the root of the false transcendence offered by the movies. It is here that the real shift occurs. Themes of incest and sex (particularly homosexuality) are downplayed; the possibility of non-normative sexual expression is generally eliminated in favor of heterosexual unions. By changing the "objectionable" elements and removing "objectionable" characters, these movies shift the focus away from the idea of the small town as a threat. In the novels, the town is a force that bears down on its inhabitants and condemns them to isolation. Where the existential and the political are fundamentally united in the original novels, in the films the link is severed. The resulting suggestion is that protagonists simply need to work harder to be integrated with their benign community. The characters are isolated because they do not fit in, but they *can* fit in, if only they make an effort.

The ethos of these films is, thus, individualist—that is to say, the onus of transcending the small town (and the failure to achieve such transcendence) falls entirely on the individual characters. There is no social guilt, only personal failure. This individualism is seen in three key ways, illustrated in each of the films discussed below. First, in *Kings Row*, the death of Drake is replaced by a triumphant scene in which he overcomes his disability through sheer force of masculine will. His tragedy is transformed into a wrestling match. In *Peyton Place*, the gay Norman is heterosexualized and becomes a man because of his service in World War II. And in *Raintree County*, Johnny Shawnessy finally finds happiness in the arms of his childhood sweetheart Nell. In all of these cases, the needs of the characters are met, not through a difficult act of transcendence, but by fitting into the society around them and engaging in socially-approved relationships. The implicit critique of America found in the source material is leeched in the film versions, giving them a sense of false transcendence.

Kings Row (1942) transforms the novel's tragedy into a straightforward tale of grit overcoming obstacles. The movie is, as far as it goes, a straight adaptation of the novel, within the parameters of the medium; where the film diverges from the novel is in minimizing the cast of characters (for instance, combining Renée and Cassandra Tower, eliminating Jamie, and so on). In the process, however, the film loses the bite that characterizes the novel. In "Where's the Rest of *Kings Row*: Hollywood's Emasculation of a 'Grand Yarn,'" Mark Scherer gives a detailed account of the changes made—and the reasons for those changes—in adapting the book to screen. He calls the process "an illuminating case study in the powerful emasculating effect of Hollywood's self-censorship mechanism."[4] The adaptation was produced at a time when studios felt the need to put out more stimulating material in order to compete with independent producers. At the same time, the censorship board loomed over every film made.⁵ A series of negotiations led to the decision to insert "compensating moral values" in the form of a scene in which Parris is implicitly blamed for the tragedy that destroys Cassandra.⁶ The result, according to Scherer, is a film "sadly disjointed and quite confusing in many key respects."⁷ Scherer's account of the process of adaptation is concise and complete and therefore need not be repeated. Of most interest here are two alterations: the elimination of characters and the removal of key plot elements.

Taking characters out of a novel or combining them is a standard practice, particularly in the case of longer books such as the novels examined here. It is simply impossible to replicate on the screen the expansive cast of characters found in a novel. In the case of *Kings Row*, most of the eliminations are of this simplifying type. Thus, Benny—a mentally retarded boy whose execution is a setpiece late in the novel—is shown in one scene, right at the very beginning, as part of the introduction to the town. He is not seen afterward and, though his removal does eliminate some of the narrative's texture, the movie is not substantially different for his absence. More significant is the loss of Jamie Wakefield, who never shows up at all. As Scherer points out, much of the concern from the Censorship Board involved questions of sex, and Jamie—as the novel's explicitly homosexual character—could not be reconciled with the demand to convert the novel into a narrative of moral uplift. Jamie's removal throws off the delicate balance between Bellamann's three-man friend-group. In the novel, Parris, the protagonist, is flanked by Drake McHugh as the symbol of his heterosexual side and Jamie as the symbol of his poetic (and queer) side. The effect of this particular elimination is farther-reaching than a question of character-dynamics, however. The movie heterosexualizes Henry Bellamann's implicitly queer small town. Jamie Wakefield, an explicitly gay character who at one point attempts to seduce Parris, serves in the novel as a way of understanding the absolute loneliness enforced by the town. Writers of this period such as Henry Bellamann and Grace Metalious often use queer characters as symbols of the ways in which small towns (and, therefore, America at large) crush and destroy their citizens. Jamie sees earlier and more clearly than Parris that Kings Row is a monstrous place that will admit no trace of difference, and this is what makes him such an important character in the novel, even though his presence is less marked than that of Drake. The movie eliminates Jamie and so attempts to un-queer Parris and Drake, though as Levy observes, the "homoerotic undertones" between Parris and Drake are still present, even if audiences did not notice them.⁸ By removing Jamie, the film removes the most dominant outsider voice and paves the way for a conventionally happy ending.

The process of adaptation also shifts the gender-critique of the novel from blaming victimizers to blaming victims. In this sense, the loss of Jamie is nothing compared to what happens to Cassandra Tower. In the novel, Cassandra is a nymphomaniac, but her nymphomania is revealed to be the result of repeated and sustained abuse by her father. The novel does not allow readers to simply write Cassandra off as insane. In contrast, the movie—again, at the insistence of the censors, who feared any suggestion of nymphomania, let alone incest—diagnoses Cassandra with "dementia praecox."[9] Rape is never even broached as a possible cause of this condition. Instead, viewers are told that Cassandra was insane, that her father took her out of school when she was a child because he recognized her insanity, and that his eventual murder is motivated by a desire to keep Parris from suffering the same fate he did—that is, having an insane wife and being forced to live in a small town. The murder becomes, as Janet Walker observes, "a kind of mercy-killing."[10] For Walker, this suppression turns the film adaptation of *Kings Row* into a "post-traumatic text," in which the trauma of incest is sublimated and emerges between the lines rather than occurring as part of the main narrative.[11] According to Walker, these gaps still speak in spite of their enforced silence. This may well be true, but in terms of the text itself, incest is thoroughly erased in favor of moralizing. As Scherer points out, Parris is at one point made to feel guilt over his affair with Cassandra and suffers a kind of premonition of her impending fate.[12] Thus, the guilt for Cassandra's condition is shifted. Indeed, it is doubly shifted: first onto Parris, but ultimately onto her mother. While the novel suggests that Cassandra's emotional and mental instability is the result of years of abuse at the hands of her father, the movie claims that Cassandra inherits a form of madness from her mother—the descent of madness is matrilineal rather than patrilineal. It is her mother's fault that Cassandra is crazy. Guilt is shifted away from the patriarchal structures that enable abusers like Dr. Tower and is placed instead on women. The message is not that women are abused, but that they are irrational and prone to hysteria.

The world of *Kings Row* is flattened in adaptation. In the cases of Jamie and Cassandra, the streamlining of characters does violence to the original point of the story. Where the original novel is a queer take on small-town life, one in which the very assumptions of heterosexual, patriarchal, "normal" society are called into question, the film adaptation reinforces the heterosexual normativity current at the time. This shift is particularly apparent in the ending. The novel *Kings Row* ends with Parris forced to euthanize his best friend Drake, who has contracted cancer after having his legs removed by the sadistic Dr. Gordon. Parris is then able to find some measure of relief in the arms of a young German girl who now occupies his old estate, but the suggestion is that this peace is tentative and passing (as the sequel reveals, it is very passing indeed). *Kings Row*, like most small-town novels written during this time, is not exactly pessimistic about the possibility of human flourishing in small-town environments, but it is decidedly grim in its estimation of that possibility. In the movie, however, the town can be overcome through pure force of will. The film ends with Parris telling Drake that his legs have been needlessly amputated. As Levy observes, Parris and Drake are thus twinned symbols of manhood: "Parris teaches Drake what he needs most: spiritual strength to meet his new, painful reality [...] and Drake brings real joy to Parris's life. They are presented as two complementary facets of ideal masculinity."[13] In the novel, Parris carefully keeps the knowledge of Drake's useless surgery from his friend, believing that the knowledge would crush him. As he tells Randy, "we have brought Drake back to himself and to ourselves—but he is not quite the same Drake. If it should ever enter his mind that his own catastrophe was anything but an accident—."[14] *Kings Row* is a novel about revelation, but it is also about concealment. Parris, for Drake's own good, conceals from his friend the truth that Dr. Gordon performed a needless amputation.

In contrast, the film climaxes with Parris telling Drake everything. At first, he is inclined not to, but Elise—the German girl who now lives in his grandmother's old house and who will be his future bride—convinces him that it is better to tell Drake. She functions as the voice of conscience. This revelation at the end of the film is staged as a battleground of masculine striving. The form the conversation takes is particularly telling. Parris warns Drake that he (Drake) is about to receive a "wallop." The language is important. A wallop is, of course, a punch; he is using the language of pugilism, of fighting. He dares Drake to turn away. Drake needs to man up in order to overcome his disability. This performance is not *wholly* alien to the novel; in the book, Parris is careful to make Drake's business seem like his idea, and Randy is forced to play the servile woman in order to convince Drake that he is needed, to "make him feel that he is the chief and moving force" in the couple's endeavors.[15] And so there is, even in the novel, a kind of gender-mechanics at play. At the same time, Drake's healing occurs as Parris adopts a feminized, caring role alongside Randy. Moreover, as mentioned above, Parris is careful to limit the boundaries of Drake's performance. Drake may feel like he is "the chief and moving force" in business, but Parris acknowledges that this authority is essentially a sham.[16] Drake cannot perform the exertion that he would have been able to before his accident; his personality is so fragile that both Parris and Randy must carefully shield it from the truth.

The movie's assertion that all Drake needs to do is stick his chin out and tough it through is, thus, a radical reversal of the novel. Drake laughs—laughs at Dr. Gordon for daring to try to intimidate him, laughs at the town for trying to press him down. Ronald Reagan plays the scene with characteristic gusto; this is no fragile, tentatively-restored Drake, but a full return of the carefree roustabout of earlier in the movie. Moreover, the movie's version of Drake does not die, as he does in the novel. He ends the film hugging Randy as Parris walks back across the field to meet Elise, his wife-to-be, who serves as his moral conscience in the film. Levy claims the movie suggests that "[a]s much as reality may be painful, coming to terms with the 'truth' is essential for the individual's as well as community's welfare."[17] This ending is structured in such a way as to reinforce rather than call into question the heteronormative, patriarchal superstructures that hold up the small town. By the movie's reckoning, Drake needs to be a man—to tough it through the bad news about Dr. Gordon and embrace his no-longer-tomboyish bride Randy. What Parris needs is a beautiful wife who will provide him with the moral strength to confront his friend. The town is, ultimately, only destructive if the characters cannot fill their heteronormative roles as man and woman. The small town is revised into a place where happiness is possible, if only the characters are conventional enough.

For these film adaptations, heterosexual coupling is central to the idea of the happy ending. Though Levy suggests that a 1950s version of *Kings Row* would have featured the protagonists leaving the town, the *actual* 1950s version of *Kings Row*—*Peyton Place* (1957)—reenacts this demand for conformity to heterosexual norms. At first glance, *Peyton Place* may seem to be a more faithful adaptation of its source material than *Kings Row*. Certainly, fewer characters are condensed or removed outright, and those characters who *are* removed are deleted for the purposes of efficiency rather than ideology. Again, though *Peyton Place* is a long movie, the novel is longer. Simplification is not only necessary but desirable. In many ways, as Levy observes, *Peyton Place* is "[t]he quintessential small-town movie of the decade."[18] Indeed, Levy regards the movie as an important entry in the canon of small-town film:

> This melodrama captured better than other films the narrative conventions and value elements of small-town films. It is arguably one of the best small-town films ever made in Hollywood, blending together the thematic and stylistic elements to form a coherent work.[19]

In other ways, however, *Peyton Place* makes precisely the same moves that the earlier adaptation of *Kings Row* made. Though "civilization is too repressive and demanding,"[20] the movie cleans up the town considerably. Ardis Cameron observes, for instance, that the filmmakers rejected the New England town of Gilmanton as being unsuitably unattractive. As Cameron puts it, "[w]hat the regionalists began, Hollywood continued: the imaginary heart of New England drifted Down East, where *Peyton Place* morphed into picturesque Camden, Maine."[21] This picturesqueness is central to the film's aesthetic; it is certainly a beautiful movie, with vibrant colors and striking costume-work. But this beauty serves to conceal as much as it reveals.

In fact, the film version of *Peyton Place* is sentimental is a way that the novel is not. The movie opens over a long series of shots of the seasons passing, while "Season of Love"—the movie's theme as well as that of the eventual TV series—plays. In part, this notation of seasonal passing is rooted in the novel itself; Metalious (like Bellamann) begins her book with nature-writing. On the other hand, Metalious' opening description invokes the themes—particularly feminine sexuality—that she later explores in the novel.[22] In contrast, the opening montage of the film is distinctly picture-postcard. For Metalious, the beauty of the New England setting is intended as a counterpoint to the rot and despair she sees operating beneath the surface. In the film, however, the surface is everything. There is no sensuality here, but Currier & Ives visual pleasure, far removed from the passionate, feminine natural world of the novel. More than that, Allison's opening narration lays out the four seasons and concludes by saying that there is a fifth season, "a season of love," that exists beyond the normal four. This conclusion is an even bigger step away from the unsentimental prose of Grace Metalious. The novel shocks with its dour view of village life; its opening paragraph suggests sensuality and roiling desires beneath the bucolic surface—certainly one of Metalious' most consistent themes. In the movie, however, the viewer is promised a *love* story, not a tale of frustration but one of satisfaction.

As a result, sex is evacuated from the narrative in favor of emotionalism. The film also continues the emphasis on masculinity and heterosexual coupling seen in *Kings Row*. This shift is particularly striking. Certainly, more than *Raintree County* or *Kings Row*, *Peyton Place* is a woman-centered movie, one which is far more respectful of the perspectives of Allison and Selena and Constance than it is toward male characters. Nevertheless—and paradoxically—it is precisely in its handling of male characters that the movie reverts to the patriarchy. The biggest change is seen in the film's the treatment of Norman Page. The 1957 movie *Peyton Place* reduplicates *Kings Row*'s systematic silencing of queer characters. In *Kings Row,* Jamie Wakefield, Parris' gay friend, is simply eliminated; in *Peyton Place*, the filmmakers carefully de-queer the queer character. The character in question is Allison's friend and would-be-lover Norman Page. In the novel, Metalious makes it clear—without saying as much—that Norman is gay. Norman is introduced as "Little Norman Page," and he is said to be "pretty in the way a girl is pretty, and his voice, too, was like a girl's, soft and high."[23] This is, however, as far as Metalious gets in explicitly naming Norman's sexual orientation; though she provides numerous clues, she cannot seem to bring herself to be explicit about *this*, of all the sexual matters she deals with in the book. However, Norman fits all the midcentury stereotypes of the homosexual man: effeminacy, mother-fixatedness, and antipathy toward heterosexual sex. Norman's interest in sex with Allison is academic; when he kisses her, it is "softly, without touching her except for raising his other hand to her cheek."[24] His attitude when describing the sex-act is telling: "Norman put his arms up behind his head and crossed his legs. He began to speak as if he were explaining a troublesome problem in algebra to someone who had no inclination toward mathematics" and Allison responds "with the exact tone she would have used if she had been the dull math student whom Norman was trying to help."[25] Norman, that is to say, doesn't care about sex so much as the *concept* of sex. Later, when he witnesses a married couple having intercourse, he is filled with fear and loathing that will forever afterward mar his understanding of heterosexual pairing.[26] Norman goes to fight in World War II and returns "as a hero, with a chestful of campaign ribbons, medals, and a stiff leg on which he walked with the help of a crutch."[27] But these are all pretenses forced on him by his mother, a "little subterfuge" that she "never meant to carry [...] so far."[28] In fact, Norman was never wounded in the war and is not a hero. Norman is reduced, is symbolically castrated by his mother, and ends up a sexless shell of his former self.

The movie eliminates these elements of Norman's character. In the novel, Norman is a sexually repressed boy who is raised by his mother. His fate is an essentially tragic one because he is not saved from the predations of his mother; instead, he becomes a husk of a man with no sexual desire to speak of (and, for Metalious, this means he might as well be dead). The movie follows Metalious a certain distance. It presents Norman as an awkward boy with an unhappy home life. There are indications that his mother holds as much sway over him in the movie as she does in the book. Much of the movie continues in the same way that the novel does—there is, for instance, a kissing scene in the woods, though there is no indication Allison is sexually frustrated by it; indeed, she seems rather to enjoy it. Norman becomes her project—she is going to help him shake off his mother's influence. The language she uses would be familiar to any queer youth who encounters social disapproval—she suggests that he simply hasn't found the right girl (and that, implicitly, *she* is the right girl). However, while in the real world such language is pure fantasy on the part of the speaker, in the film version of *Peyton Place* it is exactly right. As in the novel, Norman goes off to war. But, whereas in the novel Norman never sees much action and spends most of his time in a mental ward, in the film Norman enlists in the paratroopers and becomes (as it is later revealed) a hero. The mythical medals given him by his mother in the novel are transfigured into the real thing. The war makes Norman a man.

The circumstances of Norman's reintroduction reinforce the transformation that has taken place in his character—both within the film's narrative and in its adaptation from the source material. While on a train returning to Peyton Place, Allison meets Norman. He is covered with medals. He is a highly decorated paratrooper. Immediately, viewers notice that there is something different about the formerly awkward and shy boy. He is more self-assured as he asks his fellow soldiers to leave him and Allison alone; he lights a cigarette for her and talks about the war. He says that being in the war has allowed him to come to terms with his mother and that he is returning to Peyton Place to confront her. Norman has become a man. A character who once stood for the ways in which the small town will destroy sensitive young people has now become the avatar of the ways in which sensitive young men can be incorporated into the heteronormative patriarchy through masculine self-exertion.

The film adaptations of *Peyton Place* and *Kings Row* reinforce stereotypes of masculine striving. Just as Drake overcomes his disability through sheer gusto, so Norman can now confront his mother because he has become a man. And just as the elimination of Jamie from *Kings Row* allows the filmmakers to imagine a world in which the small town (and, therefore, America) is not unrelentingly hostile to outsiders, so the heterosexualization of Norman Page allows *Peyton Place* to suggest that it is possible for Norman, and therefore Allison, to be incorporated into the heterosexual economy of the town. The movie ends with Norman walking across the street into the house shared by Constance, her husband, and Allison. Thus, the movie gives viewers a happy ending that reinforces heteronormative assumptions. Allison will not have an affair with several men, as she expresses the wish to do earlier in the film; instead, she will now settle down with the straight Norman Page. Norman, meanwhile, having worked through his issues with his mother and earned an array of medals (though not, importantly, being castrated symbolically—there is no wounded leg), is now prepared to accept the love of a good woman like Allison. This point is emphasized by Allison's closing monologue, speaking again of the "season of love" that she has found with her family. The season of love, in this case, is explicitly heterosexual and patriarchal.

These changes mark a shift from harsh critique to celebration. The novels *Kings Row* and *Peyton Place* are both highly critical of the ways in which the small town represses and shuns difference. Jamie Wakefield and Norman Page are victims of that repression, and as such their existence throws into question the possibility of ever reconciling with society. As ever, the small town here stands in the place of America itself; Metalious and Bellamann are writing, ultimately, about the conditions prevalent in America during their time. By removing Jamie and by heterosexualizing Norman, the movies suggest that the town is not so bad after all, that it is possible to come to terms with it. The people in it, in spite of the hours spent analyzing their hypocrisy, are essentially good. The protagonists are easily and seamlessly integrated with their society. Transcendence—redemption—which is the core of the small-town novel's use of the Eden-myth—comes easily. Energetic (and masculine) effort is all that is required to force a way through difficulties. The movies, in contrast to the books, can be read as regressive and reactionary, drawing back from the darkness revealed in their text and retreating to a false transcendence symbolized by the restoration of the (heterosexual) family-unit.

The result of all this revision is finally a self-contradictory text. The film cuts against itself. Its conclusions are not supported by the narrative it presents. Ryan Poll points out the ways in which *It's a Wonderful Life* is riven by a fundamental tension: the choice is between a good banker and a bad banker, but both are still bankers.[29] The myth of "friendly capitalism," in Poll's formulation, is the contradiction embedded in the myth of the small town as a welcoming community. The stress of adapting the text and also of heterosexualizing/homogenizing it causes the movies to break apart in unexpected ways. *Raintree County* offers a particularly striking example of this breakage, since the process of revising the source text is at once more radical and far less fully integrated than it is in other examples analyzed here. *Raintree County* differs from *Kings Row* and *Peyton Place* in its ambition, but the alterations to the source material follow the same pattern. At the same time, the change is more extensive. If *Kings Row* and *Peyton Place* streamline their narratives, *Raintree County* hacks away over three quarters of it. If the other two movies attempt to corral the source novels' subversive sexual forces (queer men and other sexual undesirables), *Raintree County* eliminates the novel's exploration of sexuality and replaces it with a conclusion that reinforces, rather than subverts, the heterosexual patriarchy.

The film version of *Raintree County* is the most radically altered of the movies examined here. In one sense, *Raintree County* is by necessity a different sort of experiment because the book is so long and covers such a large amount of history. The novel is comfortably over a thousand pages long. Though its immediate action—what might be called its present—occurs over the course of a day, its numerous flashbacks take readers into the distant childhood of its protagonist, John Wickliff Shawnessy. An attempt to outline the novel's numerous digressions would be an extensive narratological process; Lockridge clearly owes a debt both to James Joyce and—behind Joyce—to Laurence Sterne. Indeed, the best outline of the novel would look something like the one sketched by Tristram Shandy regarding *his* book: a line, bending back onto itself, diverging at sharp angles at some points and bulging into rotund orbs at others. That anyone thought to make a film of *Raintree County* is a minor sort of miracle in itself. There is no way the novel's extensive digressions and pseudo-philosophical reflections could fit into a movie. The filmmakers attempt to convert the novel into a kind of second-tier *Gone with the Wind*: an extravagantly mounted costume melodrama with enormous battle scenes and many heaving bosoms. The narrative is condensed down to the Civil War portions dealing with Johnny's experience in the war (though

FIVE • *False Transcendence* 109

it eliminates the death-and-resurrection subplot that makes Johnny into a kind of Midwestern Messiah). The entire movie labors in the shadow of *Gone with the Wind*, even featuring the aftermath of the sacking of Atlanta—hardly an accident, given how pivotal that event is in the Selznick movie.

The movie also re-invents the central characters as figures in a melodramatic love triangle, altering their fates substantially in the process. In this telling, Nell—the girl Johnny loves as a teenager—becomes his lifelong romance. In the novel, Nell is his adolescent sweetheart and dies after marrying his arch-rival Garwood Jones. She does not vanish from the narrative after that; she haunts it. Certainly, Johnny never forgets her:

> He opened the cardboard box and laid a handful of cut flowers, roses and lilies, on the mound. Backing away, he gazed at the stone. Its stately form tranquillized the emotion of farewell. Curved whiteness from the river became a lapidary attitude. By Ovidian magic, young love was changed to stone.[30]

But the point of Nell in the novel—as with the titular Raintree—is that this "young love" is lost. She marries Garwood Jones, Johnny's childhood rival, who is the very symbol of everything wrong with late-nineteenth century America. For Lockridge, the truth of the past is that it is preserved in memory but never obtainable in fact. Nell is important as a symbol of impossibility. Even Johnny's wet dreams make this point. In them, Nell becomes "the goddess of the river" whose body he seeks only to become "entangled in the rushes" shortly before the orgasm.[31] Nell is "nothing if not Raintree County."[32] As such, she is elusive, never grasped, always held in the memory and in the heart as a kind of tragic ideal. In the movie, however, Nell never dies, and she certainly never marries Garwood Jones—she is always there, just outside of Johnny's reach, as a very real potential love-match. Bringing these two lovers together becomes the movie's central project.

Because of this shift, Johnny's first wife Susanna is also reconfigured. In the novel, Susanna is introduced while Shawnessy is looking at photographs with his daughter Eva. The photographs show a "very pretty" woman and a boy. Shawnessy implies that they are both dead.[33] Within the present of the novel, insofar as a novel so digressive can *have* a present, Nell and Susanna are both absent; any rivalry between them is a thing of the distant past. Susanna is a Southern girl who takes Johnny's virginity and then falsely claims to be pregnant. In the novel, Susanna's ersatz pregnancy certainly divides Johnny and Nell, but she is more than simply an obstacle in the lovematch. Like Nell, she is also a symbol—a Southerner obsessed with race and race-mixing, a woman possessed of "a hidden scarlet mark."[34] Lockridge leaves open the possibility that Susanna is herself mixed-race. Every stage of her relationship with Johnny is carefully tied to events leading up to and occurring within the Civil War. The pregnancy crisis occurs at the same time as John Brown's raid on Harper's Ferry, for instance, and Johnny and Susanna wed on the occasion of John Brown's execution.[35]

Eventually, Susanna dies when she burns down the Shawnessy house, an event that is recounted through the memories of his second wife Esther (nonexistent in the film). Esther remembers the fire as an event in her childhood, when "a big house close to the square [...] was on fire, burning like a tall torch at night," and "a woman and a little boy had got burnt."[36] Susanna is tied to the madness of Southern slavery and the Southern obsession with race-mixing, and she dies in a highly symbolic fire that lights the way for John Shawnessy's second bride. All of this symbolism is eliminated in the movie in favor of melodrama. Susanna (Elizabeth Taylor) is simply the woman who comes between Johnny and Nell. Her insanity is no longer a symbol of the madness engulfing the South, its hysterical denial of race-mixing and the desperate need to maintain the *status quo*. Instead, it is simply a melodramatic beat in a movie full of melodramatic beats. The focus, thus, is shifted away from the mythic interests that motivate the novel. Instead, viewers are expected to invest in this love triangle. Such a shift creates demands within the movie. The love triangle, not central to the novel, now must be resolved, and resolved happily.

This new narrative demand has implications for the real core of the novel—that fecund, sexual symbol of life, the Raintree. In the novel, the Raintree represents the lost Eden. It represents love and happiness. The Raintree itself doesn't matter as much as the journey to the Raintree. That is to say, as Johnny himself does, the Raintree is a mythic symbol:

> [T]he tree is not the secret, but is itself [...] part of the secret only. There *are* secret places in the earth. Every county in America has its secret place and every American life is its Delphic cave.[37]

In the novel, the Raintree functions to point out the impossibility towards which all humans strive in their quest for fulfillment or happiness. To find the secret of happiness, each person must look inward to his or her own "Delphic cave," where the Divine will speak truth to them face-to-face. The movie, in contrast, retains the language but jettisons the substance. Several times, Susanna blames herself for keeping Johnny from finding his Raintree. Johnny protests that the Raintree does not exist, that its only importance is as a symbol of human striving. What matters (says Johnny) is what is found along the way to the Raintree. This language is lifted directly from the novel. But while the novel confirms Johnny's insistence that the Raintree does not exist, that it does not matter, except as a mythic symbol, the movie subverts that insistence. The decision to focus on the love triangle makes such an inversion inevitable.

The love triangle also drastically changes the way women are treated in the move from page to screen. The trend in these adaptations is to shift responsibility away from patriarchal social forces and onto individual women. Thus, Cassandra's insanity in *Kings Row* is inherited from her mother and Norman in *Peyton Place* simply needs to confront *his* mother. The film adaptation of *Raintree County*, with its insistence on the love triangle plot, converts Susanna from a symbolic character into an obstacle to Johnny's happy (heterosexual/patriarchal) union with Nell. Susanna herself recognizes this fact and expresses it to Johnny, using the language of the Raintree. The Raintree, in this context, is Nell—or, rather, a love-match with her, without any indication that these are both symbols for something else. The Raintree is not national-mythic; it is personal. In Susanna's understanding, she has kept Johnny from ever finding his own personal Raintree. Again, using language from the novel, Johnny insists that this is not the case—that the Raintree means only the human search for happiness, that it can never be found. True satisfaction is discovered in the *quest* for the Raintree. However, the way in which the movie presents its central crisis—the love triangle—means that Johnny's words have less weight than Susanna's. Structurally, if there is a love triangle it has to be resolved. And in order to provide Johnny with a "happy" ending, Susanna must be gotten rid of in such a way that reinforces the fact that Johnny always belonged with Nell.

Susanna's fate is therefore reconfigured to emphasize the fact that Johnny belongs with Nell. In the novel, Susanna dies in a fire with their son. In the film, on the other hand, Susanna takes their child and decides to go into the swamp to find the Raintree for Johnny. This is the climax of the film. The entire town turns out and searches the swamp for Susanna and the boy. Eventually, they find Susanna dead. She has sacrificed herself for Johnny's happiness. Johnny sheds the requisite tears, but the narrative trajectory, which places Nell at his side during this pivotal scene, suggests that these tears are needless. Since the child has not been found, Johnny and Nell return to the swamp together to look for him. Eventually, in the final moments of the movie, they find the boy alive—he has been sleeping at the foot of a tree with golden flowers. The boy, considering he has spent the night alone in a swamp, looks remarkably angelic. Johnny takes him in his arms and he and Nell, together, walk toward the swamp's exit. The camera does not follow them. Instead, it pulls back slowly until the audience is shown what they could have guessed all along—that the boy was sleeping underneath the Raintree. Susanna has helped Johnny find his Raintree, and this glimpse of the physical tree is the movie's sanctification of Johnny's happy future union with Nell (a union notably untainted by sex, since they have a family already-formed). Johnny's journey ends with a perfect, pure family unit.

This ending introduces an irresolvable tension into the movie. In spite of the film's use of Lockridge's mythic language, the climax indicates that

Susanna is correct. When she says it would be better if Johnny had never married her, she is correct. When she insists that Johnny would be happier if she died so that he could be with Nell, she is correct. By the same token, Johnny is wrong. The Raintree is not some sort of mythic symbol that allows people to make their way in the world. It is, rather, an actual tree in the middle of an actual swamp. Actual salvation is to be found there, rather than the tentative transcendence spoken of the in the novel. And this salvation is precisely the sort of happily-ever-after that Johnny claims does not exist. This move is a fundamental subversion of the novel. It reinforces patriarchy in a way that the novel does not. Lockridge's book has its own complex of gender-issues, but it never suggests that salvation lies in the direction of content heterosexual coupling. If anything, the novel is interested in some form of heterosexual *polyamory*. The Raintree is a symbol of fecundity, of sex in its rawest and most indiscriminate form. The movie, on the other hand, suggests that Johnny's Raintree is the sort of happy nuclear family that dominated the imagination of post–World War II America. When the movie ends the narrative of Raintree County on a triumphant note, it validates the heteronormative demand to marry and beget children. And in this way, as with *Kings Row* and *Peyton Place*, the film version of *Raintree County* (far more than the novel itself) reinforces what Ryan Poll calls the dominant myth of the American small town.

Insofar as the mythical, comforting small town exists during the 1940s and '50s, it is at the cinema. Movies such as *It's a Wonderful Life* stage the small town as fundamentally good rather than evil, and the problem becomes how the protagonist can situate himself (or herself) within this small town. The protagonist must adapt to the small-town community. Certainly, this representation is not monolithic; such films as *Shadow of a Doubt* (Hitchcock, 1943) engage with the themes outlined elsewhere in this study—particularly, in the case of *Shadow*, with incest and small-town depravity. However, cinematic adaptations of the period tend to smooth out the critiques embodied in small-town literature. By moving the focus away from the social forces that cause loneliness in the protagonist and, instead, insisting that personal happiness is best found through masculine effort and in a romantic (heterosexual) union, these movies offer easy transcendence. Thus, in *Kings Row*, Drake overcomes his disability in a scene that is written as a contest of masculine strength. In *Peyton Place*, Norman Page is heterosexualized and becomes a man through his experiences in World War II, turning him into a suitable love-match for Allison. And in *Raintree County*, the Raintree becomes a symbol of Johnny Shawnessy's personal desire for his childhood sweetheart Nell. His wife is removed from the equation and he forms a pure heterosexual union with Nell, a union that symbolically takes place under the shadow of the Raintree. All of these changes undercut the social commentary of the source material and reinforce heteronormative patriarchy. The chief insight of small-town literature in this period is not that protagonists just need to learn how to fit in. Rather, they *cannot* fit in because ultimately everyone is an outsider. Which is not to say that these novels offer no visions of transcendence. The church and the courthouse both offer alternative routes. These are difficult routes, and often involve the process of abandoning both religion and law in order to push beyond the isolation of the small town and touch something resembling the metaphysical. The next two chapters will examine these alternate routes.

Six

Good God, Bad God
The Church

Small towns are fallen Edens and the central problem of small-town fiction is how to transcend this fallen state. Religion and law—that is to say, the Church and the Courthouse—offer two possibilities. Churches show up often in small-town literature. The church is another landmark of the small town; the village of Peyton Place is bookended by a Catholic church and a Protestant one, and a pivotal scene in *Kings Row* takes place in a church. The importance is not the building itself but the fact that the structure speaks to the omnipresence of religion in the lives of small-town Americans during the 1940s and '50s. The religious perspective conveyed in these books is anything but charming and comforting. Religion in the post-war world takes on a terrifying and forbidding aspect with which authors are forced to grapple. Writers of small-town fiction of the period are interested in using transgression to move beyond the God of theology. This tension speaks to the tremendous shifts occurring in the American religious imagination at midcentury. There was certainly a "postwar revival of religion," as Kenneth L. Woodward points out in his book *Getting Religion*.[1] Revival or no, however, midcentury small-town fiction betrays a deep anxiety about religion. Contemporary anxieties pushes some writers to seek out a way of encountering the Divine that bypasses traditional religious formulations. These authors are motivated in no small way by the pressures of World War II. The Holocaust and the Atom Bomb have both shaken belief in a beneficent Deity. The new concern is that God, if such a Being exists, does not really like humanity much. In Katherine Bellamann's *Parris Mitchell of Kings Row*, Parris is forced to grapple with the idea that "there must exist in the universe a conscious and maleficent fate."[2] This fate, which Parris associates with the Calvinist God, is the image against which authors in the period rebel. In the process, they develop new ways of encountering, and grappling with, the Divine.

This rebellion takes a form that might be called the sacramental secular. Symbols of religion have no meaning anymore, but the secular world—nature, science, humanity—holds within itself its own means of transcendence. In turning their attention to the sacramental secular, these authors are not outside the mainstream of American thought during this period, nor do they offer a comforting fantasy to which middle-class readers can escape; instead, these authors use their small-town setting as a way of dealing with the problems of twentieth century life. Chester Eisinger argues that religion is an obsession of twentieth century fiction, and this claim is particularly true of small-town fiction.[3] The question of religion is intensified by the pressures facing a globe entering its second World War and, following that, trying to navigate the post-war existential malaise. The conflict between the collective demands of religious faith and the assumption of individualism as the core of American identity is particularly important here. America's individualist compact is one that is well-established in its history and literature. It has also set up some of the deepest fissures in American life and in the American psyche, since an enormous psychic burden comes along with individuality. This burden is what noted theologian Paul Tillich (speaking in existentialist, rather than material-historical, terms) calls "anxiety [which] is the state in which a being is aware of its possible nonbeing."[4] This anxiety can be spoken of in two ways: first, in the existentialist manner of Tillich; and, second, in a national sense. These two are related to each other. Tillich also speaks of "collective anxiety." The cure for this anxiety, according to Tillich, is the movement whereby Being takes into itself the condition of its own Nonbeing.[5] This taking-in is transcendence, and transcendence is a central element of small-town religiosity in fiction of the period—transcending the Calvinist God and moving toward a Divinity closer to Tillich's "God above God."[6] Thus, the small town is a site of religion, but not in a comfortable, sentimental way. It is not a place where the most traditional religious structures hold sway; rather, it is a place of deep religious uncertainty where post-war anxiety about the role of religious life in America belies the stereotype of the period as deeply and unquestioningly pious.

The small-town narrative is formed by a quest for the sacred. In his book *Sacred Land*, Mark Buechsel argues that many early twentieth century Midwestern writers consciously associate themselves with a Catholic, sacramental view of nature as opposed to the desacralized Protestant universe which was then being explored by Max Weber.[7] These authors adopt a sacramental viewpoint which, according to Buechsel, involves "[s]ubmitting to creaturely finitude and to the postlapsarian fact of living in a broken world."[8] The Midwestern modernists aligned themselves against a Protestant viewpoint which seeks to control nature, to bring it under subjection, to imprison it in the mechanistic framework of the late nineteenth century. Instead, the Midwestern authors surveyed by Buechsel—who include Anderson, Cather, and Fitzgerald—insist that mechanisms of control "will be resisted by the reality they are trying to ignore."[9] These narratives reject the Calvinist positivism of the Protestants. American religion in the years following World War II makes a similar move, as midcentury small-town literature increasingly focuses on the dangers of collective religious expression and questions the desirability of individual piety.

Though I will not lean heavily on this terminology, it should be acknowledged that this quest is recognizably Gnostic. The Protestant God—what I call the Bad God, the God of control and social manipulation—is analogous to the Gnostic demiurge, a sub-deity who creates the world of suffering. In small-town fiction, this God does not necessarily exist in a metaphysical sense, but he nevertheless exerts control in the lives of Americans. The characters in these stories must recognize the illusions created (or "created") by this demonic Father-God and, in recognizing them, achieve true knowledge of their own essentially divine selves (the Good God, Tillich's God-beyond-God). Harold Bloom, in his study *The American Religion*, lays out the coordinates of what he considers the essential American religious experience in a way that clarifies the concerns of this chapter:

> The God of the American Religion is not a creator-God, because the American never *was* created, and so the American has at least part of the God within herself. Freedom for an American [...] means two things: being free of the Creation, and being free of the presence of other humans.[10]

Bloom's comments are incisive, but I will demonstrate below that the American writers dealing with small-town fiction at midcentury are not quite in alliance with his thesis, though they are certainly concerned with the themes he mentions. Freedom from creation and from other humans are both experienced by characters in these narratives as sources of profound anxiety rather than liberation. The overwhelming sense is that humans are fallen, not because they are within nature and community, but because the world of midcentury America has substituted falsehoods in the place of true communion. Like Bloom's religious heroes—and like Whitman and his transcendentalist comrades—these characters find God within themselves by breaking the commands of the Bad God/demiurgical figure who is (in these books) associated with the Calvinist God of Protestantism. In so doing, they pierce the mask of the world and touch the divine. That is to say, they achieve knowledge.

Faith lost and found, a movement from the Bad God to the Good God (or to the Tillichian "God above God"), characterizes the religious concern of small-town fiction. Henry Bellamann's *Kings Row* acts as a distillation of the religious struggles encountered by writers of this period. Halfway through *Kings Row*, Parris Mitchell faces a crisis. His life has up until this moment been a series of losses—his first love Renée, his grandmother, and his lover Cassandra Tower, killed by his mentor (her own father). Parris has already experienced a gradual crisis of belief; at the end of Book One, he reflects that "if there was a God, who looked after everything and everybody, [...] events were strangely ordered."[11] The sermons he recalls from his visits to church are unhelpful in clearing up his confusion. Now, facing the deaths of his grandmother, his mentor, and his lover, Parris visits the Catholic church. Feeling that the world of childhood is "receding at hideous speed," he takes comfort in the strangeness of the place.[12] Parris is experiencing the crisis of individuation I outlined in my discussion of the schoolhouse. He is growing up, falling out of the prelapsarian state of childhood and into adulthood, and this fall is a crisis since he does not feel that religious expression is helpful in reconciling the tensions roiling within him. In the church, Parris encounters Father Donovan, the local priest of the small Catholic congregation, and the two engage in a brief conversation. Parris is desolate and disoriented, about to leave Kings Row for Vienna (where he will remain, off-stage, for much of the rest of the novel). Meanwhile, Father Donovan is representative of the kind of ordered life that Parris can no longer have. In the middle of this exchange, Parris abruptly says, "I don't believe in God."[13] Indeed, he cannot; his certainties about the world around him have been shaken and he stands on the brink of a new life—and God, who was never very close anyway, does not speak.

Father Donovan's response reinforces the centrality of alienation in mid-century small-town literature. The priest remarks that "[i]t must be—pretty hard going sometimes. It's so hard to be alone."[14] If, as per Tillich, "religion is the state of being grasped by the power of being-itself," that power is most often manifest in a desire to become embedded in a particular community or location.[15] Characters in small-town fiction of this period desire a rooted place, a home that is organic and life-giving. Religion gives a sense of belonging to a rooted reality. The metaphorical and concrete natures of space become conflated in the presence of the sacred symbol. In *Kings Row*, Father Donovan explains to Parris his own religion by speaking in terms of location. His experience in the (local) church ties him into the (universal) Church centered in Rome:

> I come here sometimes and then I can see [Rome] and hear it all again. It's like feeling the pulse in your wrist that tells you you are alive. I come here and I can hear the beating of the great heart of Rome. It makes me feel that I'm a part of something—far away as it seems to be sometimes—but a part of something. Yes: I can understand that it must be very hard not to believe in God.[16]

For Father Donovan, the Church offers a solution—partial though it is—to the tripartite estrangement mentioned above. This solution is, importantly, bodily in nature, "like feeling the pulse in your wrist"—and, therefore, incarnational. Father Donovan's beating heart becomes "the great heart of Rome" and he is united with the Church Universal. For him, this unification provides a means of transcendence—of being grasped by the power of Being-itself. For Parris, however, this approach is not useful, which is why Bellamann suggests another path for the disillusioned twentieth-century nonbeliever.

Nature itself conveys grace, as is demonstrated by Father Donovan's own faith. As a Catholic priest in a predominantly Protestant town, Donovan is seen by the locals as "a somewhat sinister figure."[17] He is isolated from them. Nevertheless, it is Donovan who offers the most wholesome vision of the town of Kings Row; the second section of Book One is given over to an account of Donovan wandering around town and out of it into the surrounding countryside, where he is consumed by the beauty of nature as he reads *The Little Flowers of Saint Francis*.[18] Once again, the boundary between the small town and the natural world is permeable. They become closely identified one with the other. So, too, is there a slippage between the past and the present. Donovan "remembered that this feeling for nature was a modern one. Perhaps a very old one, he amended—some sort of paganism that might even be dangerous."[19] The sense that nature conceals the sacred is at once the result of modern alienation and possibly the remainder of an ancient sense of pantheism. It transcends temporal markers. In any case, this sense gives Donovan more confidence in his work as a priest. Because he feels the Divine so strongly in nature, Donovan is perfectly comfortable with the new sciences, which he views as "consonant with one's ideas of an infinite God, the infinite power of Deity, and that sense of the infinite which he could always feel in the finite moment."[20] These words are recognizably continuous with the sacramental Modernism outlined by Buechsel. Nature becomes a church, in a tradition stretching back to Emerson and beyond.

In the sacramental world of nature, the priest and the nonbeliever find a common religion. They share a faith that transcends doctrine. Parris Mitchell never recants his statement to the priest in the Catholic church. Late in the novel, however, Parris and Father Donovan become walking companions, each finding in the other an outlet for his loneliness. Though Parris has not developed a faith in God, his relationship with the priest is nevertheless wholesome and redemptive. Donovan still expresses hope that Parris will eventually come to religion—not so much because he believes Parris will go to hell otherwise as because he desires Parris to be "a happier man than I think you are."[21] The two men are able to bond because both of them believe, as Parris says, in "some sort of relationship with the transcendental *order* of mathematics."[22] At the conclusion of this conversation, Father Donovan offers words that will propel Parris to his epiphany, assuring the other man that intuition—both Parris' and Donovan's—should be trusted. After years of working as a priest, and therefore of witnessing the worst of his parishioners, after years of considering "the order of the universe," Father Donovan feels prepared to say that he and Parris have no reason to differ on points of theology. The two of them "stand, now and then, on common ground."²³ This common ground is precisely a faith that, deep down in the structure of the universe, there is some transcendent Word giving order to it—a logos, which draws philosophical implications from Pythagoreans and religious implications from the Gospel of John. Immediately after this conversation, Parris walks through the pastoral countryside surrounding Kings Row and, coming near his grandmother's old property, he encounters Elise, the young woman who will in the final pages of the book offer him a respite from loneliness. That the meetings parallel each other is not an accident; at the end of the book, Parris once more encounters Donovan, who offers a prophecy of "the new world—the next Kings Row" which is defined by "[a] dance-like [sic] of angels on everlasting guard over the people of this world. Good angels, and evil angels, too, contending with them for dominion."²⁴ Parris realizes that Elise is his good angel. The novel ends with Parris hurrying to meet Elise and thereby to escape the estrangement that he has experienced for the whole novel.²⁵ Though authors of the midcentury were almost universally skeptical of the ability of conventional religion to absolve the tripartite estrangement spoken of by Tillich, they did not give up a religious hope rooted in the material world and in concrete human relations.

The struggle between good angels and evil angels is a shadow of the larger struggle of midcentury religion between a good God and an evil one. Ellery Queen's *Ten Days' Wonder* (1948) examines the tenuous place of religion in the post–World War II world by bringing Ellery face to face with a maleficent Father-God. Ellery's pathway to Wrightsville in this novel, Howard Van Horn, is closely associated with World War II, though he is not himself a soldier. Ellery first encounters Howard immediately before the invasion of France. Howard is a deeply disturbed individual. He is subject to blackouts, during which (he comes to suspect) he is guilty of unspeakable crimes. When Pearl Harbor is bombed, Howard hopes "to get into uniform, get going, do things."²⁶ The war seems to offer Howard a way of escaping his demons; however, the military doesn't "have much use for a guy who [stages] his own private blackouts," and so Howard is rejected, much to the derision of his hometown.²⁷ Howard is defined by the war precisely because he was not a soldier. His failure to serve in the war marks him out, separates him.

Ten Days' Wonder uses religion in its very structure. Ellery, as is his wont during this period of his career, is at first resistant to the idea of getting involved in an investigation. Eventually he relents, however, and goes to Wrightsville to stay with Howard's father, Diedrich Van Horn. As in *Calamity Town*, the actual crime is displaced to late in the novel. Instead, the reader follows Ellery as he begins to piece together the details of a blackmail plot being leveled against Howard. Howard, as it turns out, has been conducting an affair with his father's much younger wife Sally and the couple is being blackmailed. As the novel continues, a pattern emerges. Ellery discovers that Howard seems to be systematically breaking every one of the Ten Commandments. The novel climaxes when Sally Van Horn is murdered. Ellery, thinking that Howard in his depressive and obsessive state has killed his lover while mistaking her for his father, reveals all he knows—at which point Howard commits suicide. The case concluded, Ellery returns home. At a much later period, however, Ellery discovers an accidental piece of evidence in the pocket of coat he once loaned to Howard. He realizes that the real mover behind the entire plot was not Howard at all. Diedrich, knowing of his son's affair with Sally and determined to punish the boy, has forced him to commit or seem to commit a crime against every one of the Ten Commandments, culminating in the murder of Sally. Ellery confronts the patriarch, who has become a withered old man in his dilapidated mansion, and offers him a choice: exposure or suicide. The old man chooses the latter, and Ellery leaves him and walks back into Wrightsville.

This novel is thick with Biblical allusions. As is common in Queen novels, *Ten Days' Wonder* is a highly patterned book. Recurring numerical patterns are standard in the Queen books. Other novels, such as *A Fine and Private Place* (1971), make use of similar strategies. Here, the number ten recurs throughout the novel. The primary point of reference, as shown in the obsession with the Ten Commandments, is the Old Testament, and particularly the books of the Pentateuch. The title itself is such an allusion. Most directly, the title references to the *Proverbes* of John Heywood, which speak of a *nine* days' wonder. But the addition of a tenth day points toward the Old Testament theme of the novel. Moreover, though the Biblical days of creation number seven rather than ten, the practice of patterning the book according to a certain number of days is an allusion to the book of Genesis. Key moments are tied to specific days. Immediately at the end of the seventh day, Diedrich's plan comes to fruition when Ellery reaches his first (incorrect) solution. The opening chapter, "The First Day," begins with an explicit invocation of the biblical text. The first sentence reads, "In the beginning it was without form, a darkness that kept shifting like dancers."[28] The first three words echo the book of Genesis, when the Spirit calls form out of formlessness (similarly, this is the moment when Diedrich's plan begins to take its final shape). The rest of this sentence, and indeed this whole first paragraph, is also an invocation of the Jewish creation myth; in Job 38:7, God demands to know where Job was "[w]hen the morning stars sang together, and all the sons of God shouted for joy?" That is, he demands to know where Job was at the moment of creation. Howard is an Adam-figure, tasked with obeying impossible commands and then punished for failing to obey them. But he is also a Job figure. Job was tested by God and passed the test by patiently waiting for vindication. Howard, on the other hand, is tested by his father and fails the test. The allusion to Jewish creation myths is especially telling since, as the novel will show, Howard is himself a creation of his demonic father-god.

The figure of the father and the figure of the Father-God are closely related to each other. American literature is awash in diabolical father-figures: Huck's pap, Thomas Sutpen in *Absalom, Absalom!*, Humbert Humbert in *Lolita*. Deidrich Van Horn, a self-made man who now controls Wrightsville, fits within this tradition. It takes very little work to imagine the Freudian subtext of these figures. Freud asserts that the (male) child first directs his sexual desire toward his mother and so desires to kill his father. A key factor of early development is successfully transferring affection from the mother and repressing or overcoming the desire to kill the father.[29] This Oedipal complex is a shadow of an older (and, ultimately, more philosophically interesting) conflict. Freud later read the murder of the father back into prehistory with his myth of the primal father in *Totem and Taboo*. The father, for Freud, becomes the Father-God.[30] The Oedipal complex is thus a matter of symbolic importance: the father becomes the Father and by refusing to die he comes to wield, as Slavoj Žižek points out, a godlike power of Law.[31] Žižek, in his gloss on Freud's story, observes that "after the parricide, the [father] reigns as Name-of-the-Father, the agent of the symbolic law that irrevocably precludes access to the forbidden fruit of *jouissance*."[32] The word *jouissance* has a particular meaning in Lacanian theory, but for the purposes of this story it can be simply be glossed as pleasure. Žižek asserts that the father becomes a law-giving force after death and so precludes certain pleasures (such as incest) from his guilt-stricken sons. In effect, the father becomes God the Father.

In *Ten Days' Wonder*, the demonic-divine father is explicitly tied to mid-century capitalist expansion. The Van Horns are "the industrial element, the tycoons, the Mitsubishis of the community."[33] The bank, which in *Calamity Town* belonged to the patriarch John F. Wright, is now "no longer John F.'s but Diedrich Van H.'s."[34] The union between the Divine and the dollar represents a movement recently recognized by Kevin Kruse in his book *One Nation Under God: How Corporate America Invented Christian America*. Kruse argues that the conventional historical understanding of American religion in the 1950s is flawed because it does not take into consideration the social movements of the previous two decades:

> [T]hroughout the 1940s and early 1950s, [James] Fifield and like-minded religious leaders advanced a new blend of conservative religion, economics, and politics that one observer aptly anointed "Christian libertarianism." [...] [T]hey saw Christianity and capitalism as inextricably intertwined and argued that spreading the gospel of one required spreading the gospel of the other.[35]

Kruse's book delineates the union of the commercial and the Christian, and particularly the union of conservative capitalism with conservative Christianity. By 1925, the vision of Jesus as "a glad handing host, Rotarian, speculative promoter, and canny businessman"[36] was well-established, and it is this typology that Kruse shows continuing in the anti–Roosevelt, anti–New Deal religiosity of the 1930s and '40s. The Van Horns are the new aristocracy of post-war America, an aristocracy that unites capitalism with conservative religion to an unprecedented degree. Diedrich Van Horn is the son of a firebrand preacher; he was not born to wealth but acquired it. And his wife, Sally Van Horn, is herself a product of Low Village, where the "foreigners" live.[37] Van Horn is rich from industry, not heredity, and steeped in a particularly fundamentalist kind of religion. His ascendancy is explicitly compared to a dictatorship. It is also tied to the war, since "[t]he great upsurge in the Van Horns' fortunes seemed to have come just before during and since World War II."[38] Thus, *Ten Days' Wonder*, even more than *Calamity Town*, is deeply tied to its historical moment. By the end of World War II the demonic-divine Father God has merged with the forces of industry in a way that was hinted at in pre-war literature.

If *Calamity Town* is about Ellery Queen discovering America, *Ten Days' Wonder* is about the newly Americanized Ellery Queen examining the place of religion in a post-war America. Ellery's relationship with Howard is explicitly said to begin before the war and continues after the war has concluded. Shortly after Howard Van Horn first contacts Ellery, the detective has a brief flashback to their first meeting in "prewar Paris: Paris of the Cagoulards and the *populaires;* of the incredible Exposition, when Nazis with elaborate cameras and guidebooks infested the right bank, shouldering their way *Uebermensch*-wise through pale refugees from Vienna and Prague."[39] Howard is working in Paris as a sculptor, carving "such looming deities of maleness as Zeus, Moses, and Adam."[40] Howard's obsession with masculinity is directly tied to his obsession with his father. What is telling here is the fact that Queen directly invokes two Jewish figures (who are not deities) and one Greek god— indeed, *the* Greek god, Zeus himself, Lord of thunder. These are also all figures associated with lawmaking and lawbreaking. Zeus, of course, is the father of the gods. Moses brings the Ten Commandments down from the mountain. Adam, in the Christian tradition, is responsible for the damnation of his children.

Thus, Ellery in this novel goes up against God himself. The post-war setting of the novel is significant. A God who allows his chosen people to be slaughtered, who saddles them with unreasonable demands and then punishes them for failing to meet those demands, is no God at all. He is a powerful malevolence more akin to Lovecraft's Cthulhu than to any sort of beneficent Divinity. Howard's obsession with divine father-figures provides a psychological clue to the mystery. Though the Biblical figures Queen evokes are Jewish, Van Horn's upbringing was Calvinist. His dead father was a preacher who "believed in a God you could see and feel—especially feel" and who "had created God in his own image."[41] At first, Diedrich Van Horn seems to have escaped his father's influence—he is a vast godlike man who has provided for his own son the image of God. Ellery recognizes Diedrich's godlike qualities early on, and wonders "if Diedrich had the gods' vices as well as their virtues. Whatever his vices might be, they would be anything but trivial; this man was quite above pettiness."[42] Of course, like many murderers in crime stories, Diedrich is ultimately revealed to be pettiness itself, in spite of the grandeur of his methods. Nor is he quite as removed as he seems from the old death-dealing religion of fire and brimstone, of hell and destruction. Shortly after Ellery arrives at the Van Horn mansion, he has a bizarre encounter with a mysterious figure wandering the grounds and murmuring "*Yea, though I walk through the valley of the shadow of death....*"[43] This phantom is Diedrich Van Horn's mother, a woman who has lapsed into senility and now haunts the estate like a wraith.

I have mentioned before that the author-figure Ellery Queen was a construct, the product of collaboration between Frederic Dannay and Manfred Lee. Thanks to Joseph Goodrich's *Blood Relations: The Selected Letters of Ellery Queen, 1947–1950*, it is possible for readers today to glimpse the often-fractious process by which these two men constructed their stories. *Ten Days' Wonder* proved to be a particularly difficult story for the men to agree upon. Their correspondence allows us to see the thinking behind such odd figures as the mother. Frederic Dannay considered the mother important as "a psychological 'plant'—she prepares the way for the acceptance of the Biblical theme."[44] In fact, Van Horn's mother is a key to the thematic substructure of the mystery. For Van Horn is closely allied to a particularly puritanical form of American Christianity, and that Puritanism continues to haunt him, as it haunts America, long after it has lost its wits. Though he designs the Ten Commandments murder as a way to draw Ellery into the case and to convince him that Howard is the killer, Ellery recognizes at the end of the novel that Van Horn has been shaped by his own upbringing. Van Horn's father, as a fire-and-brimstone preacher, "*preached the anthropomorphic, personally vengeful, jealous God of the Old Testament*" (italics original).[45] According to Ellery, Van Horn's elaborate plot is a way to "kill [the father] fifty years after" his death.[46] Again, the demonic-divine Father appears; religion is, for Queen, a matter of fathers all the way down. The father has died and assumed the role of Law, while the mother remains as a physical reminder that the New England Puritanism of the region has warped her son, has created him just as he creates his own son.

Revivalism offers one escape from this crisis by focusing on the ecstatic and the experiential, rather than the legal and the theological. However, revival carries with it its own danger—the risk that the urge to submerge in the collective will lead to dangerous fanaticism. Writers about small towns during this period cast the revival as a bizarre, and probably dangerous, phenomenon. Lillian Smith's 1944 novel *Strange Fruit* is most often discussed as a problem novel about racism in the segregated South. In this novel, Tracy Deen—the son of a leading family in the town—conducts an affair with an African American woman named Nonnie. At first content with their secret passion, Tracy is gradually convinced to give Nonnie up—after which he is murdered by her brother, who then leaves town. The novel climaxes in the lynching of the African American Big Henry, Tracy's childhood playmate, for the murder. The novel is recognizably about race. Though some critics, such as Cheryl Johnson, have attempted to interrogate the queer subtext that undergirds the narrative,[47] the race-based reading of the book holds the most sway. However, the racial aspect cannot be separated from anxieties about religion in the 1940s and '50s. While it would be incorrect to argue, as Edwin Bergum's mythical critic does, that Smith lays the blame for racial intolerance and racial violence at the feet of Southern religion, she certainly sees religion as complicit in the murders that make up the novel's core.[48] The ecstatic revivalism of the small town functions to maintain a racially unjust *status quo*.

Historically, religion in America was explicitly invoked to maintain group cohesion. Paul Conkin, in his book *A Requiem for the American Village*, discusses Thomas Jefferson's "very general theism" as a unifying factor in early American thought.[49] Tocqueville argues that "men cannot do without dogmatic beliefs" and that "the most desirable seem to me to be in matters of religion."[50] Religion, for Tocqueville, is important because of its social utility. He argues that religions "impose upon each man certain obligations toward the human race or encourage a shared endeavor, something drawing him away from a contemplation of himself."[51] As such, he argues that religions are chiefly interested in the demand "to purify, govern, and restrain the overly fervent and exclusive taste for comfort which men experience in times of equality."[52] Religion functions as a stop-gap between democracy and mass tyranny. In the twentieth century, the growing awareness of American diversity, together with the experiences of a depression and two world wars, led to a re-evaluation of this religion-as-referee ideology.

Religious thinkers divided broadly into two camps: the fundamentalists and the liberals. For fundamentalists, religion served as a bulwark against the godlessness of modernity. For liberals, religion provided a way by which the world could be improved; the expansion of charity—the purification and governance spoken of by Tocqueville—was regarded as the chief concern of religion. Walter Rauschenbusch, writing in the early part of the twentieth century, argued that "[i]t is one of the most pressing duties of religious men to insist on [the] fact of solidarity and press its ethical importance home to the conscience of every man."[53] Against such a viewpoint, Reinhold Niebuhr warns in his 1932 book *Moral Man and Immoral Society* "that a sharp distinction must be drawn between the moral and social behavior of individuals and of social groups."[54] Because of this distinction between the individual and the group, Niebuhr argues that there are necessarily boundaries beyond which religious love cannot move. These boundaries are related to the size of the collective, with the result that "religion may increase the power and enlarge the breadth of the generous social attitudes, which nature prompts in the intimate circle; but [...] there are definite limits to its power and extension."[55] Those who argue otherwise are, to use Niebuhr's dismissive phrase, "moralists," not having "an understanding of the brutal character of behavior of all human collectives."[56] Niebuhr's argument is that religion may encourage individuals to behave better, but there is no guarantee that this positive effect will be extended to all of society.

Revival is, in *Strange Fruit*, the domain of white privilege. Periodically—as with, for instance, the Great Awakening—America has been swept by a wave of religious revivals. Revivals—tent-meetings in which people come together to "get religion"—feature in several midcentury small-town novels. For Lillian Smith, revivalism is a uniquely white phenomenon. The African American characters in *Strange Fruit* view revivalist religion as a pastime for the white citizens of the town. Puritanical focus on propriety and the *status quo* must have some sort of safety-valve and religious revivals provide that valve just as surely as the lynching later in the novel does. The African American characters in *Strange Fruit*, outside of one minister and his wife, are not interested in religion at all; they are much more interested in keeping out of the way of white people. Because the revival is a domain of privilege, the revivalist minister Dunwoodie is a servant of the *status quo* and so ultimately does far more harm than good. The Reverend Dunwoodie exemplifies muscular Christianity. His revivalism is enthusiastic and masculine; in private, he tells Tracy that men need a God who is their "own Kind"—that is, male.[57] Dunwoodie is, in fact, a close representation—not even a parody, but something much closer to a portrait—of the type of 1920s revivalism exemplified in Billy Sunday. Anthony Channell Hilfer sums up Sunday's depiction of the Christian as "a fighter, and his enemy [...] anyone who was 'immoral,' theologically unorthodox, or 'un–American'—to sum it all up, a nonconformist of any sort."[58] Dunwoodie seeks to break Tracy's nonconformity and return him to traditionally white ways of being-in-the-world. Dunwoodie's appeal to Tracy is twofold. In the first place, he offers a strong masculine presence that has been lacking in the younger man's life. That is, he offers a father. While Tracy is at first dismissive of the preacher, in short order he falls under the other man's spell.

In the second place, Dunwoodie offers Tracy a means by which he can re-integrate with his community after being so thoroughly separated from it under the dual pressures of World War I and his love affair with Nonnie. It is Dunwoodie who insists that Tracy must reject his own inclinations to treat Nonnie as a human. Dunwoodie tells Tracy that "you have to keep pushing them back across that nigger line."[59] This line is at once metaphorical and literal; Smith makes much of the very literal boundary running through the town separating the races. Dunwoodie's words are, thus, designed to maintain not only the ideological *status quo* but also the concrete-material separation of the races.

Religion is a tool of in-group maintenance, and as such is directed against in-group members who have deviated in thought or action. In the case of the white revivalism of Smith, the primary deviant is Tracy Deen, a soldier recently returned from the First World War. During World War II and in the decades immediately following it, estranged characters are often soldiers who in the process of their experiences overseas have come to view their own essential nature as separated from itself. Though *Strange Fruit* is set before World War II, that conflict's predecessor is key in differentiating Tracy from other members of his community. It is during his wartime experiences that Tracy first realizes that he is in love with Nonnie.[60] The difficult experiences in Europe grant to Tracy, if only briefly, a new perspective on race relations in the South. Upon his return, Tracy experiences dramatic estrangement from his hometown:

> The South was a picture full of things, people, smells, deeds, sounds. But no feeling. Things have changed, folks said. You won't know the place. Niggers all going North. Hard to get help. Everybody biggety. War's ruined em. Won't work. Cotton slumping. Boll weevil been terrible.
>
> He listened. There were words as familiar to them as his own name, but words with which he now refused identification. It was as if he were the only thing real. The rest was made up.[61]

Smith illustrates Tracy's distance by conveying the words of his fellow countrymen in telegraphic language. The sentences are not even sentences. They are flashes of thought, like a montage in a film. Nor is Tracy the only estranged character. His distance from his hometown parallels that of his eventual murderer Ed, one of the African Americans who has gone up north (to Washington) to escape the racist hegemony of the region.

Dunwoodie uses religious revival to socialize Tracy back into conformist white society. Under the influence of the preacher, Tracy decides to join the church. Immediately, he finds himself re-integrated into the community in a way that he has not experienced since returning from the war. He gains the approval of the men of the town, the affection of its women, and—perhaps most important of all—he gains the whole town's approval of his future "fine little wife."⁶² But in doing so he must reject Nonnie, and so reject the better part of himself. He attempts to pay her off, leaving the money on a fence post. Immediately after this act of final renunciation, Tracy is killed.⁶³ His soul has died already, and so it is only natural that his body should follow. In Smith's world, religion holds no promise of redemption; indeed, it is ultimately responsible for destroying Tracy. The point is not that religion is actively evil but that it is passively so. It is incapable of restraining the evil of society—it is even a silent (and often unsilent) partner to those evils. Religion is not a tool for democracy; it is a palliative designed to reintegrate people into the *status quo*.

The salvation offered by Dunwoodie is revealed to be damnation itself. The minister uses the saccharine vision of the mother's heart, broken by the wild living of her son, to convince Tracy to abandon Nonnie.⁶⁴ Just as in *Ten Days' Wonder*, the mother is a physical manifestation of spiritual control. The difference is that in Smith she is wholly normalized, part of the fabric of the community, while Queen allows her to exist only as an obscene residue. When Tracy decides to break with Nonnie, it is precisely this sentimental identification with the injured mother that he cites as a primary motivation, saying that he has been in the process of "ruining her whole" life.⁶⁵ Tracy says that he has determined that he must come to terms with his effect on other people. These other people notably do not include Nonnie; he has successfully pushed her back across the color line, dehumanized her according to Dunwoodie's suggestion. The preacher may talk about hell and heaven, but his interests are ultimately this-worldly. He wants to maintain social order, not disrupt it. His response to Tracy's murder is, thus, telling: he is more worried that it will disturb his revival than he is about the dead man's immortal soul. So, too, with his discussion of the lynching, in which he agrees with Brother Saunders that "it doesn't do any good to criticize people—not at a time like this. Only stirs up more bad feelings between the races. A servant of God has no business mixing in such matters. Our job is the winning of souls to Christ."⁶⁶ The bitter irony here is that Smith presents all of Dunwoodie's work—including his failure to condemn the murder of Henry—as actively damning the souls of people around him.

There is, thus, a deep anxiety about religion in midcentury small-town fiction. This anxiety is often secular; God, if he exists, is not present in religious observance. When the literature admits the Divine, the results are as often destructive as they are redemptive, as is the case with Flannery O'Connor's *Wise Blood* (1952). *Wise Blood* tells the story of Hazel Motes, a soldier returned to his homeland with the determination to not only *not* become a preacher, but to establish a church whose basic tenet is that God does not exist. Over the course of the novel, Hazel is humiliated and frustrated by a Deity who will not allow himself to be ignored. The book ends when

Hazel blinds himself—in imitation of the fraudulent preacher Hawks—and performs other acts of physical self-torture as a means of penance. *Wise Blood* is populated by characters who are at odds with the community around them, at odds with themselves, and at odds with God. They are examples of the tripartite estrangement described by Tillich in his sermon "To Whom Much Is Forgiven…."[67] Tillich argues that humans are estranged from God, the Ground of Being Itself, who "appears to us as an oppressive power," from others, in whom "we find hidden hostilities," and from the self.[68] In *Wise Blood*, the failure to resolve such estrangement may lead to the worship of obviously false gods (as with Sabbath Hawks) or the final loss of all humanity (as with Enoch Emery). Sabbath, the oversexed daughter of a fraudulently blind preacher, sets out to seduce Hazel Motes (in spite of Hazel's own stated disinterest) and becomes O'Connor's secular Madonna when Enoch brings her a shriveled mummy from the local museum. She is, in her own words, "a bastard," which is telling because bastardy cuts (or cut, particularly at this time) the child off from the normal ties of community.[69] She wants Hazel, implicitly, so that she can settle down, become rooted, and leave her father's wandering lifestyle.[70] The fact that Hazel prizes mobility so much should be a warning sign; so, too, should the fact that he is in many ways a reiteration of her father (and becomes literally that and more when he actually blinds himself, in contrast to Hawks' failure to do the same). In the end, once Hazel has blinded himself, Sabbath leaves, saying that "she hadn't counted on no honest-to-Jesus blind man."[71] The joke in this line should be self-evident; Hazel is, in the end, genuinely honest to Jesus.

For O'Connor, fanaticism cut off from any sort of signified Transcendent ultimately leads to dehumanization. Tillich calls fanaticism "the correlate to spiritual self-surrender: it shows the anxiety which it was supposed to conquer."[72] *Wise Blood* presents readers with Enoch Emery as a particularly poignant (and viciously funny) example of estrangement. When he first meets Hazel Motes, Enoch claims to have been in the city two months after having escaped (Huck Finn–like) from a school where he was sent by a "Welfare woman."[73] In spite of his residence in the town, Enoch has no friends and immediately fixates on Hazel. The desire to belong, to be a part of something, is central to the boy's story; in this same passage, one of his first statements is that he works "for the city," a claim that indicates a longing for communal affiliation. Hazel's atheistic sermons inspire Enoch to bring him a mummy as the "new jesus" (the proper name, tellingly, not capitalized) and Enoch expects to be rewarded; he desires "to become something."[74] There is an ambiguity in this phrase, which O'Connor exploits: to become something means, on the face of it, to become famous, well known, loved. This is the desire of the human laboring under Tillich's tripartite estrangement. But Enoch does not desire to become some*one*, but some*thing*—and that is, of course, exactly what happens to him. Enoch sees an advertisement for "Gonga, the Giant Jungle Monarch" and quickly declares, "I know what I want."[75] Enoch has previously met Gonga, a movie publicity stunt—really, a man in a gorilla suit who stands outside the cinema shaking the hands of children. Enoch slips into line and shakes the gorilla's hand and the narrator tells us that "[i]t was the first hand that had been extended to Enoch since he had come to the city. It was warm and soft."[76] The touch of the hand represents contact, community (thus, "the right hand of fellowship" is a standard phrase for religious communities). Enoch decides that he wants this community—more properly, he wants to be a bearer of this community, to have people want to shake *his* hand in the same way he shook the gorilla's hand (he wants, in fact, to become a minister of the church of Gonga). He slips into the truck transporting the actor in the gorilla costume and overpowers the men inside, then rushes to the park where he ceremonially buries his old clothes and dons the Gonga costume. In O'Connor's prose, Enoch's transformation is signified by a change in pronoun: "he" becomes "it."[77] Its "god had finally rewarded it."[78] But the reward comes at a price. Having sought community in this inhuman messiah, Enoch is stripped of his humanity and exiled from the world of humans; the first couple he encounters runs from him, and he is left sitting, staring alone at the lights of the city.[79] This, then, is the awful price of estrangement for Enoch—the thing he worships ultimately dehumanizes him.

The ghosts of dead fathers (and, therefore, of dead gods) haunt these anti-religious protagonists. In *Wise Blood*, an important combatant in the battle for Hazel's soul is the ghost of his grandfather, "a waspish old man who had ridden over three counties with Jesus hidden in his head like a stinger."[80] It is against the redemption promised him by the old man that Hazel struggles, against the assurance that "Jesus would have him in the end."[81] A central joke of O'Connor's novel is that, the more he kicks against the goads, the more like a preacher Hazel becomes. His clothing indicates that he is already far along this path; after all, he is introduced carrying "a stiff black broad-brimmed hat."[82] Even the work he finds for himself is that of an itinerant preacher. His gospel is irreligion, but it is a gospel all the same. Moreover, he insists that the fraudulent preacher Hawks try to save him.[83] Even his blasphemy has an air of desperation about it. Jonathan Baumbach has observed that "the commission of sin becomes for Haze [sic] a kind of ritual declaration of freedom from God the Father's authority."[84] When Hazel strikes out against the God preached by his grandfather—a God in whom he insists he does not believe—he simply confirms the power of that God over his life.

Even if a character happens to finally reach what O'Connor regards as true contact with the Divine, this achievement comes at a terrible price. He must be stripped, slowly and systematically, of all pretense to self-determination. Hazel is a soldier lately returned from combat. While in the war, Hazel experienced a crisis of faith; during his time in the military, "[h]e had all the time he could want to study his soul in and assure himself that it was not there."[85] Hazel's experiences in the war separate him from his fellow humans (he is forgotten), from himself (he despises his own lapses), and from God (he begins preaching a new atheistic religion). Hazel echoes the effects of World War II on the American psyche. This crisis of faith motivates Hazel throughout the novel. The Army follows him, both literally in the case of his recurring checks and figuratively in his duffel bag[86] and his army shoes[87]— shoes that ultimately become tools in his self-immolation. Rather than having his horizons expanded by his experience in the Army, Hazel has found them limited; he is now subject to monomania, to a desperate desire to prove that Jesus doesn't exist. His attempts to avoid becoming a preacher ironically lead to precisely that end, suggesting that Hazel does not know himself as well as he thinks he does.

The truth is, as Sabbath tells him, he "don't want nothing but Jesus."[88] As is often the case, O'Connor is punning. In the immediate sense, Sabbath is saying that Hazel doesn't *desire* anything but Jesus; his monomaniacal preaching of the church without Christ is a symptom of his own deep need for Christ. Moreover, in a world of postwar prosperity, the automobile has become a marker of social stability. Hazel has a car (albeit a terrible one) and puts faith in this machine to free him.[89] Hazel wants for nothing: sex, a car, even a sense of purpose—but what he doesn't have (not yet, anyway) is Jesus. But that very lack indicates that there is something there to lack, just as Hazel admits that you cannot blaspheme unless something exists to be blasphemed against.[90] The biggest joke in all of this is that no one else in the novel cares. When Hazel stands on a street corner, desperately blaspheming, rather than being upset with him for calling into question their deepest spiritual beliefs, the people of the city are annoyed that he is getting in the way of their pleasure-seeking.[91] In his act of bearing anti–Christian witness, Hazel is the only true believer in a town full of Christians. The crazed old grandfather was right all along. Jesus gets Hazel in the end. And in the beginning; if Hazel's street-corner sermons are attempts at desperate blasphemy, they are also the words of a prophet, of a man who negatively testifies to the continued relevance of religion in the lives of a populace that has forgotten. Hazel Motes is, as Robert Detweiler asserts, the postwar prophet of God:

> [O'Connor's] art illustrates the observation of Paul Tillich that "now, in the old age of our secular world, we have seen the most horrible manifestation of the daemonic images; we have looked more deeply into the mystery of evil than most generations before us; we have seen the unconditional devotion of millions to us a satanic image; we feel our period's sickness unto death."[92]

In World War II, a tremendous attempt was made to unify concerns about democracy with concerns about religion. The end of the war brought a recognition and a crisis: a recognition that a whole century of bloodshed on this scale was untenable, and a crisis of faith. What authors of this period seek, then, is a manner of belief that would not lead to violence but to redemption, and they found this belief in an incarnational mode. O'Connor, as the most traditional believer discussed in this chapter, presents the most traditional solution. The human must encounter the Divine and lose himself, must die literally and spiritually to his own pride, in order to be born again. But O'Connor's solution is tempered by the horrific years preceding the composition of *Wise Blood*. Hazel is a minister despite his attempts to avoid that fate. In the end, Hazel finds a kind of family with Mrs. Flood, his landlady. Certainly, it is not an ideal family, and not one free of exploitation on her part, but it is nevertheless a family, a communion of two lonely people. Moreover, Hazel embodies within his own flesh the self-abnegation required by the fact of being grasped by Being Itself. And so Hazel becomes an ironic Christ-figure, a way by which Mrs. Flood is able to transcend her own loneliness and reach some measure of the Divine, though O'Connor is typically elliptical in what exactly Mrs. Flood perceives in the "pin point of light" in the dead man's eyes.[93] Hazel has fulfilled his calling at last; he has become a minister, one who conveys grace.

Not all authors saw traditional religion as offering the hopeful, albeit painful, transcendence of O'Connor. They were obliged to look elsewhere. *Raintree County* stages the standard midcentury conflict between metaphysically-grounded religion and religion as a means of control. As in *Strange Fruit*, a central setting of *Raintree County* is a revival. But this revival is different because it is not (or is not *only*) a means of social control. The revival is often, explicitly or implicitly, compared to a carnival. Revivals are carnivalesque in that they call for participation outside of the standard pulpit-congregation dichotomy. Bakhtin observes that "[c]arnival is not a spectacle seen by the people; they live in it, and everyone participates because its very idea embraces all the people."[94] In the same way, revivals and other forms of ecstatic religious experience seen in Protestant evangelical religion in the United States encourage mass participation on the part of the audience. The Dionysian excesses of the revival may be oppressive, but they may also unexpectedly lead to actual rebirth. While these fervors can often be used to serve the *status quo*, they can just as easily turn around and co-opt the *status quo* itself. *Raintree County* contrasts its protagonist's pantheistic religious experience with revivalist religion, but the novel also suggests that both can be means of accessing something divine.

As in *Strange Fruit* the revival in *Raintree County* is an outlet for the pent-up tensions native to small-town life. Every year, the women of the town go back to the tent to be converted, and these conversions are spoken of in sexual terms, indicating that it offers the women a way of experiencing satisfaction that their husbands cannot or will not give them. Esther Shawnessy, John Shawnessy's wife, is one of only two women in the town who does not compulsively seek satisfaction in the preacher's tent; on her first visit with Preacher Jarvey, he asks whether she has been converted and she recalls that "her conversion at age sixteen had been a dreadful and exhausting experience. She had been broken up for days before and after. She never expected to be converted again, and didn't understand people who got converted over and over."[95] The symbolic link between Esther's first conversion and her first sexual experience could hardly be more explicit. Preacher Jarvey is a sexual being in a way that *Strange Fruit*'s Dunwoodie is not. The scene in which preacher Jarvey attempts to convert Esther is rife with sexual subtext, with the preacher persisting "with a force that she would have deemed brutal except for the holy purpose behind it," a force that culminates in the preacher attempting to convert her with "his godshout."[96] This revivalist Jarvey is popular with the ladies of the town because (it is implied) the experience of being converted by him gives them a sexual satisfaction that they, in their puritanical society, cannot otherwise have. Thus, he offers a carnivalesque escape from propriety. As it develops, preacher Jarvey is conspiring with Esther's father to expose a purported affair between Shawnessy and Evelina Brown, a local freethinking woman. Lockridge soon reveals that preacher Jarvey is (predictably) motivated less by a concern for purity than by "a whip of shrewd lust."[97] That is, he is getting off on the idea of Shawnessy and Evelina getting it on.

For Lockridge, sex is divine and cannot be denied even by the most puritanical of revivalist preachers. Unlike the Reverend Dunwoodie, Jarvey is himself deeply conflicted precisely because he is making a tremendous effort to deny the lifegiving spirit that runs through him. This spirit is sexual and fecund, and so is tied to Lockridge's mythography of Raintree County itself. Jarvey's rhetorical style and methods of salvation are highly sexualized, but he is obliged to sublimate that sexuality to an uncomfortable extent. For Preacher Jarvey, sex is so strongly denied that even an accidental encounter with nude statues in a garden is likely to confuse and terrify him.[98] Over the course of his activities leading up to the night on which he will assemble a mob to burn Evelina Brown's house and expose Shawnessy as an adulterer, Jarvey has a sexual encounter with a local woman, the Widow Passifee. As the preacher and the widow drink dandelion wine together, their discussion turns to Shawnessy's purported affair—an affair to which the Widow Passifee claims to be a witness. Jarvey declares that the two of them should pray. Again, the sexual and the religious are deeply united here, with the widow telling the preacher that he should "go on and pray as hard as you want, Brother Jarvey. My daughter Libby's down at the school and nobody'll bother us."[99] Jarvey makes love to the widow while having visions of "Cretan lawns"— indicating that, beneath even the puritanical religion of Brother Jarvey is a wilder, pagan belief in life itself. The dandelion wine, associated with wildness and nature, moves him into a position of encountering the sacred-sexual, but he cannot remain there. The preacher's lapse does not keep him from his self-righteous and erotically charged mission, but it does prove to be his undoing when two small children who witnessed the act tell Jarvey's assembled mob. The result is, surprisingly, not violence, but laughter.[100] The laughter of the mob in this context is redemptive because it is a laughter that exposes hypocrisy while not condemning the natural urges that motivate the preacher. Jarvey exits the narrative running "down the road into Waycross, with short steps, hands before him like a man half-blind and beset by pestering sprites."[101] This revivalist minister, incapable of understanding or interacting with the sacred world, blinded by his focus on holiness, is offered a moment of redemptive laughter. Instead, he makes his way blindly back toward Waycross in disgrace.

The dandelion wine and the redemptive laughter of the mob figure into Lockridge's broader purpose in *Raintree County*. Lockridge is seeking a new language for religious experience. *Raintree County* portrays redemption as a union of the sacred and the secular—of nature and Divinity. It is, thus, dramatizing a fundamental midcentury shift. Faced with the prospect of a malevolent deity, authors of the period make a turn toward what Tillich calls "the God above God." For Tillich, theism itself must be transcended.[102] In *Raintree County*, John Shawnessy decides that the true religion of America is politics—that is, Puritan systems of control—and attempts to create a new religion. This religion is characterized by a sacramental view of nature. In Shawnessy's view, Christianity rejects humanity. His new religion celebrates it. There is no afterlife, only the present; there is no miracle more wonderful than life itself. Accordingly (in another Whitmanesque twist), "every human life is sacred because it is the whole of life and [...] in the continuity of being, no life is lost."[103] The new religion discussed here is, in fact, quite an old religion. Shawnessy's faith is essentially sacramental, according to the terms defined by Buechsel. The sacramental bespeaks "the inextricable inter-fusion of the physical and the spiritual [...] crucial values seen as inherent in the natural order and learned from encounters with the often mystically depicted Midwestern land."[104] Because of his unconventional religious beliefs, Shawnessy is branded as an atheist—atheist being "anyone who didn't believe in the stern old God of Raintree County and in the literal truth of the Bible."[105] But in Lockridge's cosmos Shawnessy is more religious than any of his peers because he is able to tap into the mystic unity at the heart of the county—typified in the Raintree and the pastoral/Edenic world.

The key to understanding *Raintree County* is sexuality—not just the act itself but the ways in which it becomes a signifier for prosperity and fecundity. Because sex already exists in the very language used to describe Paradise, sex is one of Lockridge's central thematic concerns. The story of the Garden of Eden is introduced early to John Wickliff Shawnessy by his father (a preacher). Young Johnny thinks of this tale as "the oldest story in the world, sealed with the seal of primal mystery."[106] This idea of "primal mystery" is important for Lockridge because he believes that the small town—really, the land surrounding the small towns of Raintree County—holds within itself a sort of mystery, the same mystery that is found in sex and procreation. Mark Buechsel's description of the attitude of the Midwestern Modernists applies equally well to Lockridge. These authors "portray the fecund Midwestern land as a spiritually significant, highly sexual, and sacramental realm at odds with the New England-derived [...] culture."[107] The mixture of the sacred and the secular (which might be called incarnation, a putting-on-of-flesh) is central to Lockridge's artistic and philosophical project in *Raintree County*.

Accounts of religion in midcentury small-town fiction offer in miniature the larger struggle in American religious thought in the years during and following World War II. Writers, faced with the prospect of a demonic-Divine, sought to escape the shadow of traditional Protestantism by killing this Divine father-figure and replacing him with something else, something more pantheistic. Most often, traditional conceptions of God—both the Calvinist and the Revivalist—are seen as tools for maintaining social order. The revival needed is, thus, one that focuses on the incarnational aspects of religion, divorced from dogma or superstition. This is the kind of religion that O'Connor and Lockridge pursue in their portrayals of belief in the small-town setting. In light of post-war realities, O'Connor presents in *Wise Blood* a kind of dark incarnation: the Word must be made flesh, but that flesh will inevitably be offensive and suffering, as with the final state of Hazel Motes' corpse. Lockridge sees the Divine as already incarnated in nature, to be accessed by a carnivalesque, sexual leap into community. In either case, what these authors of the 1940s and '50s are seeking is a form of transcendence—a movement beyond the superficial pieties of religion in order to touch the throbbing heart of Being Itself.

Seven

Fortunate Fall
The Courthouse

The small town's status as a fallen Eden opens it to the question outlined by Jeffrey Miller in *The Structures of Law and Literature*. Miller asks readers "in a post–Eden world, is earthly justice impossible? Is there a [...] Promised Land, a new Eden?"[1] For Miller, the fact of the fall requires the institution of law, such that "Eden—the earthbound utopia—is the beginning and end of the law."[2] Eden is the beginning because the fall occurs in Eden, and it is the end both in the sense of being a goal (thus, an end-point, a *telos* or eschaton) and in the sense that the law is not needed in whatever future glorified state the law might restore. The courthouse provides the small town with an identity because it constitutes the town as an entity bound by laws. But in midcentury small-town fiction, law proves to be an inadequate dam between evil and the world. Rather, law*breaking* is the redemptive act within small-town fiction—going against legal and community norms to access the lost Eden. Midcentury small-town fiction represents the breaking of legal and social norms as a potential source of transcendence. Small-town narratives of the period are not, despite some appearances to the contrary, interested in preserving the *status quo*. They are part of a broader post–War trend that would culminate in the sixties—a trend of distrusting authority figures and seeing real liberation in the breaking of laws. To transgress the law of the community is to assert one's own ability to discover The Good for oneself. This Law that must be broken is not just the established legal code but the situational and social norms of the community. Midcentury small-town narratives are stories about breaking the law as a positive good.

The law is most frequently represented in small-town fiction—naturally enough—by the figure of the lawyer. In James Gould Cozzens' *The Just and the Unjust* (1942), a young(-ish) lawyer named Abner Coates is attempting to make his name in the small town of Childerstown by trying a number of cases, including a murder trial. His father—once himself a lawyer, now a judge—offers a dash of cold water to the young man's idealistic hopes regarding social change. He observes that the law, in spite of its drawbacks, is "the stronghold of what reason men ever get around to using. [...] It gives you a groundwork of good sense."³ Cozzens' understanding of the law, at least as presented here, is that it is the only stop-gap between humanity and mass chaos. The lawyer manages expectations to achieve the best results for the whole community. The lawyer is a lonely figure because he is a man set apart. This alienation is central to his function in the town; one of the reasons that authors of small-town fiction often choose lawyers as their protagonists (in addition to detectives, poets, and so on) is precisely the fact that these characters are alienated. Lawyers are alienated in that they are fundamentally aristocratic characters. Distance permits authors to examine the ambiguities of democratic life in midcentury America, with the protagonist entering the fray and commenting upon it rather than being caught up in it. However, the side-effect of this removal is that the lawyer-protagonist is lonely; Richard Weisberg, in delineating the six traits of the lawyer-protagonist, places "*Frugality (and bachelorhood)*" at number five, saying that "the fictional lawyer's lack of interest in personal comforts frequently extends to his remaining a bachelor; storytellers do not permit accomplished lawyers to have personally fulfilling lives." (italics original)⁴ Alienated from his society, the lawyer experiences the full pain of tripartite alienation while trying to restore Eden for his fellow-citizens.

Abner's relationship with the *status quo* demonstrates the troubling aspects of the lawyer's position. He must uphold the high moral standards of the law while at the same time recognizing that the law, as a human instrument, is fallible. This fallibility extends to Cozzens himself. As an author, Cozzens reflexively falls back on misogynistic assumptions, but locating his works within the context of the small-town fiction provides a tool with which to engage the problematic aspects of his work without neglecting the very real strengths that critics have noticed in him. His verbal portrait of Mary Beach, a schoolgirl who (in a minor subplot) accuses her teacher of seducing her, will help to illustrate both aspects of Cozzens' reactionary stance and his concern with the ambiguities of life. Abner thinks of Mary Beach as advanced for her age and speculates that she had understood that her teacher was attracted to her and so "she kept signaling little invitations, making them, if Sam [the teacher] pretended to ignore them (as he very likely did at first) bolder each time and more alluring."⁵ This paragraph is typical of Cozzens, demonstrating both an astonishing reflexive misogyny *and* moral complexity. It is needless, I think, to say too much about the perils of shifting the blame from the male offender onto the female victim. Cozzens' anxiety about the ability of the law to discern wrong from right is, however, equally apparent. The law is an imperfect tool for establishing a perfect society.

There is, for Cozzens, an eternal conflict between legal-ideal norms of right and wrong and the material (incarnate) world surrounding his characters. Abner's internal meditations are characteristic of his profession as a lawyer and should be read as such. For Dwight Macdonald, Cozzens' fascination with the law is a problem, since "to Cozzens a trial is reality while emotional, disorderly life is the illusion. He delights in the tedious complications of lawyer's talk, the sort of thing one skips in reading the court record of even the most sensational trials."[6] The fact that Macdonald contrasts life and law is particularly suggestive, since other critics have also observed Cozzens' fascination with legal procedure and argue that, on the contrary, this fascination is based in the author's respect for the complexity of life. Louis Coxe credits the author with "a ratiocinative technique superimposed upon a dramatic, almost melodramatic, subject matter," and says that this contrast provides much of the pleasure to be derived from Cozzens.[7] According to Coxe, Cozzens recognizes "that life is a tragic affair. The novels move outward with the quest for reality, vision, and direction."[8] The central burden of all of Cozzens' fiction is that "life consist of messes; it is the job of some to make them, that of others to clean them up. An impossible task and we do it every day."[9] The world of James Gould Cozzens is a fallen (imperfect, alienated) world, in which fallen (imperfect, alienated) persons attempt to maintain some semblance of order. That is to say, Cozzens portrays his small town as an already-fallen Eden.

The tension at the heart of *The Just and the Unjust* is that the law pretends to absoluteness, but it must be enacted in a world where the truth is far from clearly discernible. As an author, Cozzens' respect for the law and his fascination with the details of legal procedure cause him to reflexively side with lawyers, and particularly with lawyers representing the interest of the state. Thus, for Cozzens the danger is that a small town may be swayed by emotion or by unreason and allow the guilty to escape punishment entirely. After all, according to Cozzens, the only way that someone comes before the court is if they have already been determined to be guilty.[10] Abner in *The Just and the Unjust* is an ideal representative of the lawyers discussed by Tocqueville: aristocratic, conservative, contemptuous—often openly so—of democracy. The resolution of the murder trial at the center of the novel demonstrates the dangers of democracy; while the jury does find the defendants guilty, the verdict rendered is second-degree murder rather than first-degree murder. After the trial, while Abner reflects on the results, he attributes the verdict to the talent of the defense for making "the proper appeal, the appeal to vanity and sentimentality, and plain bone headedness."[11] Fallen persons can never enact true justice.

Fallenness, as a state, means that tidy judgments of right and wrong are impossible. Abner must take upon himself the responsibility of judgment without a clear-cut guide. A world filled with fallen people cannot be neatly divided into saints and sinners, just and unjust. Law (ideally considered) impartially judges between equally weighted elements to achieve the proper assignment of guilt and innocence. The law must arbitrate; this is its purpose. However, when a society is not an undifferentiated mass—when it is a collection of individual persons, all butting up against each other and interacting in different and unexpected ways—the impartial assignment of guilt and innocence becomes a much more fraught endeavor. Once again, the problem confronting the lawyer here is that law is only necessary in a fallen world—a world in which individuals are divided from each other and from themselves. What Cozzens sees is that humans are complex and that neat legal formulas do not often work. This ambiguity is heightened in the case of Mary Beach by the nature of the crime under consideration. For statutory rape is *statutory*—it is a legal construct, not an eternal verity. The letter of the law demands punishment, but for Cozzens that letter may well cut against the grain of actual justice. As such, it is possible for Cozzens' protagonist to throw some doubt upon the victim's story to highlight the gap between the legal and the moral.

As Cozzens presents it, the novel's central conflict is ultimately between youthful idealism and seasoned wisdom. Facing this gap is the task of Cozzens' lawyer-protagonist. Coxe considers the acquisition of wisdom to be a central theme of Cozzens' career. Idealism is not enough; wisdom is essential, because "in so far as a man lacks the capacity to enter into another's nature and understand it, at least partially, he lacks heroic stature."[12] This demand for wisdom is illustrated in the final pages of *The Just and the Unjust*, when Abner speaks to his father. In this conversation, Abner is made to see how much growth is required to be, not only good, but effective in a fallen world. Abner gradually develops into the kind of person who can understand and work with men he hates. This development is important. The young man's initial starting-point is rigidly moralistic. When he is encouraged to seek a high position by a man he considers corrupt, Abner refuses—not because he does not want the position, but because he dislikes the man making the offer. At one point, Abner says, "I don't give a damn whether anybody is looking or not. I'm looking. I care whether I look like a louse," to which his father responds "Well, we all have our pride. It does a good deal to make us fit for human company. But I don't know how far the world at large [...] is in duty bound to minister to yours."[13] It is one thing to have strong ethical or moral convictions, but Cozzens insists that these convictions should never get in the way of actual effectiveness

The search for justice in the small town must be tempered with pragmatism; learning to act pragmatically in such an environment is, for Cozzens, deeply tied to the reality of World War II. *The Just and the Unjust* was published in 1942, shortly after America's entry into the war. Although the novel is set in 1939, its date of publication suggests that Cozzens has in mind broader world-historical circumstances. These circumstances are not immediately apparent, since the bulk of the novel is concerned with small-town politics, Abner's romantic confusion, and the complexities of the murder trial. Unexpectedly, however, on the final page Abner abruptly makes a leap from the local to the global, observing that someone seems to be "cooking up another war for us in Europe."[14] The sudden insertion of the oncoming Second World War recasts the preceding pages. They are no longer simply about the ambiguities of small-town life; they are, rather, a meditation on proper action in a world gone mad. Abner's father's response shifts the burden of the novel's weight onto the problems of maintaining American democracy in the face of total world war. War is a central element of the trials of life, and there is no guarantee of a simple solution; only the law, combined with the efforts of lawyers, enables ordinary citizens to continue with their lives.[15] When Abner responds by asking what is wanted of him, the judge responds that "[w]e just want you to do the impossible."[16] The arduous task of navigating competing demands between private idealism and public action is not one that Cozzens will allow to pass lightly, particularly in a time of war. A sense of fallenness is the root of democracy, a belief that only by muddling forward can any sort of justice be done. Thus the need for compromise, which Miller says "is the lot of the responsible person, doing his best in a fallen—imperfect—world."[17] As Chester Eisinger observes in *Fiction of the Forties*, "the hard recognition of the limitations of reason and of man's institutions is a logical consequence of the recognition of human shortcomings generally and of the futility of any absolutes promulgated by human beings."[18] The individual must move forward with a full, tragic awareness of the ambiguities involved in each decision.

 Cozzens, far from mystifying or concealing the tensions at the heart of the small town, uses problems of justice to sharpen them. Cozzens, thus, anticipates Reinhold Niebuhr's sense of the irony of American history. For Niebuhr, writing after World War II, the irony of American history is that the United States is obliged to act in precisely those ways that seem to be antithetical to its self-fashioning in order to keep peace, since "dreams of a pure virtue are dissolved in a situation in which it is possible to exercise the virtue of responsibility toward a community of nations only by courting the prospect of guilt of the atomic bomb."[19] The highest error would be to try to avoid guilt by calling for nuclear disarmament or total pacifism. Niebuhr, writing after the cataclysm of World War II, argues that in the face of such powerful threats as fascism and communism, the only move that responsible American intellectuals could make would be to accept that the bomb cuts against deeply held American ideals *and* to accept that it is impossible to have world peace without the potential use of the bomb. Thus, it is essential for the "American nation, involved in its vast responsibilities, [to] slough off many illusions which were derived both from the experiences and the ideologies of its childhood. Otherwise we will seek to escape from responsibilities which involve unavoidable guilt."[20] The move that Niebuhr makes here is precisely the same move that Cozzens makes at the conclusion of *The Just and the Unjust*. It is a move that, according to Niebuhr, is essential to the maintenance of democracy. He evokes wisdom just as Coxe does *vis-à-vis* Cozzens when he says that "the triumph of the wisdom of common sense over [ideology] is, therefore, primarily the wisdom of democracy itself," since democracy by its very recalcitrance prevents ideology from manifesting itself in its pure state.[21] Pragmatism is the way to justice. But pragmatism is another term for fudging the rules. Law—pure law—is incapable of returning the small town to its Edenic state.

William Faulkner's series detective Gavin Stevens illustrates the failure of the lawyer-figure to establish justice. *Intruder in the Dust* (1948) features Stevens as one investigator among many. Lucas Beauchamp, an African American man, is accused of murder. Stevens' young nephew Chick Mallison begs Stevens to prove that Beauchamp is innocent, but Stevens is convinced that Lucas is guilty. Chick and two other characters—his African American friend Aleck Sander and the spinster Miss Habersham—investigate and prove that Lucas is innocent by demonstrating that the murdered man's body has been removed and replaced with another corpse. Only then does Stevens agree to help Beauchamp. He has to be coerced. Thus, in *Intruder in the Dust*, Gavin is the defender of the *status quo* even in the face of Lucas Beauchamp's self-evident innocence. Michael Wainwright suggests that Gavin is indebted to the hard-boiled heroes of Hammett and Chandler—particularly in his knight-like devotion to truth.[22] In fact, the lawyer is hobbled as a detective by his own devotion to the way things are. Moreover, Stevens is less Chandlerian than he is Doylean. *Intruder* is a detective novel in which Faulkner plays many types of investigator off of each other—the boy detectives Chick and Aleck Sander, the spinster detective Miss Habersham, the man-of-action Lucas Beauchamp, and Gavin Stevens. In many ways, Gavin Stevens is the most "classical" detective of the many investigators in the novel. Certainly, he fits the Philo Vance mold, as Mick Gidley has observed.[23] Stevens' features—"the too-thin bony eager face, the bright intent rapid eyes"—closely echo the conventional image of Sherlock Holmes.[24] Furthermore—like other lawyer-protagonists and detectives—Gavin is a bachelor.[25] Stevens is not a man of action. Where the other investigators in the novel tend to rely on grunt work (following suspects, digging up graves), Stevens demonstrates a talent for analyzing a problem based on the facts alone.

Once he is convinced of Lucas' innocence, Gavin moves to clear the accused man's name. He fetches the sheriff and together they go to the grave where the victim is interred, only to find that the plot has been dug up again and both corpses—the original and the one the boys found the previous night—are now missing. The sheriff and Gavin reconstruct the crime:

> "We're going to find out right now where to start." [The sheriff] turned to [Gavin], saying in the mild rational almost diffident voice: "It's say around eleven o'clock at night. You got a mule or maybe it's a horse, anyway something that can walk and tote a double load, and a dead man across your saddle. What would you do?"[26]

The form of this interrogation is well-known to readers of the detective novel; over the following pages, Stevens and the sheriff play with possibilities until they finally conclude that the only place to hide the body would be "in sand"[27]—that is, in a plot of quicksand that Aleck Sander had observed earlier in the night.[28] This is solid detective-work. However, Stevens is a failure in other respects, since he must be forced into defending the falsely-accused Lucas. The lawyer alone cannot pursue justice.

Justice in small-town fiction is most often something achieved by characters who act extra-judicially. Whereas Cozzens manifests the complexity of judgment by means of monologue, Faulkner demonstrates it in the very form of *Intruder in the Dust*. He suggests that the law is inadequate to the demands of true justice. By using multiple detectives, Faulkner argues for a complex, democratic approach to social problems, one in which the outcast and powerless take the lead. Peter Rabinowitz suggests that the detective story works as a tale of discovery, in which the investigator "learns something important about himself, usually something about his own guilt or [...] about the naiveté of his idealism."[29] This sort of self-discovery works differently in Faulkner, who has more than one detective at work in his novel. Rabinowitz suggests that *Intruder in the Dust* charts Chick Mallison's maturation.[30] Chick, however, needs help in the form of Aleck Sander and Miss Habersham—an African American child and an unmarried woman, respectively. Though all of the novel's detectives are marginal in some way—because of race, age, gender, or education—together they form a community that is a mirror to the larger community of the town. Instead of presenting a single detective, *Intruder in the Dust* gives the reader a whole community of detectives. Detection is a group effort.[31] *Intruder* features multiple detectives struggling with themselves—Gavin with reflexive racism, Chick with cowardice, Lucas with pride—in order to understand history. If, as Gavin asserts, murder is a communal property, the detection of murder must also be a communal property, just as the establishment of racial justice (the novel's primary theme) must be a communal effort.[32]

The community must grapple with its own ambiguity and create order from disorder. The theme of communal detection is not a new one for Faulkner. His short story "An Error in Chemistry" (in the 1949 collection *Knight's*

Gambit) offers another example of group-investigation. In this story, the murderer is impersonating a little-seen local character and nearly succeeds in the imposture—except for one small mistake while making a whiskey toddy. The mistake is immediately noticed by Stevens, the sheriff, and Chick—all of whom are present. The killer is brought to justice through a moment of group-deduction, in which, as J.K. Van Dover and John F. Jebb observe in *Isn't Justice Always Unfair?*, "[t]he revelation of the crime, recognized by *several insiders*, protects the community from further harmful incursion" (italics original).[33] In a similar way, *Intruder in the Dust* presents detectives characterized by their need for each other. Lucas needs Chick to prove his innocence; Chick needs Aleck Sander and Miss Habersham to exonerate Lucas. They all need Gavin Stevens to put the force of law behind their discoveries and bring the true killer to justice. The difference is that the gap is not between "insiders" and "outsiders"; rather, Faulkner presents a community, riven by its own internal divisions but united all the same, investigating itself and absolving itself of its own crime.

Because Faulkner positions the group as the locus of detection in *Intruder in the Dust*, Gidley's claim that the end of the novel sees Gavin safely back on "the seat of justice" is clearly incomplete.[34] Gavin has been compromised as a detective. Properly chastened, he encourages his nephew Chick to avoid giving in to the *status quo*, since "[s]ome things you must never stop refusing to bear. Injustice and outrage and dishonor and shame. Just refuse to bear them."[35] It is here—rather than in Stevens' long speech on Northern politicians—that Faulkner locates the heart of the novel. Gavin has changed because he has been forced to see the fruits of his willingness to accommodate the *status quo*. Moreover, Chick has been changed by the process of uncovering communal sins—and since he, not Gavin, represents the future of the South, Chick's moral epiphany should be given greater weight than anything Gavin says. The communal detection of *Intruder in the Dust* is begun by a wronged man (Lucas), is carried out by those who refuse to bear injustice and is legitimated (at last) when those forces join and compel powerful citizens to help their cause through weight of evidence. *Intruder in the Dust* presents a mobilized community working to absolve its own guilt. By presenting readers with multiple investigators, Faulkner makes it clear that crime (and, implicitly, racial inequality) is the property of a community and, as such, must be absolved by that community. *Intruder in the Dust* is a novel of detection, an exercise in genre that uses the central figure of the detective novel—the detective himself—to highlight Faulkner's concerns about race-relations in the American South. Though Gavin Stevens presents an argument against the legal imposition of equality, the overall thrust of the book is more biting, less safe: if justice is to be achieved, it must be by a communal effort, spurred on by those who refuse to bear injustice. Community is the core of justice, just as justice is the quest for a utopian community. As Miller observes, "[i]nsofar as 'law and literature' primarily concerns justice, it does so presuming or questing for civil—or civilized—order."[36] Civil order is a property of community; one cannot have the first without presupposing the second.

The move from communal detection to private law-breaking is not so vast as it would appear. Within the fiction of the time-period, law-breaking appears both as a horrifying specter and as a means of transcending injustice and reaching what might be thought of as true justice. In either case, however, the pathway lies through law-breaking. The primal taboo, according to Freud, is the incest taboo, and incest appears often in small-town literature as a sign of either degradation or (sometimes) dark transcendence. *Peyton Place* asserts that incest shapes the characters living in the small town and that working through or escaping from that incest is essential if the characters are to achieve wholeness. *Peyton Place* is a novel about incest at its very core. A central character, Selena Cross, is repeatedly raped and eventually impregnated by her stepfather Lucas. The incestuous text is somewhat papered over by the circumstances of the novel's production; the editors, nervous about featuring incestuous rape prominently in the novel, insisted that Metalious make Selena Cross' molester her stepfather rather than her father.[37] Incest during this time period occupied a double position, seeming "simultaneously 'unnatural' and unlikely."[38] However, around the time of World War II there was a renewed interest in "the sex offender."[39] This interest was primarily focused upon strangers—predatory men who may lure children into their webs of iniquity.[40] Cameron points out that Metalious was afraid when she changed the identity of Selena Cross' molester from father to stepfather that her book had been turned into "trash"—however, as Cameron points out, "the story of Selena Cross conforms to recent clinical and historical studies that have revealed the discrepancies between the myth and reality of girlhood sexual assault."[41] Eventually, as a result of this repeated assault, Selena is impregnated, leading her to request an abortion from the local physician, Dr. Swain. After Swain has performed the abortion, he pays Lucas Cross a visit and threatens him, extorting a confession and prompting Lucas to flee the town. At first it seems as if Lucas is gone for good, but he returns during World War II, having gone AWOL from the Navy. He attempts to rape Selena again and she kills him and buries his body in a sheep pen. The discovery of his body will later lead to her trial for murder and to Dr. Swain confessing to performing the abortion.

This scenario is the center of a tight pattern of incestuous themes webbed throughout *Peyton Place*. Allison MacKenzie's one-time beau Norman represents a young person in thrall to a parental figure—this time, his mother. He is a sensitive boy, despised by the other boys in town. Norman seems to be closely modeled on Jamie from *Kings Row*, though Metalious is far less forthcoming about his sexuality than Bellamann is in the older novel. The boy's attitude toward his mother is one of reverence mixed with fear; early on in the novel, he avoids going home because "[his mother] might even give him an enema."[42] The controlling mother raises the specter of homosexuality; Dr. Swain says that he would "like to see the boy get free of [his mother] before it's too late. Maybe if he got himself a nice girl, like Allison MacKenzie, it would counteract Evelyn's influence."[43] What Dr. Swain is worrying about here is the old Freudian idea that young men are turned gay by overprotective mothers. Tied to this psychological worry is the threat of incest. Dr. Swain makes a reference to "a young boy with the worst case of dehydration I ever saw. It came from getting too many enemas that he didn't need. Sex, with a capital S—E—X."[44] The image is that of a mother who anally assaults her son, making Norman into a parallel figure to Selena (and, therefore, it is no real accident that Allison shares a bond with both characters). It is heavily implied that Norman is radically wounded by his mother's overprotective, sexualized care.

This controlling, quasi-sexual bond continues into adulthood. Once World War II breaks out, Norman—along with most of the other young men in town—goes off to fight. In 1944, Norman returns home "with a chest full of campaign ribbons, medals and a stiff leg on which he walked with the help of a crutch."[45] He is welcomed as a hero, but in fact his heroism is (as Dr. Swain quickly deduces) a sham perpetrated by his mother. Dr. Swain agrees with the editor of the newspaper "that since they had discovered a truth which would only hurt Norman in the town [...] they would forget the matter entirely."[46] Norman is allowed to continue the charade that his mother has set up—walking with a fake limp, wearing fake medals, living a fake life. Norman's quasi-incestuous bond with his mother has made him incapable of imagining sexual congress without terror. His dreams are filled with worms spilling from the split abdomen of Allison MacKenzie.[47] The damage done by Norman's incestuous relationship with his mother is just as permanent as that done to Selena Cross.

Allison MacKenzie, the novel's protagonist, is also included in this incestuous theme, though she manages to transcend it in a less violent way than Selena does. Her closeness to her father is posthumous, since the man died many years before the novel begins. Nevertheless, its strength is suggested in the fact that Allison's very given name is shared with the dead father. Moreover, Allison is undeniably fixated on her father; at one point she says his photograph "looks just like a prince."[48] Indeed, she falls asleep referring to him as "my prince."[49] Allison's father operates as an absent yet controlling male fantasy in the life of his daughter. In Allison's case, the consequences are not as disastrous as the incestuous rape perpetrated upon Selena. Indeed, Allison is in many ways a rebuke to psychiatrists such as Otto Rank, who says that "[w]hereas the man (father) is able to live out his repressed incestuous impulses toward his daughter [...] in the woman (daughter) [...] the repression of attraction to the father [...] frequently leads to neurosis."[50] Allison does not become neurotic, though she does replicate her mother's own sexual history in her affair with Bradley Holmes, her agent, "forty years old, dark haired and powerfully built."[51] Allison remembers her mother's words about her own affair, that "I was lonely and he was there," and reflects that she (Allison) is "not alone" because she has friends with her.[52] There is a difference between mother and daughter. Nevertheless, in carrying on an affair with a married man—and then in returning to Peyton Place—Allison follows her mother's trajectory. This repetition continues the incest-theme. Holmes clearly represents a father-figure to Allison, and her affair with him not only replicates her mother's affair with the male Allison, but also provides the young woman with a way of realizing her incestuous fantasies about her father. Just after the two spend a weekend in the country together, Allison reads a newspaper headline proclaiming "PATRICIDE IN PEYTON PLACE."[53] The "patricide" referred to is Selena's murder of her stepfather, but it also refers (symbolically) to Allison's own character arc. She returns home immediately after reading the headline, thus ending the book. The repetition of her mother's affair with her father has cleared Allison's mind, has allowed her finally to leave behind her incestuous infatuation with her father. Neither Allison nor Selena are made neurotic by their experiences, in spite of Rank's assertion quoted above. Instead, both manage to escape the trap of parental incest, either by literally murdering the father (Selena) or by figuratively doing so (Allison).

Thus, incest is a central theme of *Peyton Place*. And this thematic concern is not mere prurience; Cameron points out that in this novel "incest, domestic violence, and unwed motherhood are not simply put on display; they are linked to social indifference and economic injustice, simultaneously political and private acts."[54] That is, incest is the result of conditions in the small town. Metalious suggests that small towns themselves are based upon, that they live and move and have their being within, a fetid miasma of incest. As with the small town, so with America itself. The darkest crimes imaginable, the ones most proscribed by society and most firmly punished, thus reveal the true nature of that society. Just as incest is the sublimated core of the Eden myth (the oft-repeated question of where Cain got his wife is answered simply by the fact that he married his own sister), so it is at the heart of American mythology.

The task of navigating the boundaries of the law—of determining when and how it should be broken—often falls to professionals in these novels. Law and medicine are closely related by the Edenic rift—which is to say, that both death and sin enter the world through the fall. It is the job of the lawyer to remedy the latter and the job of the physician to treat the former. Doctors are often called upon to occupy the seat of judgment. Partway through *Peyton Place*, Metalious reveals that Selena Cross' stepfather, Lucas, has been systematically raping her and that Selena is now pregnant by that rape. Selena goes to Dr. Swain, asking for an abortion. He resists the idea, telling her that "I've done a lot of things in my time, Selena, but I have never broken the law."[55] Once he learns who the father of the child is, the doctor is confronted with a crisis of conscience. He has always prided himself on hating three things: "death, venereal disease, and organized religion."[56] Now, however, his choice is not between absolutes: whichever road he takes, he will be destroying a life—either the life of the fetus in Selena Cross' womb or the life of Selena herself. The perils facing unwed mothers during this time—as well as later—were very real. Steven Mintz observes that "girls who got pregnant [during the 1950s] were often forced out of school and had their children's birth records stamped 'illegitimate.'"[57] This is the fate that Allison barely avoids, but it is one that Selena's offspring could not. And, since Selena comes from the poor side of town, the peril to her is even greater.

The abortion is, thus, a case in which Dr. Swain must make a choice beyond legal definitions—he must transcend his own legal and ethical convictions, or at least consolidate them into some decision with which he can live. At last he makes his choice, saying, "I *am* protecting a life, *this* life, one already being lived by Selena Cross."[58] Dr. Swain is making an existential choice in the proper sense of the term; he arbitrates between two conflicting fields of meaning and acts in such a way as he would desire to be a law for everyone. Once he has agreed to perform the abortion, he pulls nurse Mary Kelly into his act, a decision which will later haunt him.[59] His choice is not an easy one, nor is it without consequences. When Selena is on trial for the murder of her stepfather, Dr. Swain decides to come forward with his story. This decision adds gravitas to Dr. Swain's earlier actions regarding the abortion. Metalious refuses to permit the abortion to be an easy decision. For Dr. Swain carries with him the full moral weight of his decision, believing that he has destroyed in turn "the child [...] Mary Kelly [...] Nelly [Cross, Selena's mother who commits suicide after the disappearance of her husband...] and now Lucas [the rapist stepfather]."[60] Realizing the harm caused by his choice (regardless of whether it was the morally right thing to do), Dr. Swain chooses to put his own career on the line, confessing to the abortion in order to save the life of Selena Cross once again. The doctor's willingness to take on the moral weight of his choice qualifies him in Metalious' view to properly adjudicate the morality of Selena's abortion—that is, to take on the role of judge.

Dr. Swain has broken the laws of the community in order to achieve a greater level of justice. Judgment carries with it a tremendous moral responsibility, and as such is liable to misuse if the wrong person takes its seat. In *Kings*

Row, three of the central characters are doctors—the two quasi-antagonists, Dr. Tower and Dr. Gordon, and the protagonist Parris Mitchell. Dr. Gordon is a demonic manifestation of the town's ideology in that he maims and kills people he feels are morally inferior or socially useless. This particular aspect of Dr. Gordon's personality is concealed by the fact that he seems to be a kindly country doctor; however, in one of the first important scenes featuring him—a scene in which he does not even physically appear—he is in the process of cutting off a man's legs without chloroform because (he claims) the anesthesia will kill the patient.[61] Later, when Drake falls under a train, Dr. Gordon removes his legs, not for a legitimate medical reason, but because Drake had given romantic attention to his (Dr. Gordon's) daughter Louise. After Dr. Gordon dies, Louise claims that "he was a butcher [...] he always talked about his operations. And nearly always he said the patient's heart was too weak for chloroform. I tell you, Parris, he liked to hear them scream."[62] Symbolically, Dr. Gordon here is an embodiment of the communal will since the people he maims and kills are undesirables, people who have in some way sinned against the community. He is judge and jury and executioner. Thus, people such as "Ludie Sims. A pretty, flighty, quasi prostitute—a subject of town talk" is punished with "[f]acial paralysis."[63] The fact that Gordon acts out against people who are already looked down on by the community cannot be missed. In performing his sadistic operations, Dr. Gordon enforces the narrative structure of small-town life by eliminating undesirables.

Gordon becomes a law to himself, embodying the normal moral or legal order. Dr. Tower—Parris' mentor as well as an incestuous rapist—occupies a strange position, both within the novel and within Parris' own mind; neither wholly villainized nor wholly vindicated for his crimes, the old man takes on the form of a Gothic protagonist. Incest is the central signifier of Tower's transgression. In her book *Relative Intimacy: Fathers, Daughters, and Postwar American Culture*, Rachel Devlin proposes that "there was a pervasive cultural interest in fathers' relationships to their teenage daughters during the postwar years."[64] Devlin's book traces a genealogy of incestuous father-daughter pairings from *Kings Row* through *Peyton Place* and William Styron's *Lie Down in Darkness*—all of which use the name Peyton as a sort of genetic marker. Devlin's study is not perfect; her summary of *Kings Row*, for instance, is woefully inaccurate regarding key plot-points. For instance, *Kings Row*'s Peyton does not marry his African American lover Melissa, since he is already married to the symbolically-and-literally sterile Patty.[65] However, Devlin's broader point regarding father-daughter pairings is suggestive. After World War II, the bonds between fathers and daughters *were* emphasized, particularly in small-town literature. This interest is often manifested in the character of an incestuous bond, actual or sublimated. I have already discussed the sublimated incest at work in Allison MacKenzie's relationship with her dead father as well as Selena's rape at the hands of her stepfather. These events show the interest in incest arising at midcentury, but they do not examine it as a pathway toward dark transcendence, as Bellamann presents it in *Kings Row* through the figure of Dr. Tower. Parris Mitchell is Dr. Tower's student. The master himself is (as indicated above) a Gothic figure, complete with an insane wife and a nymphomaniacal daughter named Cassandra. Parris strikes up a relationship and then a sexual affair with Cassandra. When the time nears for Parris to leave Kings Row, Cassie begs to go with him, saying, "I don't care if you marry me or not. Just let me go away with you. I've got to."[66] Mere pages later, Parris—who is staying with his friend Drake—learns that Cassie has been murdered by her father, who then committed suicide.[67] This murder-suicide will haunt Parris, not only in this novel but also in its sequel.

Dr. Tower attempts to transcend the closed-in world of Kings Row through law-breaking. For unknown reasons, Dr. Tower leaves his entire estate to Parris, who accordingly inherits the old man's journals. While reading these journals, Parris discovers the truth: that his mentor, a man whom he respected and loved, has been for many years systematically raping his own daughter. This incestuous rape is at once a horrifying sign of the darkness lurking in the town and a demonstration that Dr. Tower has moved beyond conventional morality entirely. The doctor's obsession is "not the usual kind of crazy. He was so proud of his intelligence that he began to think he was better than anybody else, and beyond any kind of law that—you know—that keeps us all kind of in place."[68] His moral sense has become clouded. The rape "began way back there when Cassie was a little girl."[69] Incest represents a fundamental crime against the natural order of things, closely aligned with murder. Parris suggests Dr. Tower began molesting his daughter because of an overweening pride and a sense of isolation. Together, these elements of his personality drove him to commit his crimes. That is, Dr. Tower was alienated. But he was alienated because he was a symbolic judge; his taboo-breaking was the direct result of the fact that he had obtained access to hidden mysteries and was overcome by them. His failure as an arbiter of right and wrong is an inversion of the transcendence Parris must attain.

Dr. Tower represents one potential danger to Parris as the young man pursues his own quest for hidden knowledge. As a psychiatrist, Parris Mitchell seeks out the dark corners of the human psyche—motivated in no small part by his experiences with Cassandra and Dr. Tower. Parris successfully transcends legality in a way that neither of the other two doctors in the novel do. Throughout *Kings Row*, Parris is essentially a passive character—things happen to him. The only time he acts early on in the novel is when he makes love to Renée—and at that point the consequences are so horrific that he withdraws from the world of action for the entirety of the novel, with two exceptions. The first is when his grandmother is dying and—at her housekeeper's bidding—he agrees to euthanize the old woman.[70] The second is when he discovers Drake has cancer. Drake is his best friend in the town. As such, the choice is a heartbreaking one, one directly associated with both Parris' earlier actions regarding his grandmother (the only other person who ever loved him) and the actions of Dr. Gordon (the doctor who made Drake an invalid to begin with). Faced with the painful death of his best friend, Parris confronts a situation analogous to the one confronting Dr. Swain in *Peyton Place* years later, only this time it is as the climax of the narrative.[71] The death of Drake represents the final stripping away of Parris' already-limited circle of friends. He has lost his grandmother, Dr. Tower and Cassandra, and now Drake. He is totally and utterly alone. But, importantly, in this last loss—the loss of his dearest friend on earth—he is given a choice. He is compelled to judge in a situation where right and wrong are deeply muddied and implicated in each other. Unlike Dr. Gordon, who positions himself as the demonic voice of the small town, Parris Mitchell is worthy of adjudicating right and wrong precisely because he is unwilling to do so. Parris earns that right by making the hard choice and taking the responsibility into himself. Gordon and Parris are dark shadows of each other and the specter of Dr. Tower hovers behind both, terrifying and liberating because his dark transcendence removes the communal aspect of morality.

Just as Gordon and Tower provide murderous mirrors to Parris' own heartbreaking decisions, so Dr. Tower's incestuous urges mirror Parris' discovery that sex itself can provide a means of liberation. Within midcentury small-town literature, sex outside of marriage is typically thought of as an act of rebellion against society. As such, it carries with it both social consequences and metaphysical import. In *Kings Row*, sex constitutes a moment of fall from Edenic harmony to a state of responsibility. Parris Mitchell's first sexual encounter is with the girl Renée, a childhood friend with whom he swims nude in what they call "their 'secret lake.'"[72] The adolescents, having already agreed that they are a couple, consummate their relationship in a manner redolent of pastoral fantasy. The encounter is not unambiguous, however; it carries with it an uncomfortable tincture of force (particularly important in a novel that features father-daughter rape).[73] Bellamann is self-consciously evoking the Garden of Eden and its central Tree of Knowledge in this encounter, a fact which is confirmed by the consequences of this sexual union. Renée's father Sven sees the two young people and, once Renée has returned home, beats her savagely. Parris hears the noise of the beating and immediately contracts a brain fever; when he returns to consciousness, Sven has taken his family and left.[74] Parris never sees Renée again, but she will continue throughout the novel to be a touchstone, reminding Parris of the childhood innocence that he lost that day by the secret lake.

The idea of sex as the secret to life, as a transgressive means of accessing whatever divine undercurrent exists in the world, is a core idea in *Raintree County*. As with other authors in this study, Lockridge associates his small town with the Garden of Eden. As such, sex constitutes a sort of fall as well as the potential for redemption. Johnny Shawnessy loses his virginity to Susanna Drake, a young woman visiting from the South who will eventually become his (insane) wife. The tie between sex and guilt is made explicit in this passage, but "[t]he feeling of guilt came afterwards when he returned to the familiar part of the county and the effects of the cider wore off. Guilt had not been in the act itself."[75] Lockridge is careful to point out that Johnny's "sense of guilt was not religious."[76] He is not afraid of the judgment of God but of his own mother's disappointment. The act of lovemaking liberates Shawnessy from Protestant morality. Far from regarding sex as sacred, Lockridge suggests that Protestantism has reduced sex to a mere act, simply another mechanical function that must be regulated as such. Desire is denied, "there was propagation—but not pleasure. There was love—but not the act of love. Eros and his flame-tipped arrow had abdicated in favor of Jesus and the cross."[77] Within such a context, sex outside the bounds of marriage becomes a radical, even revolutionary, act. This passion is, thus, ultimately identified with love—the desire for two things to be unified. And love, as Shawnessy comes to understand it, is "the all important discovery that one is not alone in the world."[78] For Lockridge, sex—even so-called illicit sex—is a pathway to overcoming loneliness and restoring a lost Eden.

Just as religious transcendence is incarnational and sexual, so the transcendence of law has a sexual aspect. At the core of the small-town engagement with justice is sexual liberation. One of the many subplots of *Raintree County* involves an atlas of the county which is said to conceal bizarre portraits within its pages—satyrs and nymphs, obscene depictions of sexual acts, a vast pagan orgy concealed beneath the prosaic face of the land. Throughout the novel, John Shawnessy periodically returns to the book and scans its pages, trying to see these legendarily dirty pictures on the otherwise placid surface of Raintree County. They never appear; it is only at the end of the novel that the protagonist discovers the truth. He and the "Perfessor" are discussing the atlas when Shawnessy suggests that they have been "*too* subtle."[79] Suddenly, prompted by a mention of Poe's "The Purloined Letter," Shawnessy leaps forward and flips through the book until he finds "the long form of the Raintree County Courthouse."[80] He discovers that the mysterious artist who created the atlas has substituted the primal moment of fall from the book of Genesis for the image of justice at the top of the county courthouse:

> He [the artist] had unveiled the Eleusinian mysteries to the Court House Square where it would be seen by all who came there—[…] the whole lusty tide of life that pooled and poured into the foresighted enclosure of the Court House Square to appease a devout hunger as old as a gathering of mankind in crowds.[81]

The courthouse, existing as it does in the center of the town square, provides a focal point for the town. This passage argues that the courthouse also constitutes the town's identity. For community cannot exist without law and law itself cannot exist without a fall from grace; as Jeffrey Miller says, "*Law begins and ends with Eden*" (italics original).[82] The substitution of lawbreaking for the sign of judgment in *Raintree County* represents the deep springs of life from which the citizens of Raintree County draw their sustenance, whether they know it or not. As a self-consciously Romantic work, *Raintree County* embraces the idea of transgression as a way to attain one's own personal connection with the life forces that make up the universe. The fall, for Lockridge, is a *felix culpa*—a fortunate fall which, as Miller explains "makes possible the immortality of the human soul through the resurrection of Christ."[83] Lockridge's predilections are more pagan than they are Christian, but he has no less regard for the fall than those ancient theologians.

Small-town fiction in the 1940s and '50s, insofar as it deals with justice, sees it as a means of recovering a lost Eden. The law itself, imperfect because its creators are imperfect, cannot produce the liberation needed, as is seen in *The Just and the Unjust*. Accordingly, writers of the period turn to various extrajudicial means to attempt the reconciliation. Some, such as Faulkner, locate possible redemption in communal effort. Others—Metalious, Bellamann and Lockridge—position the individual law-breaker (or norm-breaker) as achieving redemption through a more fully sexual—embodied, incarnate—mode of living. But not all transgressors are so fortunate. Some, because of racial or sexual oppression, are forced to live their lives on the outskirts, and it is this group to which I will next turn my attention.

Eight

Transcending Division
The Outskirts

Like the ravine through Green Town in *Dandelion Wine*, a political and existential rift is at the core of small-town identity. The religious leap to the God-beyond-God is one method by which small-town characters attempt to transcend that division. Law-breaking is another. However, the small town never escapes its essentially alienating nature. Throughout this book I have been at pains to show the ways in which small-town literature cuts against the myth of the unified small town. Nowhere is this counter-narrative so apparent as in the literature's treatment of the marginalized, the outcast, and the oppressed. Indeed, small-town fiction typically protests the hegemony of the powerful. Much discussion of small town literature does not give enough weight to this essential point. For Ryan Poll, "[n]arratives set in a small town, more so than narratives centered either in the city or the suburb, are primarily communal narratives that foreground a sense of belonging."[1] Similarly, Miles Orvell calls the post–War small town "a place of refuge, a place of invisibility."[2] Long before either critic, Page Smith located the ideology of the small town in "[i]ndustry, frugality, equality, neighborliness, and loyalty"—that is, in precisely those values that provide a sense of belonging to the individual.[3] For Smith, as is typical of critical analyses of the small town dating back to Herron's *The Small Town in American Literature*, these "true communities" are on the verge of dying out, of being replaced by urban society with its purported disconnection and alienation—the lonely city replacing the neighborly town.[4]

More often, however, the small town is an anti-community. The language of small-town fiction always speaks to an absence of community even in the face of desire for a state of belonging, and the symbol of this absence is the outlying area where the racial and social outcasts live. As I will demonstrate in this chapter, literature of the small town during the 1940s and '50s is fundamentally concerned with difference. The *desire* to belong may well be present, and the small town may represent that desire, but it does so negatively. Fundamental to small-town fiction is the failed promise of belonging. Divisions and dislocations are at the core of small town fiction, and any attempt to critically engage this literature without taking that fundamental paradox into account is doomed. Accordingly, within this chapter I reverse the expected direction of discussion: though the psychogeographic movement of this book is now moving outward toward (ultimately) the graveyard, I have here chosen to invert my direction by beginning with the physical outskirts of the small town and moving inward toward the spiritual or existential outskirts. In this way, I will show that small towns are ultimately to be thought of as a collection of overlapping outskirts. There is, in a very real sense, no in-crowd. This is the sense in which small-town literature is protest literature. It protests the alienating nature of post-war conformity as well as the actions of classism and racism. Thus, my reading is distinct from other interpretations of the small town which see the community as reinforcing the *status quo.*

When I call small-town literature "protest literature," I do not mean that it is a protest in the sense that social realism of the 1930s was. Upton Sinclair and Sinclair Lewis, among others, wrote didactic fiction with the intention of causing concrete political change. During and after World War II, small-town chroniclers were less invested in didacticism. Tom Perrin's study *The Aesthetics of Middlebrow Fiction: Popular U.S. Novels, Modernism, and Form, 1945–75* offers a detailed and intriguing study of many of the novels discussed here. With regard to what he calls "problem novels," Perrin insists that (in contrast to Modernism), "a first principle of the social problem novel is that conventional plots and realist narration cannot be abandoned."[5] This conviction leads to a fundamental paradox, since "realist novels tend to tell the personal story of one particular protagonist and are thus fundamentally ill-suited to addressing structural social problems."[6] Perhaps this tension is why small-town fiction is seldom considered for its emancipatory trajectory. That trajectory is nevertheless present, going all the way back to Anderson's vision of the grotesque. For Anderson, the citizens of Winesburg are warped, having been made so by the inhospitable community around them. They exist in a shadowy, marginal state, picking up whatever crumbs of joy they can with little dignity and no self-respect. The grotesque is not simply mockery. To display these warped characters is to marvel in their humanity. The Andersonian grotesque is fundamentally sympathetic; the old man in "The Book of the Grotesques" views his subjects with love, marveling at their ability to find meaning in a life that dooms them to meaninglessness. Anderson's shadow falls long in small-town fiction. This literature is a fiction of the grotesque, and its broader point is that America is a nation of grotesques. As such, small-town fiction urges solidarity with the outcast and the unremembered who dwell in the midst of the community.

The myth of the unified small town is, to be sure, one with which all the fiction I consider here grapples to some extent. The small town is typically presented as a unity of parts. This double vision lends some credence to the idea that small towns are central to ideological constructions of the nation-state during the twentieth century. Ryan Poll asserts that "over the course of the twentieth century [the] small-town trope has become a material reality."[7] The reason for this manifestation is related to the conditions of Depression-era America. As the small-town environment was restructured in the imagination of the American people during the 1930s, the emphasis came to rest upon unity in diversity. In some cases, this trend continued into the 1940s, when concerns about fascism took center stage. This interest finds a parallel in other cultural productions of the period. Alfred Hitchcock's 1944 movie *Lifeboat* presents a vision of a multicultural America teaming up to take out the monocultural Germans, while platoon movies of the period emphasize racial diversity even as the U.S. Army was still segregated.[8] A similar shift occurs in the westerns of this period, as John G. Cawelti observes in *The Six-Gun Mystique Sequel*. In *Stagecoach* (1939), for instance, the travelers represent a hodgepodge of derelicts, drunks, and prostitutes, which "just as those oddly assorted bomber crews and infantry squads would redeem themselves and defeat the enemy in many later movies of World War II," succeeds at last in defeating "the enigmatic and hostile wilderness."[9] Small-town fiction, like westerns and platoon movies, places emphasis on the diversity of the small town, rather than its homogeneity. *It's a Wonderful Life*, for instance, offers a vision of the small-town as a secure, loving community bound together by ties of affection rather than of ethnicity or race. The community itself is multiethnic: the viewer is presented with the Irish cop, the Swedish immigrant, the white Anglo-Saxon Protestant protagonists, united by friendship and goodwill. This diversity is as much ideological as it is realistic; what these films offer is not America as it really was but as filmmakers and audiences liked to imagine it.

The claim made by all these works of self-construction is that America, unlike Nazi Germany, is not culturally monolithic. Read in this way, small-town fictions of the 30s and 40s seem to be a kind of propaganda for the American dream—a dream unfulfilled but aspirational. However, precisely because the picture of America is aspirational, the small town continues to exist in the literature as a space in which American ideals can be critiqued and examined. There is no point to aspiration (as there is no point to Eden or its apocalyptic twin the Kingdom of Heaven) if it does not point to a lack within the currently-existing world order. Thus, the function of the literary small town is not to mystify American imperialism and the fascist undercurrents of small town life. Rather, small-town literature exposes imperialism and demands that readers envision a better way of life. I have already touched on this theme in my chapter on the schoolhouse; if education is a method of raising up citizens, as it is in Saroyan (for instance), then part of that training is an insistent focus on the multicultural fabric of American life. If fascism insists on sameness, on uniformity, the American small town insists on diversity. Saroyan's *The Human Comedy* poses the problem is a straightforward way. The books examined here are, by and large, more elliptical. These works make their demands, not by proposing solutions, but by dramatizing oppression. Small-town fiction critiques the ways in which members of marginalized groups are oppressed by the larger society.

Race is never far from the small-town narrative, even when it might seem to be so. Ryan Poll, discussing Page Smith's *As a City Upon a Hill*, critiques what he considers to be Smith's blinkered focus on New England. "The reason Smith excludes the South," says Poll, "is because of the ideological assumption that the small town is exclusively a white space."[10] This ideology, according to Poll, is central to the small-town mythos. He says that "what makes the dominant small town a fascist form is its aesthetics of erasing racialized bodies and cultures, and instead producing and projecting an ethnically homogeneous space, culture, and people."[11] However, even a cursory examination of small-town fiction shows that whiteness is only exclusive in the sense that white citizens have exclusive power. Miles Orvell, though he does (as mentioned above) identify the small town with a sense of belonging, is careful to point out that "[i]f the small town has been a cultural symbol of 'friendly, heartwarming, social life,' it has also been [...] a symbol of prejudice, segregation, and hostility to the stranger."[12] Indeed, it can hardly be the one without at the same time being the other.

Lillian Smith's *Strange Fruit* demonstrates that the town of Maxwell is divided into two worlds: the world of the white ruling class and the world of the African American underclass. The entire novel is structured around a series of transgressions, of movements between the world of the oppressed black population and the world of their white oppressors. The struggle of individuals who find themselves in such a situation provides the motor of the book. When the Reverend Dunwoodie warns Tracy that "you have to keep pushing them back across the nigger line," he is speaking both metaphorically—in that there is a perceived need for white power structures to keep black persons in their place—and literally.[13] The town of Maxwell is divided by a color line and is in fact constituted by that same line. The communities on either side of the color line find themselves confronting the fact that they are constituted by the very thing that gives them so much anxiety. For post–Marxist psychoanalysis, as interpreted by Slavoj Žižek, the important thing is "demonstrating how [social struggles'] articulation into a series of equivalences depends always on the radical contingency of the social-historical process."[14] That is, any social struggle (against racism, the patriarchy, and so on) must first confront the fact that it is constituted by the very division it seeks to eliminate, so that "the thing to do is not to 'overcome' [...] but to come to terms with it."[15] This coming-to-terms is one version of what I call transcendence—the movement by which opposites must embrace each other in order to move beyond their constitutive division. Transcendence is never easy, and Smith seems to argue that it is wholly impossible. Smith dramatizes this dialectic in two sets of characters, with the white Tracy Deen being the uniting factor. These sets are racialized dyads. In each case they represent an instance of attempted boundary-crossing—transgression—that is thwarted by the fact that these boundaries define the relationship from the outset.

The first failed attempt at transcendence is sex—that is, precisely the mechanism that allows transcendence in other small-town fiction of the period. Smith here uses the stereotype of the light woman and the dark woman. The importance of this dyad is discussed in Leslie Fiedler's *Love and Death in the American Novel*. According to Fiedler, women in American fiction are almost always divided into two categories: the pure, blonde good girl and the dark, passionate bad girl. The clearest representation of these two women is found in James Fenimore Cooper's *The Last of the Mohicans*: the saintly Alice is contrasted with Cora, who, in Fiedler's words, "is corrupted [...] stained even before birth with the blackness of the primitive and passional."[16] Thus, racial divisions are already present in the light woman-dark woman dyad. Typically, this division is implicit; though Cora may be presumed to have mixed ancestry, Cooper does not insist upon this fact. Cooper's Cora is implicitly mixed-race, but her tragedy lies (in part) in the uncertainty of her racial makeup. Smith heightens the racial undertones by making them explicit. In *Strange Fruit*, Tracy is consciously divided between the African American Nonnie—for whom his blood burns—and the conventional, blonde Dottie, whom he has been courting since high school. Nonnie is associated with nature, and it is often in a natural setting that the reader discovers Tracy making love to her (the Edenic echoes here are unmistakable). Nonnie is also associated with passion—not, as with Cora in Cooper's novel, her own, but Tracy's. In contrast, Dottie is propriety, as Tracy reflects at one point in the novel, possessing "a life so neat, so orderly, like a folded handkerchief carried around all day and never crumpled."[17] Tracy must choose between Dottie and Nonnie, and in so doing he must choose (in his own mind) between a civilized, orderly life and a natural, passionate one. By being forced into this choice, Tracy is isolated from both women and from himself; just as the passion of Nonnie is a projection of Tracy's own passion, so Dottie's purity is a projection of Tracy's obsession with social acceptance. Both women are ultimately illustrative of the crisis within Tracy himself rather than existing as characters in their own right. Thus, the extent to which Smith confirms Tracy's understanding of his situation is open to question. On the one hand, as Johnson observes, "Nonnie's characterization fell victim to Smith's resistance to racism's lies and distortions and their impact on the hearts and souls of black and white Southerners" because she (Smith) painstakingly depicts Nonnie as essentially a white girl with black skin.[18] In Johnson's analysis, Nonnie's own sexual desires are hardly touched, so desperately does Smith attempt to avoid painting her in terms of the stereotype of the Jezebel. On the other hand, Nonnie's own lack of strong sexuality highlights the ways in which the dark woman in Fiedler's dyad is essentially a victim.[19] The injustice of Maxwell's color-line is thus dramatized in the very treatment of the character: she is different, she is defined by that difference, and yet she is written in such a way as to be incapable of transcending that difference.

If sex fails to enable transcendence, so does friendship. Smith's second dyad is Tracy and the African American Henry. Henry and Tracy were childhood playmates and even now exhibit a form of closeness. Again, Smith here plays on a character dynamic identified by Leslie Fiedler in *Love and Death in the American Novel*. Fiedler claims that—because of a flight from sexuality—American novels tend to focus on homoerotic couplings between men. These couplings are most often mixed-race in nature, "a kind of counter-matrimony, in which the white refugee from society and the dark-skinned primitive are joined till death do them part."[20] Tracy and Henry are just such a couple. Smith demonstrates this counter-matrimony in a touching scene midway through the novel when Henry drops his mask and for a moment there seems to be the possibility of genuine emotional exchange between the two men. Henry, "in a frantic gush of sympathy, half falling over his own big feet, [...] knelt beside his friend and put his arms around [Tracy], grunting out inarticulate comfort."[21] The sincerity of this moment should not be ignored. Henry and Tracy have grown up together and share a kind of friendship. In this instance, Henry is overcome by his connection to Tracy and attempts to comfort him; race seems, for a brief instant, secondary to shared bonds of friendship and mutuality. Tellingly, Smith relays this moment through Henry, for reasons that become clear when Tracy responds to Henry's gesture. For just as Tracy has dehumanized the two women in his life, he has no use for Henry's friendship. Their moment of potential connection vanishes when Tracy complains that Henry "stink[s] like a polecat." The mask goes back up and Henry resumes the posture of servitude, saying, "I washes. I sho does. Mebbe not so sufficient."[22] In Smith's novel, there can be no true equality between men where the standardized practices of racial injustice exist. They are isolated from each other.

For Smith, racial inequality prevents human contact. Smith does not hold out hope that individual attachments can transcend the racial barriers set up by society. This separation shows up most concretely in the climactic chapter when Sam, another African American character, finally decides not to palliate white feelings and gives a speech to Tom Harris, a white man who considers himself "the black man's friend."[23] Henry is soon to be lynched for the murder of Tracy (a murder he did not commit) and everyone in the town, black and white, knows what is coming. In this speech, Sam rails against an unjust society that will condone the murder of an innocent black man, demanding "what would a decent God have to do with the thing like—."[24] Tom interrupts him, saying (slowly!), "there's things no nigger on earth can say to a white man!"[25] Even the sympathetic white man is distanced from the victims of social injustice by his very whiteness—he cannot imagine a world in which it was otherwise. And even the sympathetic white man is ready, in a moment, to turn away from his black friends and reinstate racial divisions in the harshest possible way, using the vilest language. This scene illustrates what Perrin regards as the fundamental problem of *Strange Fruit*. Prejudice cannot be solved by having the right ideas; indeed, "the novel worries that encouraging readers to celebrate the bond of common humanity joining them to its characters will, in political terms, do more harm than good by blinding them to the realities of structural inequality."[26] Smith is demonstrating that all forms of interracial coupling are incapable of providing any real closure because they are both constructed and destroyed by the society around them. By the end of the novel, Tracy and Henry are dead. Nonnie is pregnant and serene, but nevertheless faces an uncertain future. Sam has had his faith in his friend forever broken.

The primary cause of this impossibility is white resentment of empowered African Americans. These symbolic resonances occur within the context of a novel whose focus is inescapably double. *Strange Fruit* is set in the 1920s, but it was published in the middle of World War II. As such, it partakes of a double reference whenever "the war" is mentioned. Nonnie's sister Bess reflects that "a war can change anything."[27] The indefinite article here suggests that Smith is in fact making a broader claim, a claim that extends out from the immediately local significance of World War I. Several of her male characters were involved in World War I. This war highlighted hometown inequality between African Americans and whites. Smith may be speaking of the 1920s in her novel, but she is speaking equally to the 1940s. World War I is most often connected with the mass exodus of African Americans from the South. At one point, one of the men conspiring to lynch Henry complains about the fact that the war gave African Americans a sense of belonging to their society. With pride, he relates how he humiliated "one fool in a corporal uniform" by making him doff his hat.[28] The war has given African American men a sense of pride, and the white establishment is at pains to remove that pride. Smith holds out little hope that these racial divisions can be overcome; in her construction, the entire town is based upon racial injustice and so inevitably works to that end. The racial divide splits the town like a ravine.

Eight • Transcending Division

In small-town literature, a sense of pride can be dangerous for racial minorities. William Faulkner's detective novel *Intruder in the Dust* explores this hatred of self-assertive African American men through the character of Lucas Beauchamp. Though Beauchamp is in some ways a marginal figure in his own story, Faulkner's original plan was for *Intruder* to feature him as the novel's primary detective. Beauchamp was to be falsely accused of murder and set about proving his own innocence.[29] That element was eventually dropped, and many of the primary investigative duties devolved onto Chick Mallison, Gavin Stevens' young nephew. Nevertheless, it is not quite correct to say that Chick is the only investigator in the novel.[30] I have previously discussed the ways in which Chick, Aleck Sander, and Miss Habersham all work together (with Gavin) as an investigative collective. Lucas also acts as a detective. Indeed, his investigation leads to the murder—it is the instigating factor in the whole plot. Crawford Gowrie and his brother Vinson—two men from Beat Four, a rural section of Yoknapatawpha County—are in business together, working at a mill. During a late-night walk, Lucas discovers that lumber is disappearing from the mill. Lucas investigates and discovers that Crawford is the thief and that he is selling the lumber to a third party. This discovery eventually leads to the murder that forms the novel's core investigation.

Intruder in the Dust is a detective story, and Lucas functions as a hard-boiled detective. John Cullen Gruesser highlights the distinction between the ratiocinative detective and the hard-boiled detective, saying that "hard-boiled detective fiction often features a lower-middle-class white male protagonist with a disdain for unmanly behavior, a suspicion of women, colorful, demotic language, and the toughness and street-smarts to operate in a corrupt and violent urban environment."[31] Leaving off the racial significance of Gruesser's identification of the hard-boiled protagonist with whiteness, Lucas possesses many of the other qualities Gruesser highlights. Beauchamp's early encounter with Chick, in which he saves the boy's life and then refuses payment, is indicative of Beauchamp's own standards of masculinity. To be paid for a service is to exist in a lower sphere; to refuse payment is to forcibly establish equality between two parties. This exchange is doubled at the conclusion of the novel, when Lucas not only insists on paying Gavin for his services, but also on waiting until a receipt is drawn up. Beauchamp's standards of masculinity mean that he cannot accept payment for a kindness. He also must insist on giving payment for being rescued from a similar—though more racially fraught—danger. Throughout the novel, Lucas is characterized by his refusal to play a subservient role to the white folks of the town; it is this, as much as anything else, that prompts the mob to turn on him.[32] Gavin derides Lucas for his pride, but there is little indication—given Lucas' positioning as a tough man in the text—that Faulkner shares his protagonist's sentiments.

Indeed, as a detective, Lucas is superior to all the other investigators in the book. Lucas is an outsider—not only in the Sherlock Holmes sense of being removed from society, but in the Raymond Chandler sense of being better than society. For Chandler, the detective must stand outside his society. He must especially be separate because, as Ernest Mandel observes, "the American crime story [presents] crime as [...] completely integrated into society as a whole."[33] If society is implicated in the crime, the detective must be separate from the society. Lucas Beauchamp's race sets him apart already, but there is more to distinguish him from the rest of the world. The reader is told constantly in the novel that if Lucas would only play by white rules, if he would only bow and scrape with the proper humility, he would be in far less danger of lynching.[34] Lucas does not bow and scrape; he is far too proud for that. And yet, for all his pride—for all the ways he exemplifies the "tough guy" archetype—Lucas still finds himself in jail. He is only saved when a coalition of detectives made up of other marginalized individuals (children and spinsters) is able to convince Gavin Stevens to look into his case. For Faulkner, the small town is founded on racism, but it also offers a mechanism by which racism can be transcended. It is precisely in the embracing of racial difference, the embracing of the fact that the small town has never been an exclusively white space, that Faulkner sees the possibility of moving on.

Far from being an exclusively white space, the small town is imagined in some of the literature as an exclusively *non*-white space. In *Yokohama, California*, Toshio Mori pushes the conception of racial transcendence to its logical end-point. Race is a central concern for Mori, even when it is not being explicitly discussed. The book's very title is designed to make a political claim: that if the European residents of Winesburg, Ohio, are American, the Japanese citizens of Yokohama, California, are as well. The radicalness of this claim, particularly in small-town literature, cannot be overstated. Asia has sometimes cropped up in small-town literature, but it primarily functions there as a sign of the exotic. When Carol renovates her house in *Main Street*, one sign of her cosmopolitanism, transplanted to the monocultural Gopher Prairie, is "a Japanese obi."[35] Her first—unsuccessful—attempt at being a society leader involves a "Chinese" masquerade where the partiers dress as "mandarins and coolies and—samurai (isn't it?)" and Carol herself is "The Princess Winky Poo."[36] This muddled attempt at high culture is very much of its time. It is also, of course, a kind of yellowface—Carol is as Asian as Myrna Loy, and she thoughtlessly collapses China and Japan into a pan–Asian stereotype. She is enacting, that is, a kind of minstrelsy. Robert G. Lee observes that "minstrelsy can be understood as a ritual response to boundary crisis."[37] That is, yellow-and-blackface performances serve to reinforce the out-ness of the outskirts even as they seem to bring them into the center of the white town. Calling herself "The Princess Winky Poo" reduces China—reduces

Asia itself, since Carol does not know the difference between China and Japan—to a childlike fairy-tale.

However, this move is not mere exoticism. Something about the small town itself invites connections—even superficial or mocking ones—to Asia, and that something is its deep identification both with America itself and (back of America) with Eden. The purpose of Carol's masquerade is more complex than Lee would suggest. For not only does the racial masquerade insist upon the other-ness of the Other, it also bespeaks a perverse kind of admiration. Blackface is embedded in "a complicated web of love and hate, fear and guilt, attraction and repulsion, mockery and mimicry."[38] Similarly, this modernist orientalism works both to maintain separation between white society and Asia and as a perverse acknowledgment that the West has much to learn from the East. As Zhaoming Qian articulates it, "China and Japan are seen not as foils to the West, but as crystallizing examples of the Modernists' realizing Self."[39] Now, certainly this form of Orientalism still insists on Asia as the Other, but Qian argues the High Culture interest in Asia was based on a recognition of similarity rather than difference.[40] In small-town literature, Asia is often inserted at the heart of the community, appearing in unexpected places. Thus, the Raintree in *Raintree County* comes from China.[41] Similarly, in the fragmentary sixth and final book of *Paterson*, William Carlos Williams speaks of "a Chinese poet who/drowned embracing the reflection of the moon in the river."[42] The poet spoken of here, as Williams makes clear, is Li Bai, also known as Li Po or Li Bo. Williams unselfconsciously inserts the ancient poet into his account of the small city of Paterson, New Jersey. The suggestion is that America, crystallized in its small towns, exists in a continuity with both Asia and with the paradise that Columbus believed he had discovered there.

Though the small town has long been associated with Asia (and, behind Asia, with the Garden of Eden), such an association can often erase the lived experiences of actual Asian-American persons. Carol's masquerade notably includes no actual Asians. In contrast, Toshio Mori works to re-present the small town through explicitly Asian eyes. Though *Yokohama, California* was intended to be published in 1942, the events surrounding Pearl Harbor caused publication to be pushed to 1949, after the war had already ended.[43] As such, the collection partakes of precisely the same double vision that is typical of small-town fiction during the period: its setting is in a past significantly removed from contemporary situations, and yet it comments upon contemporary situations. Just as an offhand mention of a woman having relations in Hiroshima acquires a new significance after that city has been bombed by the United States, so the discussion of a distinctly Japanese-American small town becomes hyper-signifying after the immense racism direct towards Japanese-American persons during World War II. John W. Dower, in his essay "Race, Language, and War in Two Cultures: World War II in Asia," observes that there was a vast disparity between the ways in which the Germans were portrayed in popular discourse and the ways in which the Japanese were discussed.[44] As Dower puts it, "Japan's aggression [...] stirred the deepest recesses of white supremacism and provoked a response bordering on the apocalyptic."[45] This racist discourse mixed elements of gender denigration as "[t]raits attributed to the Japanese often were almost identical to those assigned to women in general: childishness, irrationality, emotional instability and 'hysteria'—and also intuition, a sixth sense, and a talent for non-discursive communication."[46] On the homefront, as Reed Ueda argues, the overwhelming assumption was that Asians in general were impossible to assimilate to the broader (white) American culture.[47] The form that this assumption took was different depending on the national origin of these Asian-American persons. By and large, Chinese immigrants were viewed more favorably than Japanese immigrants, for reasons related to the war. Ueda notes that "the assumption of the profound alienage of Asians—the historic grounds of restrictive naturalization policy—appeared in justifications for denying civil rights to Japanese-American citizens enunciated during the prosecution of internment."[48] This policy of internment—by which Japanese-American citizens were rounded up and put into camps where they could be monitored—forms, thus, a subtext to *Yokohama, California*, even though only one story makes direct reference to it.

Mori's fiction includes a covert quest for racial reconciliation. The story "Tomorrow Is Coming, Children," is the first selection in the book, and so serves as a framing device for the entire collection. It is the monologue of a grandmother, immigrated from Japan, who attempts to make sense of the racism she encounters during World War II. She says that "[i]f there were no war we would not be in a relocation center. We would be back in our house on Market Street, hanging out our wash on the clothesline and watering our flower garden. You would be attending school with your neighborhood friends."[49] This passage accomplishes the same task that "Slant-Eyed Americans" does in that it emphasizes the *Americanness* of these Japanese-American persons. The grandchildren are addressed by stereotypically European-American names. Furthermore, the things the interned persons miss—living on Market Street, washing clothes, tending flowers, and going to school—are not particulars of a Japanese-American existence; rather, they are signifiers of small-town life more broadly considered. Lawson Fusao Inada, in his introduction to the 1985 re-issue of *Yokohama, California*, argues that, in spite of the story's seeming encouragement of forgetfulness, it is actually a call to remember the injustices of the camps, since "Grandma is actually teaching history, interpretation, survival tactics, strategy—in the guise of a bedtime story."[50] Inada is correct, as far as he goes, but the survival here is not simply a matter of remembering, either. It is also about redefinition.

EIGHT • *Transcending Division* 163

To understand Mori's project, it is important to notice how he repositions the citizens of the town. Specifically, it is worth noticing the precise way in which he marginalizes his few white characters. Before the section quoted above—to which Inada refers—Grandma narrates "the first time [she] began to feel at home" in America.[51] She narrates an encounter with the white wife of a Japanese acrobat. The wife exists on the margins of the narrative, like other white characters in the collection. That is to say, Mori brings persons formerly on the outskirts (racial minorities) into the center of the narrative while pushing formerly central persons onto the outskirts. He is inverting the stereotypical American small town. That most American of institutions is no longer the primary domain of white people; it is instead dominated by people of color. Importantly, however, the small town remains recognizable; structurally, Yokohama is no different from Winesburg. By implication, then, the citizens of Yokohama are just as fully American as the citizens of Anderson's small town.

Mori is also redefining the ways in which racial exchange takes place, since the medium of this friendship is not speech but silence. Grandma and the woman cannot communicate—Grandma's English is limited, and the other woman can only say the name of a town in Japan. Nevertheless, these women form a bond; at one point, the white woman's husband thanks Grandma for being a friend to his wife and, when Grandma protests that they never talk, he says, "She understands. You do not have to talk."[52] For Grandma, this friendship with a white woman allows her to feel accepted in America. But the mechanism in play here is more suggestive than that: the white woman is married to a Japanese acrobat. The unspeaking friendship between Grandma and the woman crosses racial lines in a way that is not exploitative, possibly precisely because they cannot communicate. The marriage between the acrobat and the woman, however, suggests something more—a bonding, a union, a moment of two-becoming-one. What Mori is offering here is not the idea of forgetting the past—as Inada rightly points out—but the possibility that, even in remembering the past, a fusion or union can be accomplished. The fundamental racial divisions in play may, in his view, be transcended by something as simple as friendship and love.

Mori's collection is, thus, fundamentally about accomplishing precisely that transcendence despaired of by Smith. Transcendence of injustice is a central theme of this collection. Though the internment camps and the racial injustices of the war years are elsewhere not so obviously discussed, they nevertheless form an unspoken subtext to this unapologetically Japanese-American book. Frank Chin, in his essay "Come All Ye Asian American Writers of the Real and the Fake," argues that "none of [Mori's] characters in *Yokohama, California*, written before the war, suffer the schizoid agony of being torn apart by the conflicting parties of the dual personality or identity crisis."[53]

That is to say, these Japanese-American characters are not conflicted about either being Japanese *or* American, and this is precisely the revolutionary force of the collection. Like Ted Nakashima in his article "Concentration Camp: U.S. Style," they feel themselves to be Americans and on the side of the United States rather than that of Japan.[54] Moreover, though Inada overstates the reality when he says that "there are no white people in all of *Yokohama, California*"—there is, for instance, the flower-salesman in "Slant-Eyed Americans" or the white wife of the Japanese acrobat in "Tomorrow Is Coming, Children," both stories composed during Mori's internment in World War II—it is certainly true that "the people do not define themselves as nonwhite, nor do they need to rely on whites."[55] On the other hand, Mori insists on the naturalness of this nonwhite community, and so emphasizes the role of race. He does this most notably in the title of the collection as well as the stories "Slant-Eyed Americans" and (Inada to the contrary) "The All-American Girl." These sorts of decisions are always political. Yokohama, California is a town defined by and shot through with an awareness of racial divisions just as surely as *Strange Fruit*. The point, however, is that Mori presents racial difference as being an element shared by everyone in the town. The collection incarnates an alternate vision of America.

Racial outskirts and class-based outskirts often mix. In *Kings Row* the two are explicitly tied together. Its heir *Peyton Place* is also about race. Indeed, Sally Hirsh-Dickinson argues in *Dirty Whites and Dark Secrets* that the real scandal of *Peyton Place* is racial rather than sexual: Samuel Peyton, the town's founder, was black—a fact that the white residents of the town are reluctant to admit.[56] Hirsh-Dickinson suggests that this foundational story, rather than the explicit sex, is the real scandal of *Peyton Place*.[57] This interest in race bleeds into a concern with class. Dr. Swain—one of the heroes of the novel—calls the tar paper shacks on the town's outskirts "cesspools, as filthy as sewers and as unhealthy as an African swamp."[58] The language is, tellingly, racialized here. Filth and disease are associated not only with a swamp, but with an *African* swamp. Thus, anxieties about racial purity and about class-lines are united here. Some of the more well-to-do citizens worry about the growth of the shacks, saying that they are fire hazards.[59] Notably, the discussion takes place without consulting the inhabitants of those shacks, and the only objection centers around the idea that zoning is in some way tyrannical.[60]

Gender, race, and class are all united in *Peyton Place*'s cosmos. Ardis Cameron observes that, though *Peyton Place*—like *Kings Row*—was immediately popular because of its salacious content, Grace Metalious addresses "the real class system [...] the system of the rich against the poor, and of the insiders against the outsiders."[61] This concern with class is manifested in the treatment of Selena Cross in particular. Selena is Allison MacKenzie's best friend. The two of them are a matched set, "Selena with her dark, gypsyish beauty [...] and Allison MacKenzie, still plump with residual babyhood, her eyes wide open, guileless and questioning, above that painfully sensitive mouth."[62] Again, this is precisely Fiedler's light-and-dark-girl dyad. However, over the course of the novel, Metalious undercuts the dyad in a number of ways. First, she emphasizes that Allison, no less than Selena, is a creature of passion. Second, she betrays more curiosity about Selena's plight than Cooper or Smith do about their respective dark ladies. Whereas Allison comes from a respectably middle-class family, Selena lives among the tar paper shacks with her mother, brother, and stepfather, who (Metalious says) might in another area of the country be referred to as "poor white trash."[63] It is this depressed way of life that, Metalious indicates, allows Lucas Cross to rape his step-daughter, leading to the pregnancy that forms a central crisis of the novel. Selena's one romance of the novel is with Ted Carter. Ted's parents object, because "[t]hey regarded as a failure a son who could allow himself to become involved with a girl from the shacks."[64] The Carters are themselves from the shacks, having worked (and married) their way out of them. Arguably, though Ted ostensibly breaks with Selena because of the murder charge against her, the class divisions in Peyton Place are no less to blame for his abandonment of her. The very fact that Ted is concerned about what the well-to-do citizens of the town would say indicates as much.[65] Ted has already experienced that talk; Metalious says that his parents' humiliation causes a good deal of pleasure within the town, since "[t]o see young Carter take up with a shack girl, after his people had worked so hard to escape the same environment that had spawned Selena, had a certain beauty, a poetic justice."[66] Selena's romance with Ted is doomed by class divisions even before she kills her stepfather.

Like *Peyton Place*, Grace Metalious' follow-up, 1960's *The Tight White Collar*, is centrally concerned with the experience of women in a repressive small town. Though the title would suggest that Metalious is primarily interested in economic matters, her politics are thoroughly sexual. The novel's plot can be summarized briefly: the school board of the town of Cooper Station invites Chris Pappas to teach school. This decision raises the ire of Doris Palmer, a high-ranking woman in the town, who arranges a petition to have Pappas fired. Meanwhile, Chris' wife Lisa has an affair with a member of the town's founding family, Anthony Cooper, who throws his support secretly behind the plan to have Chris fired once the relationship becomes too close. The main interest of the book, however, does not reside in this somewhat threadbare plot. Instead, Metalious structures the majority of the novel's eighteen chapters around extended flashbacks exploring the histories of the characters, including Doris Palmer, the woman who wants Chris thrown out. This construction allows Metalious to further explore the themes that interested her in *Peyton Place*: the fact that the small town's façade conceals nested sets of stories, all of which are in violent contradistinction to the wholesome small-town myth.

Doris is the novel's primary symbol of small-town hypocrisy. Upright and proper, it is she who insists that Chris and Lisa are not fit for the town.[67] As it develops, however, Doris' history is hardly so saintly. Metalious observes that "[i]f the whole truth had been known, Doris would never have been able to live in Cooper Station in the first place."[68] That truth, as it turns out, involves an impoverished girl from Ireland who moved to New York and seduced her employer's son. When her employer (tellingly named Theo) finds out, he forces Doris to perform a striptease for him while he pleasures himself.[69] After this, Doris seduces Theo and becomes pregnant. She blackmails her employer and moves to Philadelphia, then back to New York, and finally to Boston, abandoning her child along the way.[70] Using the money provided by Theo, she is able "to attach herself to the fringe that dwelt right outside" the center of Boston society.[71] That is to say, she enters a kind of outskirts within society. In this case, the outskirts become a place of inclusion; here she meets Adam Palmer and marries him, moving with him to Cooper Station, where she creates an identity for herself such that "[w]ithin ten years, there were many people who never stopped to remember that Doris had been born elsewhere."[72] So far, this narrative seems to be simply a matter of small-town hypocrisy. Doris *is* a hypocrite, true, and Metalious clearly positions her sympathies alongside Lisa Pappas and against Doris. However, both Lisa and Doris share a position in society that victimizes them. Doris is presented as being, from an early age, incredibly ambitious and willing to use her own sexuality to achieve her goals. She determines to get to the United States and she does, where "[w]ithin two days she had secured a position as chambermaid with a wealthy family."[73] While Metalious positions Doris as the representative of small-town propriety, she *also* recognizes that Doris has fought her way from a position of disadvantage to become the prominent citizen she is.

Race and gender are visibly marginalized positions; sexuality is—largely— invisible. However, it is no less subject to the alienation experienced by the previous two groups. *The Tight White Collar* features Metalious' first direct discussion of homosexuality. In *Peyton Place*, Norman Page is implicitly gay, but Metalious does not directly address his sexuality. In contrast, *The Tight White Collar* presents readers with David Strong, the local music teacher. David is marked off from the rest of the town as "a little peculiar" because "it wasn't natural for a man to wear cologne or to polish his fingernails, even if he did use colorless polish, or to be so finicky about his food," leading other men in town to conclude that David is gay.[74] For his part, David recognizes that he is different, but does not admit to himself that he is gay. Metalious' treatment of homosexuality in *The Tight White Collar* is very much of its time. She hews closely to midcentury stereotypes of how gay men are formed: a distant father and a mother who is "a frigid stick of a woman" have combined to shape David into the man he is.[75] Accordingly, David sublimates his sexual urges into the church.[76] At one point, David moves to France. While in Paris, he lives with a man named Martin Mallory. Metalious describes their domestic arrangements briefly, noting how "[w]henever David undressed in the room, he could feel Martin's eyes on him."[77] Their relationship becomes sexual, a submissive-dominant coupling; they quarrel and then David pleads for forgiveness. Finally, the relationship comes to a head when Martin beats David with a belt, filling the father's place.[78] David needs sex with men because his family life as a child has warped him. So far, so regressive.

Metalious does present a counter-narrative to the overriding Freudianism of David's past. Within the "present" of the novel itself, David makes friends with a young local man named Mark. It is clear from their interactions that Mark is sexually interested in David, and he soon tries to seduce him.[79] David at first rebuffs Mark, but his curiosity gets the better of him and he asks Mark how he can live with these desires roiling within him. Mark's response is startling:

> "David, I don't have to tell you how happy I am that you've finally admitted the truth to yourself," he said. "But accepting the truth, well, that's quite a different matter." He looked at David for a long, quiet moment and then his voice took on a low, musical, persuasive quality. "Listen, David, the first thing you must do is rid your mind of all the dreadful labels you've picked up along the way. There's no such thing as right and wrong in our case. What's 'wrong' for most people is 'right' for us so you see how little sense there is to putting name tags on anything, don't you?"[80]

The language here is recognizable even today, and it follows a particular pattern: first must come self-awareness ("admitted the truth to yourself") and then self-acceptance. The rejection of conventional morality is Metalious' gloss on the Wildean aesthete, as is clear in her invocation of Lord Henry Wotton elsewhere in the novel. Mark also invokes a history of queer characters in canonical literature. When he warns David not to allow himself "to be influenced by others. By the so-called 'normal' people..." he is obliquely calling to mind Wing Biddlebaum's words to George Willard in *Winesburg, Ohio*.[81] Queerness is set in sharp contrast to the overbearing, monstrous small town. Of course, as Metalious demonstrates elsewhere in the novel—as well as in her other work—there is nothing "normal" about the people of the town. They are all closeted in some way—that is to say, they all conceal something from the town in order to maintain the façade of normality.

Mark may have found happiness, but David remains every inch the tragic queer man. David is at first comforted by Mark's words. He discovers that "the hope that had only made itself known to him before began to burn with new vigor."[82] Metalious depicts the struggle within David in detail—he wants, he *longs*, to live in the "sin-free" world of the younger man, but he cannot help but think that Mark is "evil."[83] The crisis does not resolve happily. The two men have sex, and when David awakens it is to a "heaving sensation of sickness" enhanced by the smell of Mark's "lavender cologne."[84] Finally, David decides to kill himself. He conducts an internal monologue with his mother in which he connects his own fate with that of Chris and Lisa Pappas; indeed, he reflects (addressing his mother) "it'd be worse for me than it was for [them] and you wouldn't want that, would you? And I'd get caught, don't worry about that. Everyone knows already."[85] Finally, David dies with a prayer on his lips and he is found the next morning by his housekeeper Valerie.

The impression Metalious gives here is that queerness is part of small-town life but that anything *too* queer must be punished by death. David's suicide is thus consistent with the portrayals of queer characters elsewhere during the period, as in lesbian novels where the unhappy ending excuses the novel's queer content. In large part, Metalious is operating within the same framework that Perrin identifies with middlebrow "problem" fiction. However, where Perrin sees the genre as didactic, I maintain that, with its peculiar mixture of the Gothic and the realistic, the small-town "problem" novel stubbornly refuses to comment upon itself. In this, middlebrow literature is very like Modernist works of literature. Metalious is interested in subjectivity, not objective fact. That is to say, she is not suggesting that *all* queer men must end up like David; it is enough for her purposes that David does. Indeed, in *The Tight White Collar*, David is the anomaly. Mark, in contrast, seems reasonably well-adjusted, and though David compares Mark's words to those of Lord Henry Wotton in *The Picture of Dorian Gray*,[86] they nevertheless possess a certain power when he says "[t]here's nothing wrong in my loving you. Love is good, kind, sweet and merciful so how can you think for a minute that there's something 'wrong' about it?"[87] Similarly, David's first lover Martin observes that "[w]hat we have is exactly the same kind of love a man has for a woman."[88] Leaving aside the heteronormative assumptions embodied in Martin's words, he is arguing here for the absolute normality of gay relationships. Later, when David returns from Europe, he plays at a club where there are "languid glances […] pancake make-up and […] soft-tipped fingers that […] reached out on many occasions to stroke his arm."[89] While at this club, David "almost managed to acquire a feeling of belonging, of having his place in the world at last" before the thoughtless behavior of a couple of tourists spoils it.[90] In other words, David's inability to accept his own homosexuality is not a condition of queerness itself so much as his own religiously-warped consciousness. Mark, Martin, and the patrons of the club are all well-adjusted and happy; only David is driven at last to suicide. Metalious intends the indictment to land squarely on the town itself.

The phenomenon of outsiderliness is central to the small-town aesthetic.

Protagonists are often set apart from the community around them, but so are most sympathetic secondary characters. Because *Kings Row* is the story of Parris Mitchell, it might seem as if the small town presents a united front against which Mitchell must struggle. However, as the novel develops, it becomes clear that the pleasant, bucolic façade of the town is paper-thin. Beneath its surface lurk madness and incest and murder. Parris himself most closely identifies with two outsider characters. The one, Drake McHugh, is wealthy and a roustabout before his money is stolen by a corrupt banker and he is himself crippled by a sociopathic physician. Parris' other friend, Jamie, is soft and feminine and so definitely gay that he must always remain an outsider to Kings Row. Jamie's sexuality provides the clearest marker of his loneliness. He is first introduced through the eyes of his schoolteacher as "too pretty for a boy," dressed in a ruffled collar and distinctly un-masculine clothing.[91] Later, his mother is described as "a large gelatinous woman who seemed to be precariously held together by tight clothes and a generous amount of corseting."[92] She is an overbearing, overprotective maternal figure, which fits midcentury stereotypes of homosexuality. Jamie's sexuality is indicated from the very beginning of the novel by a series of stereotyped signs of homosexuality: he is sensitive, poetic, girlish. He also hates and fears women, having as he does an overbearing mother. These are stereotypical markers, but they should not be read as unthinkingly applied. Bellamann was apparently himself bisexual and may have conducted an affair with the childhood friend who became the model for Jamie.[93] Moreover, Bellamann was a poet, so his slip into stereotype here in describing Jamie as poetic should not be read as simply a reflexive distrust of gay people. Jamie does not function simply as a curiosity in the novel. Though he is—or becomes—a grotesque in the Andersonian sense, he also provides the clearest perspective on the fundamental alienation at the heart of small-town life.

Jamie fits well with what historians have observed about gay life in rural communities. After observing Jamie's beauty and being obscurely tempted by it, Drake attempts to convince Jamie that he "just ought to like girls. It's natural."[94] In the same scene, Drake admits that same-sex activity in Kings Row seems to be common among the boys of the town; they "kind of experimented, and played little games and all that stuff. But we got interested in girls—"[95] In his book *Men Like That: A Queer Southern History*, John Howard offers documentation of the life of queer men in Mississippi during the 1950s through the 1980s. It is Howard's assertion that critical and academic focus on cities and the post–Stonewall movement in gay rights has led to a tendency to dismiss the lives of rural gay men in the years preceding Stonewall. His study is an attempt to correct that imbalance. Howard argues that "it was in fact not the 'conformist fifties' but rather the 'free love sixties' that marked the most strident, organized resistance to queer sexuality in Mississippi."[96]

According to Howard, "Homosex between boys [during the '50s and '60s] was tolerated, expected even. To continue homosexual activity as a teen or young adult, however, was more problematic."⁹⁷ What Howard has identified in the historical lived experience of queer Southern men is precisely the argument made by Drake in *Kings Row*—teenage boys may fool around but they must eventually settle down and marry. To maintain primarily same-sex activities in adulthood hints at an over-extended adolescence.

The social stigma against adult homosexuality dooms Jamie to a colorless, unhappy existence. Drake expresses that social stigma when he warns that Jamie faces a stunted emotional life as an adult and ultimately will be driven to pederasty. Just after confessing to fooling around with Jamie as an adolescent, Drake warns Jamie that he (Jamie) is "going to go with younger and younger kids [...] you'll get in trouble about young kids. You'll get put in the pen, sure's you're born."⁹⁸ That is to say, the future that Drake envisions for Jamie is that he will become a pedophile. Within the context of the novel, Drake has some basis for this assumption; early in the book, he indicates to Parris that Jamie may be carrying on an affair with Bob Callicott, a local piano teacher.⁹⁹ When Callicott dies, a crying Jamie calls Parris and begs his friend to come to the funeral with him.¹⁰⁰ After the eulogy, Jamie curls up on the pew and refuses to leave with Parris.¹⁰¹ Jamie and Callicott clearly had a relationship of some kind, one that was likely sexual. But Drake makes a mistake here because he is (at this point in the novel) driven by a desire for sex. Jamie, on the other hand, says that he wants "somebody I can read with, and talk to, and make plans with. Somebody who knows what I'm talking about and likes the same things I do."¹⁰² Jamie does not want sex so much as he wants companionship. Sex is certainly a part of that, as seen when Jamie attempts to seduce Parris:

> [T]hey sat for a long time without speaking. Jamie unfastened Parris's wristband and slipped his hand into the sleeve. Parris was a little startled by the sensation. Jamie had strange hands—small, and plump for so slight a boy. His fingers left a tingle where they touched. But Parris felt puzzled about something, he didn't know just what. He kept trying to think his way through entangling and conflicting ideas, when—without warning—Jamie leaned forward and kissed him on the mouth. Parris was too amazed to move, too amazed to think. He felt as if a gust of flame swept him from head to foot.¹⁰³

Parris, like Drake, is not repulsed by Jamie's advances. If anything, he is turned on; the "gust of flame" and the "tingle" left by the other boy's hand suggest that Parris is, if not gay or bisexual himself, at least able to feel sexual desire for another boy. But sex is only a part of what Jamie wants. Jamie is, like Parris, an Adam in the small-town Garden of Eden, but (in *Kings Row* itself) an Adam who is destined to remain alone. By the end of the novel, he has faded into a gray shadow of his former self, working at the bank.

At its logical extreme, small town fiction does not allow for the fantasy of belonging. Rather, the genre posits a world in which everyone is an outsider. *Kings Row*, for all its melodrama and gothic flourishes, is finally a novel about loneliness: the loneliness of Parris Mitchell, to be sure, but also that of his friends Drake and Jamie, of Father Donovan (a Catholic priest in a Protestant town), of the Lutheran preacher Herr Berdorff. Cassandra Tower is victimized by her own father at an early age and forced to live in isolation until the old man at last murders her. Though on publication the novel attracted attention because of its salacious content, this content is ultimately the cover for a theme: that the small town consistently presses down upon and destroys its residents. Late in the book, Jamie has a revelation. He sees that Kings Row is "a subtle, and secret alignment of people and forces [...] arbitrary, and heartless, and impersonal." The town accepts some people, but others—Drake, Jamie, Bob Callicott—are rejected.[104] Jamie's understanding of the town is accurate, but he understates its malevolence. He assumes that Parris is part of the inner circle, but Bellamann makes clear elsewhere that even Parris does not fit in, particularly after his sojourn in Europe. Jamie's vision thus becomes a central moment in the book, the more remarkable because it occurs in the only section not centered on Parris Mitchell. The town of Kings Row takes on the aspect of a devouring monster, desperate to destroy all trace of difference. Indeed, this is precisely the fate of Jamie, who goes to work at his father's bank and loses his poetic ambitions, becoming "dry and bankerish."[105] The society around him has destroyed him.

Jamie is the central figure in a network of isolated characters, and his isolation is a type or sign of theirs. Late in the novel, Parris reflects that Jamie "like all of his kind must go on living in the strange limbo of an increasing detachment and isolation."[106] Parris here is meditating on the loneliness (or presumed loneliness, which in this context means the same thing) of the small-town gay man. Just as Bob Callicott, the music teacher, finally died alone and lonely, so Jamie is destined to end his days a shadow of his former self. But the phrase "like all his kind" obscures the fact that Jamie is not the only outsider, and his sexuality is only one marker of difference available in the small town. Jamie's loneliness is a mirror to Parris' own isolation. Indeed, immediately following these reflections on Jamie, Parris admits to himself that "[h]is own detachment followed certainly on an attitude of his own, and his isolation [...] was greater than Jamie's."[107] This awareness of a fundamental alienation radiates outward to all the characters in the novel. All of them are defined by their fundamental isolation from the people and the town around them. The characters of *Kings Row* are all outsiders. Bellamann thus offers a counter-intuitive vision of the small town: not as a community united in a common cause, but as what may be thought of as a series of nested outskirts. Dr. Tower (himself in an incestuous relationship with his daughter Cassandra) says many times that "we live in multiple worlds." Parris applies this understanding to his life in the small town, seeing it as *"multiple worlds: sometimes one inside of another, like the spheres of Ptolemaic cosmogony—encasing again a smaller world, each one complete and occupied with its own motion, and direction, and content"* (italics original).[108] The individualism that seems to promise freedom becomes instead a prison. By the same token, the community that seems to promise belonging becomes instead relentlessly isolating.

Henry Bellamann leaves Jamie there, doomed (it seems) to an unhappy life. Katherine Bellamann's sequel, *Parris Mitchell of Kings Row* (1948)—completed after Henry's death and based on notes and conversations between the husband and wife—continues Jamie's story in an unexpected way. Certainly, though the novel names Parris in its title, Parris Mitchell is barely the protagonist. Katherine does much to undermine Parris' growth in the previous novel. His marriage, which seems in *Kings Row* to promise a chance to move beyond his radical isolation, proves to be more isolating than ever and is only resolved when his wife dies and Parris finds wholeness—again!—in the arms of Drake's widow Randy. This novel is, overall, a failure; while there are one or two scenes that nearly reach the heights of Gothic bizarre that Henry mounted in *Kings Row*, *Parris Mitchell* is a less-accomplished and disappointing shadow of its predecessor. The novel is worth noting, however, because it does offer Jamie—and, therefore, the other lost and isolated characters in the world of *Kings Row*—a means of escape.

Indeed, Jamie Wakefield becomes a sort of prophetic figure. When he is first re-introduced, it is exactly as readers left him in *Kings Row*, "[t]he warm, eager personality of the young boy [...] grayed and obscured in the man of business."[109] Parris still feels warmly about Jamie, though the two men have drifted apart over the years. Nevertheless, Parris tries to counsel his friend; when Jamie speaks bitterly about the way Kings Row has worn him down, Parris suggests that "[t]he world needs poets more than it needs bankers."[110] This comment becomes the touchpoint for Jamie's storyline in the novel; where Henry left him doomed to become a dusty banker, Katherine slowly works him back into a more fulfilled life. Parris cautions Jamie that there is a difference between happiness and fulfillment. The former "is merely a temporary condition," while the latter "partakes of destiny and has the more lasting satisfactions."[111] This distinction is, of course, the core of Katherine Bellamann's project—to distinguish the happiness Parris felt at the end of *Kings Row* from the fulfillment he feels at the end of *Parris Mitchell*. And this distinction is what ultimately rescues Jamie.

Interpersonal contact is portrayed as a poetic redescription of reality. At the midpoint of the novel, Parris arranges for Jamie, in his capacity as a banker, to assist an impoverished local poet named Drew Roddy in retaining his property. This is openly a matchmaking exercise; Parris muses to Randy that he wants to "keep [Drew] from resigning himself to loneliness."[112] This loneliness is, as I have demonstrated, central to existence in small-town fiction, but here Katherine Bellamann seems to suggest that loneliness is something that can be, at least in some ways, assuaged. Unlike Jamie, Drew is not given the midcentury stereotypes of queerness (for all that both men are poets). Drew is "hollow-cheeked, and the great brown eyes, heavily smudged by illness and fatigue, were arresting; the sensitive mouth bespoke an impressionable nature."[113] Drew has been ill and is about to lose his property, a fate that will doom him since "he could find beauty somewhere else in the world—*maybe*—but to lose this [his home]!"[114] Jamie and Drew commiserate in the fact that they both "stayed too long" in Kings Row and have become tied to the place, unable to achieve their full potential. Parris asks why Drew isn't "writing poetry—instead of just thinking it like this?" and Drew responds that "all the urge went into—grubby toil right here in this unproductive spot."[115] On the surface, Drew means his land, but Jamie interprets him to mean Kings Row itself. Both men are bitter, isolated, and alone. But they find together a chance at transcendence:

> [Drew says.] "I'll be able to write something, now that I'm relieved of worry. Couldn't you come out occasionally to criticize?"
> "I'll come often—if you'll teach me some things I need to know about—just simple versification."
> "Maybe, Jamie, we can help each other."[116]

This exchange is, in fact, the last time Katherine Bellamann gives any attention at all to either Jamie or Drew. The storyline concluded, she feels no need to revisit them. But in this last exchange there seems to be a seed of transcendence. First is the fact that Jamie has finally found a person like the one he expressed desire for in *Kings Row*—someone to spend time with and talk to. Drew and Jamie are simpatico in that both are outsiders and poets. They seem to be attracted to each other, though Katherine is far less explicit than Henry in dealing with Jamie's sexuality. The em-dash separating "about" and "just simple versification" is doing heavy lifting here, like the dash that isolates Jamie in Parris' thoughts in *Kings Row*.[117] Simple versification, yes—but also all the companionship that Jamie has lost in his years at the bank, all of the ambition as a poet that he has left behind as the result of becoming so "dry and bankerish."[118] Whether or not this courtship comes to anything, it holds out the hope for some sort of revival in Jamie himself.

Poetic redescription is the mode of this transcendence. Poetry is nothing less than an incarnation (enfleshment) of the potentialities latent in the human mind. That Jamie and Drew bond over poetry is suggestive because it means that the possibility of redescription carries with it a hope for interpersonal bonding, particularly in difficult times—when the land lies barren and the forces of chaos rule. Poetry is also an apocalypse—it is a thing that reveals the hidden forces at work in society and in the human heart. Here I return to the word I applied early in this chapter: *protest*. To say that small-town fiction is protest fiction is not to claim that it proposes solutions. Solutions are not its business; incarnation and apocalypse are. Late in *Parris Mitchell of Kings Row*, Father Donovan says that "[t]he forces of greed and avarice and stupidity are loosed too often. The Kings Row that is grim and secret, dark, and retentive, must be brought out into the light. You must do your part."[119] Father Donovan is speaking here to Parris, shortly after the horrors of World War I and Parris' own personal struggles with his enemies in the town. And he is speaking partly of Parris' profession as a psychiatrist. But if Parris has always been a stand-in for Henry Bellamann (and it is interesting to speculate that he continues to be such in Katherine's continuation), then this work of revelation, of bringing "out into the light," is equally applicable to Bellamann's work as a musician, as a poet—and as a novelist. The original *Kings Row* was published in 1940, before America entered World War II but not before the war had entered the minds of Americans. Its sequel was published after the war. Thus, the saga of Parris Mitchell brackets a bloody and tumultuous period of history—surely a time, if any, when "[t]he forces of greed and avarice and stupidity are loosed." *Parris Mitchell of Kings Row* suggests that the global and personal are one, and that the job of the individual is to transcend internal divisions and counter the forces of chaos.

The mechanism for this transcendence is art—poetry, music, the novel. Small-town narratives are a form of protest against both the socially-conditioned injustices of racism and classism and the internalized isolation of the individual. In a world of chaos, a world that can end at any point, the very act of making art is a radical stance. Authors who labor lovingly over their descriptions of small towns at the midcentury are not simply escaping into nostalgia. These books are about imagining a better world. Imagining and then giving it form, shape—incarnating it. It is through this act of incarnation that Jamie and Drew bond, and it is this precise act of incarnation that Father Donovan recommends. The paradox: only by incarnation can the existential and social separations of the *carne*, of the flesh, be transcended.

Nine

In This Garden of Death
The Graveyard

The last sight of all, which ends this ramble around the literary small town, is the graveyard. It sits on a hill outside the community, a cluster of grey stones, no less a transtemporal spot than the town square. It asserts by its very presence that the small town is not disconnected from the flow of history. However, the graveyard also asserts that every person living in the town must die, that they live under the shadow of that death. The graveyard is the ultimate (in multiple senses) expression of the small-town myth, the final overcoming of loneliness and embedding in an invisible crowd. But only by *accepting* that loneliness, by embracing Non-Being, is the protagonist able to move beyond mere isolation and into a deeper community. Death and alienation are linked. The end of Eden is death—which is to say, the *point* of Eden, as a myth, is to explain the presence of death in human existence. Death is not simply a physical reality; it is an existential state which extends backward from the grave to emphasize the loneliness of human existence. Humans are imagined as having once possessed a fundamental unity one with the other, a unity that has now been fractured. Concepts of political and existential alienation often mix, particularly in the face of a catastrophe on the level of World War II. The previous chapters outlined the ways in which this mixture works by demonstrating that the small town is, ultimately, a collection of outskirts—an intersectional space in which race, class, and sexuality blur into a generalized feeling of loneliness. In the graveyard, authors attempt to mediate or resolve this alienation.

At a fundamental level, death is the ultimate form of alienation. In Christian theology, death is the result of the fall of Adam and persists in the world as "the wages of sin."[1] Sin in this context must be differentiated from mere wrongdoing. Sin is the condition of death itself; humans are in a state of "death in sin."[2] As such, they are (in Protestant, Calvinist terms) "opposite to all good, and wholly inclined to all evil."[3] In Tillichian terms, humans are alienated by sin from the Ground of Being. They are dead. Death is a fundamental human experience and occupies a peculiar, though not unique, epistemic space. As Goodwin and Bronfen observe in their introduction to *Death and Representation*, "death [...] is always only represented."[4] Like sex—the other member of Leslie Fiedler's dyad—death cannot be expressed directly, and as such isolates all who come within its purview—which is to say, everyone. The loneliness of individual death has always been recognized, but Lawrence Langer argues that "death in an age of atrocity introduces a new emphasis on loneliness."[5] The horrors of the death camps and the atom bomb brought about a new age of atrocity and so death came to occupy a new position, one that emphasized the alienation of the individual.

Existential alienation becomes closely tied to political alienation precisely because of the condition of modern warfare; Norman Mailer's hipster in "The White Negro" acts from a position of existential loneliness and isolation caused by the twin facts of the death camps and the atomic bomb.[6] The existential and the political are united. There is no death which is not existential, and no death is so political as the systematized and rationalized murder of Auschwitz or the calculated spending of lives attendant on firebombings and, especially, the atomic bomb. This reality permeates the postwar consciousness, and it distinguishes midcentury small-town narratives from their predecessors. As discussed in the first chapter of this study, the small town is identified with Eden, and therefore it is always falling, is indeed already fallen. Similarly, death haunts the small town because small towns are always dying. Ryan Poll says that "the dominant small town has become an abstract, deracinated, ideological form," designed for the promulgation of ideology, and therefore serving as a myth of an idyllic past killed by modernity.[7] This argument is sound, as far as it goes, but my own research suggests that the admitted nostalgia for a dead past is a cover for the existential crises facing American writers during and after World War II. This is certainly a concern rooted in pre–World War II literature. The small town is often seen as a collection or congregation of the dead. Edgar Lee Masters' *Spoon River Anthology* presents the reality of small-town life through the eyes of its already-dead citizens. If everyone in the small town is isolated, is cut off, then the ultimate form of cutting off—the ultimate form of isolation—is death. In small-town fiction written during and following World War II, the threat of physical death and the threat of social death are further collapsed into each other and treated as coextensive. Authors of the 1940s and '50s attempt to reconcile the existential and the political aspects of death by dramatizing various ways in which death can be transcended, for better or (often) for worse. The literature of this period charts a movement from the recognition of death as isolation through various attempts to transcend it and finally into a properly dialectic approach to the subject, expressed in Tillichian terms.

Death is the negation of life itself, not an actual thing. Midcentury thinkers—driven by the dialectic approach to philosophy—insisted that this negation is contained within the condition of life itself. For Paul Tillich, "[n]onbeing threatens man's ontic self-affirmation, relatively in terms of fate, absolutely in terms of death," and so calls the human to courage.[8] The titular "courage to be" of Tillich's book involves taking into oneself one's own negation:

> "Including" is a spatial metaphor which indicates that being embraces itself and that which is opposed to it, nonbeing. Nonbeing belongs to being, it cannot be separated from it. We could not even think "being" without a double negation: being must be thought as the negation of the negation of being. This is why we describe being best by the metaphor "power of being."[9]

If small-town fiction actively struggles with existential human loneliness, then it must at last confront the loneliness of the grave. But death comes in many forms, not all of them physical. The self can be dead—isolated—or taken over by the dead. Sometimes, as in *Kings Row*, people die to the protagonist without actually dying. Parris' childhood lover Renée, though not dead, is classed along with "Lucy, his grandmother, Robert Callicott, Dr. Tower, Cassie"—although Parris does hasten to remind himself that Renée is not dead, he attributes to her "as little seeming life as to the others."[10] Death can simply be an absence from the radically isolated individual's life. In this sense, the radically isolated individuals discussed in the previous chapters all equally hold their place among the ranks of the dead.

The dead do not always stay dead; sometimes they return to haunt the living. The theme of the small town as a location in which buried or forgotten evils emerge is deeply entrenched in the history of the genre. Nathaniel Hawthorne provided examples of hidden sins becoming manifest in, for instance, "Young Goodman Brown" and "The Minister's Black Veil." Often, too, this return is represented by the actual incursion of the dead into the world of the living. Sometimes the dead walk, or at least seem to. William Faulkner's "A Rose for Emily" features a woman who attempts to preserve her dead father and then succeeds in preserving her dead paramour. These two attempts are related in that both are rooted ultimately in a denial of death as an actually-existing reality. Miss Emily "told [the ladies of the town] that her father was not dead."[11] In her desire to keep her father alive, Miss Emily clings "to that which had robbed her, as people will."[12] It is, therefore, no surprise that her lover (or whatever Homer Barron is to her) vanishes and his corpse is only found after her death. Faulkner makes it clear that the secret here is not simply murder; it is necrophilia.[13] Emily's desire for Homer is of the same species as her desire for her father; her erotic desire—frustrated by her father and so displaced onto Barron—finds its home in another unattainable male.[14] Homer Barron, however "liked men."[15] The implication here is that Homer is gay, which is further indicated by his own insistence in that same passage that "he was not a marrying man." Meanwhile, Faulkner pictures Emily herself as a kind of corpse, "bloated, like a body long submerged in motionless water, and of that pallid hue."[16] After Homer disappears, Miss Emily withdraws, becoming at last someone only glimpsed through the windows of her house, "like the carven torso of an idol in a niche, looking or not looking at us, we could never tell which."[17]

The sight of Miss Emily framed in the window of her house brings immediately to mind another (un)dead woman, the mother in Robert Bloch's *Psycho* (1959). The connection between "A Rose for Emily" and *Psycho* (and *Peyton Place*!) has been noted by John A. McDermott in his article "'Do You Love Mother, Norman?' Faulkner's 'A Rose for Emily' and Metalious's *Peyton Place* as Sources for Robert Bloch's *Psycho*." McDermott suggests that "Norman Bates's fetish and his psychological state may be Bloch's way of paying tribute to Faulkner and Metalious the way he did Lovecraft."[18] The parallels are certainly striking. Of all the books discussed in this study, *Psycho* needs the least introduction. It is the story of a man—Norman Bates—who runs a hotel and murders people while dressed as (or inhabited by) his mother. In his 1960 adaptation, Alfred Hitchcock creates an iconic image in the silhouette of Mrs. Bates framed against her bedroom window, a sight that evokes Robert Bloch's tale of suspense as readily as a shower-curtain. The image is one of doom; the sight of Mrs. Bates draws the detective Arbogast back to be murdered by Norman.[19] Following Faulkner, Bloch doubles down on the Gothic elements; whereas Emily has not died—not physically—but merely keeps the corpse of her ex-lover in a bedroom upstairs, Mrs. Bates is *both* the revived corpse *and* (through an act of Freudian legerdemain) the person keeping the corpse. That is to say, Norman's Oedipal complex has worked itself out in exactly the way that Emily's father-obsession does in the Faulkner story: his mother, who has exerted unwonted control over his love life, has at last become his final and only object of affection. Emily's attempts to keep her father's corpse once he has died, insisting that he is still alive, have an exact parallel in Norman. Towards the end of the novel, when events seem at last to be closing in on the murderer, Norman speculates that "[t]*he Sheriff could go up to Fairvale Cemetery and open Mother's grave. And when he opened it, when he saw the empty coffin, then he'd know the real secret*" (italics original).[20] The empty coffin represents an obscene parody of the Christian hope of resurrection; in Christian theology, the hope is for eternal individual life (though what "life" means here is conveniently undefined). In *Psycho* and "A Rose for Emily," that life is transmuted into the prospect of eternal individual [un]death, much as Mme. Tarot in *Dandelion Wine* (another corpselike woman!) offers a terrifying parody of immortality. The final chapter of *Psycho* reveals that Norman Bates murdered his mother and her lover (a mirror to Emily's murder of her possibly-homosexual lover) and, while covering up the crime, "*became* his mother" (italics original).[21] A Freudian reading of *Psycho* is certainly called for by the text itself. The dead mother instantiates a return of the repressed maternal superego. For Slavoj Žižek, the maternal superego is that which threatens the phallic logic of the father.[22] The dead mother here is "the incarnation of a fundamental disorder in family relationships."[23] However, to embark on a *merely* Freudian reading of the novel is to do it a disservice, since once the psychological posturing is stripped away what remains is that most common of small-town themes: loneliness.

Everyone in *Psycho* is lonely. Norman's relationship with his mother is defined not only in terms of the Oedipal complex, but also by the fact that he has been isolated by her for his entire life. Even the location of the hotel—far off the main roads, left behind by the march of progress—underlines the fact that Norman Bates is isolated from everyone around him, even though he lives within driving distance of precisely the sort of small town that should promise community. Since the mother is a manifestation of Norman's own warped psyche, her words should be taken as a self-indictment when she says that "the truth is that you haven't any gumption."[24] Similarly, Mary Crane is literally cut off from her lover Sam Loomis by the distance between them and figuratively cut off from her sister through a complex system of family emotions. She is motivated by loneliness; her theft of the money and attempt to join Sam in Fairvale is an attempt to overcome her own isolation. Norman Bates argues in the film version of *Psycho* that everyone is trapped. Attempting to escape that trap leads to Mary's death at the hands of Norman/mother, and it leads to Norman's own psychosis.

Corpses in small-town fiction take on a life of their own. They move—into Emily's bedroom, into Norman Bates' basement and brain. They also exert an obscene influence, re-incarnating in Norman or (as I have discussed earlier) in Rhoda from *The Bad Seed*. In other novels, a grave which has been designed for one corpse becomes the receptacle for another. Most often, this sort of grave-swapping is to be found in crime novels such as *Intruder in the Dust*. To swap corpses is to swap plots; the purported victim often becomes the perpetrator and vice-versa. At other times, the terror of the grave is less horrific than the terror of belonging to the ranks of the undead. Jack Finney's *The Body Snatchers* (1955; revised and republished in 1978 as *Invasion of the Body Snatchers*) is a small-town novel in which the author suggests that loneliness and isolation can have a positive side—that they can produce the drive to improve oneself and one's surroundings. Miles, a small-town doctor, discovers that his town of Santa Mira is being taken over by seed pods from outer space. These pods replicate the residents of the small town, killing the originals and taking on their form for a limited time. That this contagion is a metaphor most critics attest; what the metaphor signifies is less certain. Brian Diemert reads it as a paranoid parable about communism.[25] Michael Rogin, on the other hand, interprets the film adaptation, at least, as a satire of McCarthyism.[26] Both interpretations suggest that the incursion of the pods could be taken as striking at the most American location of all—right at the heart of the national myth. The small town becomes a stand-in for America itself, an interpretation I favor in this study. However, the precise nature of the town's identification with the nation is more vexed than either Diemert or Rogin allow for. Read in continuity with other small-town works of the period, it seems clear that *The Body Snatchers* is engaging in a cluster of concerns that stretch as far back as *Main Street* (1920) and as far forward as *The Stepford Wives* (1972). These novels express an anxiety that the small town *itself* will destroy individuality and force a kind of mindless conformity. The small town, as an American Eden, is both a threat and a promise. *The Body Snatchers* replicates the garden imagery of *Yokohama, California*; however, in contrast to Mori's hopeful vision, the garden imagery in *The Body Snatchers* is read not in terms of rejuvenation but in terms of contagion. The seed pods are symbolic of the creeping mediocre conformity of twentieth century American life. The fact that they have their invasion-point in a small town is significant when read against other small-town fiction.

The small town, not aliens (and not Communism or McCarthyism) is the true villain of *The Body Snatchers*. Finney gives a science-fictional gloss to a long-held double understanding of small towns: they may be the essential version of America, but they are also the bearers of a deadly contagion. The idea of small-town contagion is a central theme of Sinclair Lewis' *Main Street*. At one point, Carol develops a theory of small-town literature. Carol offers a vision of the small town similar to that suggested by Finney in his novel:

> But a village in a country which is taking pains to become altogether standardized and pure, which aspires to succeed Victorian England as the chief mediocrity of the world, is no longer merely provincial, no longer downy and restful in its leaf-shadowed ignorance. It is a force seeking to dominate the earth, to drain the hills and sea of color, to set Dante at boosting Gopher Prairie, and to address the high gods in Klassy Kollege Klothes. Short of itself, it believes other civilizations, as a traveling salesman in a Brown Derby conquers the wisdom of China and tacks advertisements of cigarettes over arches for centuries dedicated to the sayings of Confucius.[27]

Here is precisely the same concern with America's place in the world that will later emerge in the 1940s and '50s. Lewis suggests that America is unfit or unready for global action, that at its base—at its most symbolically central—America is fundamentally mediocre. The small town, for Lewis, is a contagion that threatens the world. China here serves as a symbol of the farthest reach of the globe; it is also (within the symbolic world of the novel) a land of ancient wisdom threatened by American shallowness. The fact that Carol, as discussed previously, is herself ignorant about China should serve to ironize her reflections here, but the vision of the small town as the bearer of a deadly contagion is central to Lewis' thesis.

Like Lewis, Finney envisions the small-town contagion as a global threat. Late in *The Body Snatchers*, the protagonist encounters several of his former friends who have been replaced by the mysterious pods. One of them, Budlong, explains the nature of the pods by referencing evolution. The pods, he explains, are "the perfect parasite, capable of far more than clinging to the host" since they replicate the host exactly.[28] The global takeover of the pods is explicitly compared to the gradual domination of humanity over the earth, and the protagonist is assured of the end-game: "This county, then the next ones; and presently northern California, Oregon, Washington, the West Coast. Presently, fairly quickly, the continent. And then—yes, of course, the world."[29] Only if *The Body Snatchers* is recognized as fundamentally a small-town novel can its full meaning be appreciated. Far from being symbols of creeping communism, the body snatchers are something much more insidious: they are the fruit of small-town America—conforming, sterile, dying. The pod-people have lost all ability to love, to desire. They have lost all the old interests that used to concern them. They argue that "[a]mbition, excitement—what's so good about them? And do you mean to say you'll miss the strain and worry that goes along with them? It's not bad, Miles, and I mean that. It's peaceful, it's quiet."[30] But because drive and desire have left these pod-people, the ability to reproduce has also been taken from them and they are fated to live "five years at the most."[31] The pod-people number among the walking dead; they have transcended ambition—the need to be different from others, to assert individuality—but they have given up life itself. The town, as the result of these interlopers, has lost all ambition:

> We might have been on a finished stage set, completed to the last nail and final stroke of a brush. Yet you can't walk ten blocks on an ordinary street inhabited by human beings without seeing evidences of, say, a garage being built, a new cement sidewalk being laid, a yard being spaded, a picture window being installed—at least some little signs of the endless urge to change and improve that marks the human race.[32]

These little signs are missing now because the small town is dying—is indeed already dead, although it does not yet realize that fact. The description of a small town dying by degrees echoes observations of other writers from Anderson to Lockridge: the happy community has curdled, has gone bad, and its death betokens the death of a larger American community. Indeed, the language employed by Finney—both in this passage and elsewhere—pales beside the declarations of Henry Bellamann in *Kings Row*. By the end of that novel, the town has been isolated from the outer world because "the huge trunk lines ... were thirty miles away."[33] As a result, the town is withering away, dying by degrees even as its residents boast of its newfound modernity. The surest sign of the death of Kings Row is "[c]onformity—yes, and mediocrity. It was the way of the wilderness. To run with the pack one must not wear spots and streaks differently at the risk of being torn to pieces."[34] Bellamann here turns the pioneer spirit on its head; where many early Regionalists praised the pioneers as trailblazers and innovators, Parris Mitchell sees them only as a mediocre assemblage.

The body-snatchers alone do not bring alienation; it has always been part of the small-town reality. Fractured social ties often indicate loneliness: the orphan, the spinster, and the widower are all cut off from the world around them. Miles in *The Body Snatchers* is a divorcee. Moreover, because he is a doctor he has no time for a private life. The novel begins with him ruminating that he "wished [he] had some fun to look forward to that evening, for a change."[35] Though he has friends, Miles is still isolated. And he becomes more so as, one by one, the people around him succumb to the pods. The process of enpodment is itself a type of loneliness—if not for the victims, then for their friends and families. The horror of *The Body Snatchers* is rooted in the fantasy (or nightmare) of one day waking up and discovering that loved ones have become strangers. Such a discovery has an intolerably isolating effect. When Miles is first approached by his old flame Becky and her friend Wilma, they tell him that Wilma's Uncle Ira has been altered somehow. Miles does not believe Wilma—even after a conversation with Uncle Ira—and recommends that Wilma see a psychiatrist.[36] Later, when Wilma is herself taken over, Miles experiences the same dizzying terror that he dismissed as neurosis in her.[37] The incursion of the pod people—what is, in one light, a depiction of conformity and, in another, a dramatization of the wholly other-ness of the Other—eventually pits Miles against men he has known all his life; he and Becky are isolated and alone. And what is important to this discussion is that they are alone because of the conditions arising from the small town itself.

The pod people are vegetable; that is to say, they are the obscene incarnation of the small-town Edenic myth. Finney conveys the monstrosity of conformity by means of the garden. Toshio Mori envisioned small towns as gardens that would spread freedom and life across the United States. In *The Body Snatchers*, however, the vegetable growth of small towns bespeaks the ultimate demise of humanity itself. Running from the (literally!) mindless mob, Miles and Becky stumble upon a field of seed pods. The description focuses on the mundane nature of the scene that confronts them; they might be looking at any field of "cabbages, perhaps, or pumpkins, though neither were grown here, not in this area," but the protagonists realize that these crops are "the new pods, as large already as bushel baskets, and still growing; hundreds of them, in the dim, even light of the moon."[38] Here is the obscene garden of the American small town—not the hopeful seed-bed envisioned by Toshio Mori, but the very locus of a contagion that threatens to destroy the world with its soulless conformity. The novel ends with the pods defeated and leaving earth. Miles sets the field on fire and the pods—sensing that Earth is not as hospitable a target as they anticipated—lift off and return to space. Finney evokes World War II and Winston Churchill: "*We shall fight them in the fields, and in the streets, we shall fight in the hills; we shall never surrender*" (italics original).[39] The fact that Miles and Becky refuse to be absorbed into the pod collective suggests that other humans have as well, and that together they have managed to push back the invader.[40] Thus, the novel seems to end on a far more positive note than its film adaptation.

Ironically, though the pods have left, they have not taken with them the conformity—and corresponding loneliness—that is central to small-town life. The town itself returns to normal. Miles marries Becky and continues to live in Santa Mira, "a town, shabbier and more run-down than most others, but—not startlingly so"—so normal that even Miles is inclined at times to doubt his own story.[41] Mortality is high, but the dying pod-people are quickly being replaced by newcomers. The town is becoming typical, and Miles speculates that "[i]n a year, maybe two, or three, Santa Mira will seem no different to the eye than any other small town. In five years, perhaps less, it will be no different."[42] The town may have escaped the conformity of the pods, but it is conforming to the idea of the small town, with all the mediocrity highlighted by Sinclair Lewis in *Main Street*. The wheel has come full circle; the cycle of small-town life has reasserted itself.

Death is ever-present; loneliness, too, is ever-present. And characters in small-town fiction must overcome that death and loneliness through transcendence. Here I mean transcendence in the Tillichian sense of Being taking Non-Being into itself. The mechanism by which this transcendence takes place is memory. *Raintree County*, in one of its frequent lyrical passages, describes John Wickliff Shawnessy's visit to the abandoned cemetery in the abandoned town of Danwebster. As he walks, he is overwhelmed, not (as might be imagined) by death (he is, after all, in a place of death located in a dead town), but by the overpowering force of life:

> He stopped and shaded his eyes, looking for familiar stones. In the place of death he felt overwhelmed by life. Life rushed up from the breast of the dead in a dense tangle of stems that sprayed seeds and spat bugs. As he thought of other memorial journeys to the graveyard, the stones seemed to him doomed and huddled shapes around which green waters were steadily rising. He stood up to his knees in grass and weeds, holding in one hand a box of peaceful cut flowers and in the other a sickle, his eyes hurting with sunlight.[43]

In this graveyard, a place of death, Shawnessy finds himself surrounded by life. Indeed, life emerges from death, and is described in typically Lockridgian terms—that is, in sexual terms; the stems "sprayed seed and spat bugs," mirroring the seed that covered the young man's hair when he was lost in the swamp.[44] Death is tied to fecundity, and therefore to the garden imagery that makes up a central thematic node of small-town literature. Humans and the natural world exist in an uneasy alliance. Nature is envisioned as a flood, inevitably encroaching on the domains of humanity (already Danwebster is abandoned and soon the graveyard will be forgotten as well). This reversal is typical of Lockridge's work, with its juxtaposition of life-giving paganism and (allegedly) cold, dead Christianity. Like the Midwestern authors discussed in *Sacred Land*, Lockridge portrays a world in which "the culturally Calvinistic heritage of the settlers is seen as clashing with the intensely fertile, intensely sexual, alive, and abundant Midwestern land."[45] Lockridge characterizes the graveyard as "a formal garden of death," a phrase which in the context of the novel—as well as small-town fiction of the period—takes on an Edenic cast.[46] In the case of Lockridge, the meaning of these words is that death is ultimately swallowed up by the earth; the human mark upon the soil lasts only as long as human life and after that is absorbed in the pantheistic divinity that is nature.

Lockridge is positioning himself in a direct lineage from Walt Whitman. In this passage, as well as later when Lockridge speaks of "beautiful, springing hair from the flesh of the dead," the author mirrors Whitman's sexualized vision of nature.[47] The immediate reference of the "beautiful, springing hair" is to "Scented Herbage of My Breast," with its "[t]omb-leaves, body-leaves growing up above me above death."[48] The individual becomes absorbed into Nature, and so his individuality is made to contribute to the universal flowering all around him. The broader movement within Whitman—toward an inclusive, radical democracy that unites all people within himself—is no less present. Just as the town square functions as a transtemporal location, a place outside of time, so the graveyard functions as a way in which the dead and the living can touch each other, if only through the medium of the springing grass. Individuality—loneliness—is overcome, and Shawnessy communes with the dead in a mystical, even erotic, fashion. This is the ultimate hope offered by small-town fiction.

Epilogue
The Train, Again

While I was preparing to send this manuscript to the publisher, I paid a visit to a friend in North Carolina. On my way home to Alabama, rushing so that I could catch that night's new episode of *Twin Peaks*, a traffic incident forced me off the interstate. My diversion took me through Canton, North Carolina. Canton is a small town whose chief industry is paper. Perhaps it was the fact that *Twin Peaks* was on my mind, but as I followed the cars ahead of me, I was intensely aware of being in a place outside of time. The road I was following took me directly within view of the paper mill and then veered off to the left. I saw the bucolic storefronts, some with the legend "Papertown" over them, and thought—in a variation of the academic's recurrent fantasy—that it would be possible to settle here, to give up academia and make my life in this village nestled in the mountains of North Carolina. The impulse was a momentary one; I rolled down the windows to enjoy the mountain air and was immediately assaulted with the powerful stench of the paper mill. I fumbled for my pipe, loaded it with cheap tobacco, and began puffing furiously in a futile attempt to drown out the smell. It was only later that it occurred to me that in its own way, Canton, North Carolina, represents much of what I have discussed in this book. The town's website—for today, in this Internet age, all towns must have a website—declares it to be "WNC's hometown." The same website offers on its front page a photo gallery displaying what, presumably, it means to be "WNC's hometown." These photos offer no glimpse of the mill, whose stacks were the first thing that greeted me as I drove into the town and whose existence seems to provide the town with its very reason for being. Instead, visitors see the main street, quaint midcentury homes, a shot of the town nestled in the mountains. The emphasis is on coziness, tranquility, belonging.

No doubt many or even most of the people who live in Canton experience the town as such. The fact that they are self-consciously marketing themselves in this way does not mean that the marketing has no basis in reality. However, it is the image of the place, the mythology, that interests me—in fact, it is what drew me to this project from the beginning. Historical facts have little bearing on mythology, as the powers-that-be of Canton seem to recognize; when I clicked over to the "history" section of the website, it was blank save for a terse note informing visitors that the page was being worked on. Looking to Wikipedia, it seems that nothing particularly mysterious happened in the history of the town—this is no small town with a dark secret—so perhaps the lack of a town history indicates that there is no history worth speaking of. I do wonder about those people who worked in the mills all their lives. I wonder what sort of tranquility exists under the powerful stench of that paper mill around which the town clusters.

This book has been centrally concerned with the Janus nature of representations of small towns. It has been my intention to demonstrate that the small town operates on a double register in midcentury fiction. In one voice, the small town seems to offer a place of escape, a bucolic, comfortable, communal experience that stands in sharp contrast to the pressures of a world facing total war and total modernization. This is the voice most often focused on by critics such as Ryan Poll, for whom the small town is an obfuscation concealing the predatory nature of American imperial capitalism. But there is another voice at work as well, operating alongside and within these saccharine images. Like the mill stench floating over Canton, there is always within small-town literature a recognition that the town does not insulate its residents from the pressures of war and modernity. It depends upon both for its existence. It is precisely within this already-fallen Eden that existential and political pressures are felt most acutely. The small town becomes for authors of the period a testing-ground by which they can examine the tensions all around them.

This contrast between the mill and the community—their intricate interdependence—recurs constantly in small-town literature. As John Wickliff Shawnessy stands in the Danwebster graveyard, he hears a train. This juxtaposition inevitably calls to mind the contrast that Leo Marx has described as a central pastoral theme in American literature. Marx says that the contrast of the garden and the machine—specifically the train—embodies "a powerful metaphor of contradiction—a way of ordering meaning and value."[1] This metaphor of contradiction is very much present in *Raintree County*:

> He watched for the first appearance of the train. Standing among the stones of the Danwebster Graveyard, he was in the attitude of one who listens, a little fearful, for a necessary thing. His heart beat quick and hard, he felt as though the visual impact of the train would be an unendurable violation.[2]

That this is an essential scene in the novel itself and its understanding of the experience of small-town America—and, therefore, of America itself—

is evidenced by the fact that each of the major sections of *Raintree County* concludes with a small etching of a train trundling past the graveyard. The machine has entered the garden (it is only paragraphs before that the "garden of death" sentence occurs). *Raintree County* itself is concerned with the contrast between the mechanistic movement of society—embodied in Shawnessy's childhood friend Garwood Jones—and a desire for an older, pagan reality, one that is in touch with sexuality and with the earth and with the primal forces that drive all of nature. The fact that Garwood Jones is seen as the sign and signifier of the new American century suggests the elegiac quality to Lockridge's novel.[3] As Shawnessy's cynical, hypereducated mentor "the Perfessor" observes, "our old America" has been destroyed because "[t]he Declaration of Independence and the Constitution never foresaw the Modern City."[4] Though the novel is set in 1892, the concerns voiced by the professor seem strikingly consonant with concerns that were very much in the air when the novel was published in 1948. The death of the small town has been forecast since the Revolt from the Village and has become a recurring theme in criticism. Page Smith's study of small towns in American life argues that "[t]he small town as an independent, self-reliant, vital, optimistic social entity, as the classic American social entity, has disappeared [...] it is no longer available to the writer as a symbol for America."[5] Smith wrote these words in 1966 and has been proven wrong. Nevertheless, Smith expresses the same expectation offered by other critics before and after him: that the small town is an endangered space in American life. Of late, critics have begun to view this elegy for the passing of a small town with a jaundiced eye; small towns, it seems, like the South or nationalism, are always doomed. For Ryan Poll, this notion of the small town as a dying space serves to cover American imperialism. The task of this study has been to demonstrate something quite different: that the small town functions as an Eden and so *must* be dying. And, as an Eden, it also serves as a space to reflect upon the increasing loneliness of American life in the twentieth century.

    I wrote this conclusion in late 2017. I am revising it at the midpoint of 2018. Insofar as all scholarship is a product of its time, this book is the result of living for nearly three years in an American political environment which featured one candidate demanding a return to a time when America was "great." This phrase implicitly refers to the America of the 1950s, and particularly the America popularly associated with small towns: monocultural, monoreligious, quaint. The lure of this nostalgic vision cannot be denied. But such a demand rests upon a rejection of a half-century's worth of progress in defense of the rights of women, racial minorities, and LGBTQ people. The myth of the small town is used to attack multiculturalism and cosmopolitanism. But my study has shown that this is not the only direction careful thought upon the American small town can take. Authors writing during the very decades toward which this nostalgia points expressed the contradictions embodied in the American small town—and, therefore, within America itself. They did not seek to return to an idealized world or to roll back the march of modernity. Rather, they used the small town as a field in which to test and explore the multiple contradictions of existence in the mid-twentieth century.

The reemergence of the train here at the graveyard of the small town suggests a kind of cyclical return. The small town need not be simply a mystification or an idealization of America. Henry Bellamann and Grace Metalious demonstrate that fact. But even if the town is an idealization, it is vital to define the word *ideal*. If the ideal is a fantasy that removes the understanding that America is and always has been deeply flawed, then critics like Poll are correct to turn a jaundiced eye upon it. However, *Raintree County* posits the small town in a different light; Raintree County is a "mythical America" containing within it all the hope *and* despair of the American experiment.[6] This is nostalgia, to be sure. Lockridge's novel portrays a desire for belonging, a desire for a home, and above all a desire for an America that can fulfill the deepest spiritual needs of its populace. But not all nostalgia is reactionary or regressive; a case can be made that what the narratives I have examined here represent is a kind of *redemptive* nostalgia. The Edenic imagery in *Raintree County* and *Kings Row* and *Yokohama, California*—the anti–Eden of Jack Finney's body snatchers—the hard won, hard-fought justice of Faulkner and the anti-justice of Lillian Smith—and the deep sympathy of Ellery Queen—all point to the loneliness enforced by the nature of small town life, by the nature of American life at midcentury. But these portrayals also highlight the promise of transcendence. As such, they seem to urge readers onward in a progressive movement toward a better realization of the failed ideal.

Proposing a cure is not the business of small-town fiction, but every critique presupposes a solution. The train here at the end of our small-town ramble offers the chance to analyze some radical directions small-town fiction (and the critical discourse surrounding it) might take. For if the train is a symbol of connection between the outside world and the world of the small town, it is also a symbol of connection between persons. On the train, people from all walks of life are thrown together and forced to interact in a friendly manner. Mijuskvic suggests that the only true way to endure loneliness—not eliminate it, but endure it—is friendship.[7] Fromm, for his part, posits love as the proper way of escaping alienation, since "[l]ove for one person implies love for man as such."[8] Love for humanity as such implies love for oneself. Love is—as Tillich and others argue—the perfect form of transcendence. It is, indeed, the very "kelson of the creation," as Whitman says—a structural element pulling the whole together.[9] But, as my analysis has shown, transcendence—of commercial, racial, sexual, and other forms of alienation—is not an easy thing. It is not rendered inevitable by the existence of the small town *as* a small town. The small town carries within itself all the contradictions that these authors seek to resolve—if they are to attempt any sort of resolution at all, then the town must be as internally inconsistent as America itself. Thus, small-town fiction should not be looked at in a binary way as either wholly given over to nostalgia or to critique. By using the small town as a model of America, authors of this period attempt to affect a redemptive work in society. This is the real task of small-town fiction in the years following World War II.

Chapter Notes

Introduction

1. Hugh Kenner, *A Homemade World: The American Modernist Writers* (New York: Alfred A. Knopf, 1975) 12.
2. Benedict Anderson, *Imagined Communities: Reflections on the Origin and Spread of Nationalism* (London: Verso, 1983) 6.
3. Ryan Poll, *Main Street and Empire the Fictional Small Town in the Age of Globalization* (New Brunswick: Rutgers University Press, 2012) 9.
4. Poll 8.
5. Richard V. Francaviglia, *Main Street Revisited: Time, Space, and Image Building in Small-Town America* (Iowa City: University of Iowa Press, 1996) xxiii.
6. Miles Orvell, *The Death and Life of Main Street: Small Towns in American Memory, Space, and Community* (Chapel Hill: University of North Carolina Press, 2012) 1.
7. Wyn Wachhorst, *The Best of Times: Motifs from Postwar America* (Bloomington: Author House, 2016) 1.
8. Susan Stewart, *On Longing: Narratives of the Miniature, the Gigantic, the Souvenir, the Collection* (Durham: Duke University Press, 2012) 23.
9. Jennifer K. Ladino, *Reclaiming Nostalgia: Longing for Nature in American Literature* (Charlottesville: University of Virginia Press, 2012). Kindle edition. Loc. 139.
10. Ladino loc 287.
11. Sinclair Lewis, *Main Street* (New York: Signet, 1961) 153.
12. Robert L. Dorman, *Revolt of the Provinces: The Regionalist Movement in America, 1920–1945* (Chapel Hill: University of North Carolina Press, 1993) 24.
13. Dorman 25.
14. Mark Buechsel, *Sacred Land: Sherwood Anderson, Midwestern Modernism, and the Sacramental Vision of Nature* (Kent: Kent State University Press, 2014) 74.
15. Dorman 23.
16. Dorman 304; italics original.
17. John T. Cacioppo and William Patrick, *Loneliness: Human Nature and the Need for Social Connection* (New York: W.W. Norton, 2008). Loc. 927.
18. Ben Lazare Mijuskovic, *Loneliness in Philosophy, Psychology, and Literature* (Bloomington: iUniverse, 2012) lvii. NB: Though originally published by an academic publisher, this book is now self-published, a fact whose irony should be noted.
19. Poll 25.
20. Thomas More, *More: Utopia*, edited by George M. Logan, translated by Robert M. Adams (Cambridge: Cambridge University Press, 2016) 89.
21. More 87.
22. More 113.
23. Robert Nisbet, *The Quest for Community* (Intercollegiate Studies Institute, 2014). Loc. 274.
24. Nisbet loc. 513.
25. Fredric Jameson, *Postmodernism, or, the Cultural Logic of Late Capitalism* (Durham: Duke University Press, 1991) 281.
26. Guy Debord, "The Situationist International Text Library/Introduction to a Critique of Urban Geography." Par. 17.
27. Elizabeth Sandifer, *TARDIS Eruditorum—An Unofficial Critical History of Doctor Who Volume 1: William Hartnell* (CreateSpace Independent Publishing Platform, 2014) 1–2.
28. Laurence Sterne, *The Life and Opinions of Tristram Shandy, Gentleman* (New York: Macy, n.d.) 63.
29. See, for instance, Paul Parthun, "Concord,

Charles Ives, and Henry Bellamann," *Collected Work: Student Musicologists at Minnesota. Centennial Ives Issue Celebrating the USA's 200th Birthday.* University of Minnesota (Department of Music), 1975–1976. (AN: 1975–00297) 6 (1975): 66–86. Print.

30. Tom Perrin, *The Aesthetics of Middlebrow Fiction: Popular U.S. Novels, Modernism, and Form, 1945–75* (New York: Palgrave Macmillan, 2015) Loc. 74.

31. Orvell 35.
32. Francaviglia 130.
33. Poll 49.

Chapter One

1. Ellery Queen, *Calamity Town*, in *Wrightsville Murders* (Boston: Little, Brown, 1956) 9.
2. Queen, *Calamity* 197.
3. Anthony Channell Hilfer, *The Revolt from the Village 1915–1930* (Chapel Hill: University of North Carolina Press, 1969) 22.
4. Tom Lutz, *Cosmopolitan Vistas: American Regionalism and Literary Value* (Ithaca: Cornell University Press, 2004) 30.
5. Christopher Columbus, *The Four Voyages*, translated and edited by J.M. Cohen (New York: Penguin, 1969) 64.
6. Columbus 70.
7. Columbus 220–222.
8. Columbus 218.
9. Walt Whitman, *Complete Poetry and Collected Prose—Leaves of Grass (1855 & 1891–92), Complete Prose Works (1892), Supplementary Prose* (Library of America, 1982) 266–267.
10. Queen, *Calamity*, 10.
11. Ellery Queen, *Double, Double* (Boston: Little, Brown, 1950) 15.
12. Queen, *Double Double* 15.
13. Queen, *Double Double* 135.
14. Queen, *Double Double* 16.
15. Queen, *Double Double* 31.
16. Leo Marx, *The Machine in the Garden: Technology and the Pastoral Ideal in America.* (Oxford: Oxford University Press, 2000) 10.
17. Marx 25.
18. Marx 26.
19. R.W.B. Lewis, *The American Adam: Innocence, Tragedy, and Tradition in the Nineteenth Century* (Chicago: University of Chicago Press, 1966) 91.
20. Daniel G. Hoffman, "Fable as Reality," in *Pastoral and Romance: Modern Essays in Criticism*, edited by Eleanor Terry Lincoln (Englewood Cliffs, NJ: Prentice-Hall, 1969) 275–276.
21. Robert Harbison, *Eccentric Spaces* (New York: Alfred A. Knopf, 1977) 3.
22. Harbison 19.
23. Marx 277.
24. Cornell Woolrich, *I Married a Dead Man* (New York: Penguin, 1994) 7.
25. Woolrich 7.
26. Woolrich 8.
27. Francaviglia 152.
28. Miles Orvell, *The Death and Life of Main Street: Small Towns in American Memory, Space, and Community* (Chapel Hill: University of North Carolina Press, 2012) 37.
29. Poll 62.
30. Poll 81.
31. Ross Lockridge, Jr., *Raintree County* (New York: Penguin, 1994) 126.
32. Ima Honaker Herron, *The Small Town in American Literature* (Durham: Duke University Press, 1939) xiii.
33. Poll 13.
34. Poll 58.
35. Poll 62.
36. Woolrich 24.
37. Brevda 332.
38. Francis M. Nevins, *Cornell Woolrich: First You Dream, Then You Die* (New York: Mysterious Press, 1988) 117.
39. Nevins, *Dream* 359.
40. Nevins, *Dream* 358.
41. William Brevda, "'Is There Any Up or Down Left?' Noir and Existentialism," *Soundings: An Interdisciplinary Journal* 89.3/4 (2006): 330.
42. David Castronovo, *Beyond the Gray Flannel Suit: Books from the 1950s That Made American Culture* (London: Bloomsbury Academic, 2004) 80.
43. Woolrich, 23.
44. Woolrich 35.
45. Kenneth Payne, "'This Dark Thing, This Other Self': Character and Self-Distantiation in Cornell Woolrich's I Married a Dead Man (1948)," *Papers on Language and Literature: A Journal for Scholars and Critics of Language and Literature* 34.1 (1998): 95.
46. Woolrich 69.
47. Woolrich 77.
48. Payne 95.
49. Payne 98.
50. Woolrich 210.
51. Woolrich 213.
52. Woolrich 198.
53. Woolrich 172.
54. Woolrich 216.
55. Woolrich 217.
56. Woolrich 218; italics original.
57. David Palumbo-Liu, "Toshio Mori and the Attachments of Spirit: A Response to David R. Mayer," *Amerasia* 17.3 (1991): 42.
58. Palumbo-Liu, 43–44.
59. Palumbo-Liu, 42.
60. David R. Mayer, "Toshio Mori and Lone-

liness," *Nanzan Review of American Studies* 15 (1993): 24.

61. Toshio Mori, *Yokohama, California* (Seattle: University of Washington Press, 1985) 45.

62. Malve von Hassell, "Ethnography, Storytelling and the Fiction of Toshio Mori," *Dialectical Anthropology* 19.4 (1994): 405.

63. Mayer 28.
64. Mori 127.
65. Mori 128.
66. Mori 49.
67. Mori 128.
68. Mori 129.
69. Mori 129.
70. Mori 132.
71. Mori 134.

Chapter Two

1. Ladino. Loc. 397.
2. Henry Bellamann, *Kings Row* (Garden City, NY: Sun Dial, 1946) 6.
3. Bellamann 5.
4. Steven Mintz, *Huck's Raft: A History of American Childhood*. (Cambridge: Belknap Press, 2004) 219.
5. Mintz 264.
6. R.W.B. Lewis 1.
7. Lewis 5.
8. Gen. 2:18, KJV.
9. Lewis 49.
10. Lockridge 95.
11. Lockridge 44.
12. Lockridge 45.
13. Gen. 3:5, KJV.
14. Lockridge 4.
15. Lockridge 98.
16. Genesis 2:25; KJV.
17. Lockridge 155.
18. Leslie Fiedler, *Love and Death in the American Novel* (New York: Meridian, 1964) 142.
19. Fiedler 443.
20. Ray Bradbury, *Dandelion Wine* (New York: Bantam, 1976) 5.
21. Bradbury 6.
22. Bradbury 10; italics original.
23. Lewis 6.
24. Lewis 58.
25. Bradbury 102ff.
26. Bradbury 102.
27. Bradbury 103.
28. Bradbury 104.
29. Bradbury 107.
30. Bradbury 105.
31. Bradbury 109.
32. Bradbury 110.
33. Bradbury 110.
34. Bradbury 186.
35. Mijuskovic 79.
36. Reinhold Niebuhr, *Nature and Destiny of Man, Vol. 1: Human Nature* (New York: Scribner, 1949) 17.
37. Niebuhr, *Nature* 22.
38. Niebuhr, *Nature* 23.
39. Buechsel 10.
40. Dorman 24.
41. Bradbury 42.
42. Bradbury 43.
43. Bradbury 172.
44. Bradbury 172.
45. Bradbury 176.
46. Bradbury 178.
47. Bradbury 189.
48. Bradbury 188.
49. Bradbury 195.
50. Bradbury 200.
51. Bradbury 203.
52. Bradbury 237.
53. William March, Notes for *The Bad Seed*. No date. William March Campbell Papers. Hoole Special Collections, University of Alabama, Tuscaloosa.
54. See Alistair Cooke, "William March: A Trial Balance," *Manchester Guardian* June 8, 1954, p. 4.
55. William March, *The Bad Seed* (Hopewell, NJ: The Ecco Press, 1997) 26.
56. March, *Bad Seed* 49.
57. Bradbury 10; italics original.
58. Chuck Jackson, "Little, Violent, White: The Bad Seed and the Matter of Children," *The Journal of Popular Film & Television* 28.2 (2000): 68.
59. Jackson 68; italics original.
60. Jackson 71.
61. Slavoj Žižek, *Violence: Six Sideways Reflections* (London: Profile, 2009) 137.
62. Jackson 71–72.
63. Jackson 66.
64. William Saroyan, *The Human Comedy* (New York: Dell, 1966) 27; italics original.
65. Saroyan 28.
66. Saroyan 33; italics original.
67. Saroyan 34.
68. Saroyan 12.
69. Saroyan 103.
70. Saroyan 104.
71. Saroyan 106; italics original.
72. Saroyan 12.
73. Grace Palladino, *Teenagers: An American History* (New York: Basic Books, 1996) 89.
74. Saroyan 34.
75. Saroyan 47.
76. Saroyan 56.
77. Saroyan 59.
78. Saroyan 59.
79. Saroyan 60.

80. Saroyan 123.
81. Saroyan 59.

Chapter Three

1. Palladino 52.
2. Perrin. Loc. 1623.
3. Bellamann, *Kings Row* 1.
4. Grace Metalious, *Peyton Place* (Boston: Northeastern University Press, 1999) 1.
5. Metalious, *Peyton Place* 38.
6. Metalious, *Peyton Place* 371.
7. Lockridge 368–369.
8. Lockridge 295.
9. Franco Moretti, *The Way of the World: The* Bildungsroman *in European Culture* (London: Verso, 1987) 5.
10. Moretti 23.
11. Moretti 228.
12. Perrin. Loc. 1624.
13. Perrin. Loc. 1623.
14. Perrin. Loc. 1740.
15. Perrin. Loc. 1753.
16. Perrin. Loc. 262.
17. Palladino 64.
18. Palladino 71.
19. Palladino 89.
20. Palladino 101.
21. Norman Mailer, "The White Negro," in *Advertisements for Myself* (New York: Putnam, 1959) 338.
22. Palladino 56.
23. Palladino 57.
24. Beaty Beaty, *Twelve-Cent Archie* (New Brunswick: Rutgers University Press, 2015) 34.
25. Beaty 30.
26. Beaty 16.
27. Bellamann, *Kings Row* 81.
28. Bellamann, *Kings Row* 409.
29. Bellamann, *Kings Row* 385.
30. Bellamann, *Kings Row* 6.
31. Bellamann, *Kings Row* 107.
32. Bellamann, *Kings Row* 19.
33. Bellamann, *Kings Row* 96.
34. Bellamann, *Kings Row* 96.
35. Bellamann, *Kings Row* 454.
36. Bellamann, *Kings Row* 468.
37. Bellamann, *Kings Row* 521.
38. Bellamann, *Kings Row* 108.
39. Bellamann, *Kings Row* 109.
40. Bellamann, *Kings Row* 110.
41. Bellamann, *Kings Row* 110.
42. Bellamann, *Kings Row* 111.
43. Bellamann, *Kings Row* 149.
44. Bellamann, *Kings Row* 150.
45. Bellamann, *Kings Row* 268.
46. Katherine and Henry Bellamann, *Parris Mitchell of Kings Row* (New York: Simon & Schuster, 1948) 145.
47. Bellamann, *Parris Mitchell* 146; italics original.
48. Fromm 161.
49. Canetti 15.
50. Canetti 18.
51. Canetti 20.
52. Fromm 152.
53. Riesman 20.
54. Mills 122.
55. Poll 89.
56. Poll 90.
57. Metalious, *Peyton Place* 371.
58. Grace Metalious, *Return to Peyton Place* (New York: Dell, 1965) 61.
59. Metalious, *Return* 72.
60. Metalious, *Return* 87.
61. Metalious, *Return* 197.
62. Metalious, *Return* 255.
63. Lockridge 103.
64. Lockridge 102.
65. Lockridge 103.
66. Lockridge 103.
67. Lockridge 105.
68. Lockridge 104.
69. Lockridge 400.
70. Lockridge 402.
71. Lockridge 402.
72. Lockridge 403.
73. Lockridge 404.
74. Lockridge 405.
75. Lockridge 407.
76. Lockridge 294.
77. Lockridge 295.
78. Lockridge 193.
79. Lockridge 886.
80. Lockridge 887.
81. Lockridge 889.
82. Whitman 5.
83. Lockridge 745–746; italics original.
84. Lockridge 746.
85. Lockridge 769.
86. Lockridge 770.
87. Lockridge 295.
88. Lockridge 887.

Chapter Four

1. Poll 54.
2. Poll 56.
3. Thomas Wolfe, "The Lost Boy," in *The Complete Short Stories of Thomas Wolfe* (New York: Simon & Schuster, 1989) 359–380.
4. Wolfe 359.
5. Wolfe 359.
6. Queen, *Calamity* 10.
7. Poll 58.
8. Poll 105.
9. Queen, *Calamity* 197.
10. Lockridge 3.

11. William Faulkner, *Intruder in the Dust* (New York: Vintage, 2011) 23.
12. Robert Bloch, *Psycho* (New York: Tor, 1989) 149.
13. Herbert Marcuse, *One-Dimensional Man: Studies in the Ideology of Advanced Industrial Society* (London: Routledge, 2002) 257.
14. Poll 96.
15. Sinclair Lewis, "Introduction to Main Street," in *The Man from Main Street* (New York: Random House, 1953) 215.
16. Sinclair Lewis, *Main Street* (New York: Signet, 1961) 6.
17. Sinclair Lewis, "The Long Arm of the Small Town," in *The Man from Main Street* (New York: Random House, 1953) 272.
18. Orvell 35.
19. Orvell 36.
20. Poll 49.
21. Poll 48.
22. Lawson Fusao Inada, "Standing on Seventh Street: An Introduction to the 1985 Edition," in *Yokohama, California* (Seattle: University of Washington Press, 1985) ix.
23. Margaret Bedrosian, "Toshio Mori's California Koans," *MELUS* 15.2 (1988): 48.
24. Mayer 24.
25. Mayer 28.
26. Janice Tanemura, "Race, Regionalism, and Biopower in 'Yokohama, California,'" *Discourse* 29.2/3 (2007): 315.
27. Tanemura 317.
28. Mori 35.
29. Inada ix.
30. von Hassell 408.
31. Mori 35.
32. Mori 38.
33. Mori 78.
34. Mori 79.
35. Mori 80.
36. Mori 81–82.
37. Mori 82–83.
38. Mori 97.
39. Mori 97.
40. Mori 101.
41. Mori 99.
42. Mori 99.
43. Mori 102.
44. Mori 103.
45. Mori 106.
46. Mori 56.
47. Mori 55.
48. Mori 57.
49. Mori 62.
50. Bedrosian 48.
51. Mori 144.
52. Mori 145.
53. Mori 146.
54. Mori 147.
55. Mori 87.
56. Mori 88.
57. Mori 87.
58. Queen, *Calamity* 10.
59. Whitman 372.
60. Poll 73.
61. Poll 74.
62. Dorman 84–85.
63. Queen, *Calamity* 11.
64. Francaviglia 97.
65. Francaviglia 98–99.
66. Bloch 154.
67. Queen, *Calamity* 188.
68. Queen, *Calamity* 188.
69. Queen, *Calamity* 197.

Chapter Five

1. Emmanuel Levy, *Small-Town America in Film: The Decline of Community* (New York: Continuum, 1991) 16.
2. Poll 80.
3. Poll 49.
4. Mark R. Scherer, "Where's the Rest of 'Kings Row'? Hollywood's Emasculation of a 'Grand Yarn,'" *Literature/Film Quarterly* 27.4 (1999) 255.
5. Scherer 257.
6. Scherer 259.
7. Scherer 260.
8. Levy 88.
9. Scherer 259.
10. Janet Walker, "Textual Trauma in *Kings Row* and *Freud*," in *Endless Night: Cinema and Psychoanalysis, Parallel Histories*, edited by Janet Bergstrom (Berkeley: University of California Press, 1999) 176.
11. Walker 181.
12. Scherer 259.
13. Levy 86.
14. Bellamann, *Kings Row* 434.
15. Bellamann, *Kings Row* 386.
16. Bellamann, *Kings Row* 434.
17. Levy 87.
18. Levy 122.
19. Levy 123.
20. Levy 124.
21. Ardis Cameron, *Unbuttoning America: A Biography of "Peyton Place"* (Ithaca: Cornell University Press, 2015) 154.
22. Metalious, *Peyton Place* 1.
23. Metalious, *Peyton Place* 7; 63.
24. Metalious, *Peyton Place* 135.
25. Metalious, *Peyton Place* 193.
26. Metalious, *Peyton Place* 253.
27. Metalious, *Peyton Place* 305.
28. Metalious, *Peyton Place* 307.
29. Poll 80.
30. Lockridge 232.
31. Lockridge 115.

32. Lockridge 155.
33. Lockridge 241.
34. Lockridge 266.
35. Lockridge 288, 331.
36. Lockridge 370.
37. Lockridge 407; italics original.

Chapter Six

1. Kenneth L. Woodward, *Getting Religion: Faith, Culture, and Politics from the Age of Eisenhower to the Era of Obama* (New York: Convergent Books, 2016) 46.
2. Bellamann, *Parris Mitchell* 253.
3. Chester E. Eisinger, *Fiction of the Forties* (Chicago: University of Chicago Press, 1963) 171–172.
4. Paul Tillich, *The Courage to Be* (New Haven: Yale University Press, 1980) 35.
5. Tillich, *Courage* 34.
6. Tillich, *Courage* 186.
7. Buechsel 10.
8. Buechsel 15.
9. Buechsel 72.
10. Harold Bloom, *The American Religion* (New York: Chu Hartley, 2013). Loc. 1676.
11. Bellamann, *Kings Row* 81.
12. Bellamann, *Kings Row* 234.
13. Bellamann, *Kings Row* 235.
14. Bellamann, *Kings Row* 236.
15. Tillich, *Courage* 156.
16. Bellamann, *Kings Row* 236.
17. Bellamann, *Kings Row* 9.
18. Bellamann, *Kings Row* 12.
19. Bellamann, *Kings Row* 13.
20. Bellamann, *Kings Row* 13.
21. Bellamann, *Kings Row* 492.
22. Bellamann, *Kings Row* 494; italics original.
23. Bellamann, *Kings Row* 496.
24. Bellamann, *Kings Row* 535.
25. Bellamann, *Kings Row* 536.
26. Ellery Queen, *Ten Days' Wonder* (Boston: Little, Brown 1948) 17.
27. Queen, *Wonder* 17.
28. Queen, *Wonder* 3.
29. Sigmund Freud, *The Interpretation of Dreams* (New York: Macmillan, 1913) 223.
30. Sigmund Freud, *Totem and Taboo*, translated by A. A. Brill (Digireads.com, 2009) 190.
31. Slavoj Žižek, *Looking Awry: An Introduction to Jacques Lacan through Popular Culture* (Cambridge: MIT Press, 1995) 23.
32. Žižek, *Looking Awry* 24.
33. Queen, *Wonder* 26.
34. Queen, *Wonder* 97.
35. Kevin Kruse, *One Nation Under God: How Corporate America Invented Christian America* (New York: Basic Books, 2015) 7.
36. R. Laurence Moore, *Selling God: American Religion in the Marketplace of Culture* (New York: Oxford University Press, 1994) 211.
37. Queen, *Wonder* 35.
38. Queen, *Wonder* 46.
39. Queen, *Wonder* 11.
40. Queen, *Wonder* 12.
41. Queen, *Wonder* 44.
42. Queen, *Wonder* 41.
43. Queen, *Wonder* 57; italics original.
44. Joseph Goodrich, *Blood Relations: The Selected Letters of Ellery Queen, 1947–1950* (Lexington: Perfect Crime Books, 2012) 25.
45. Queen, *Wonder* 262; italics original.
46. Queen, *Wonder* 262.
47. Cheryl L. Johnson, "The Language of Sexuality and Silence in Lillian Smith's 'Strange Fruit,'" *Signs* 27.1 (2001): 17–18.
48. Edwin Berry Burgum, "The Sociological Pattern of 'Strange Fruit,'" *Science & Society* 9.1 (1945): 77–78.
49. Paul K. Conkin, *A Requiem for the American Village* (Lanham: Rowman & Littlefield, 2000) 112.
50. Alexis de Tocqueville, *Democracy in America and Two Essays on America* (New York: Penguin, 2003) 510.
51. Tocqueville 512.
52. Tocqueville 517.
53. Walter Rauschenbusch, *The Righteousness of the Kingdom*, edited by Max L. Stackhouse (Nashville: Abington, 1968) 245.
54. Reinhold Niebuhr, *Moral Man and Immoral Society* (New York: Touchstone, 1995) xi.
55. Niebuhr, *Moral Man* 73.
56. Niebuhr, *Moral Man* xx.
57. Lillian Smith, *Strange Fruit* (Athens: University of Georgia Press, 1987) 90.
58. Hilfer 178–179.
59. Smith 88.
60. Smith 50.
61. Smith 53.
62. Smith 184.
63. Smith 227.
64. Smith 99.
65. Smith 224.
66. Smith 358.
67. Paul Tillich, "To Whom Much Is Forgiven…," in *The New Being* (New York: Charles Scribner's Sons, 1955) 3–14.
68. Tillich, "To Whom" 10, 12.
69. Flannery O'Connor, *Wise Blood*, in *Three by Flannery O'Connor* (New York: Signet, 1983) 62.
70. O'Connor 56.
71. O'Connor 111.
72. Tillich, *Courage* 49.
73. O'Connor 22.
74. O'Connor 98.

75. O'Connor 99.
76. O'Connor 92.
77. O'Connor 101.
78. O'Connor 102.
79. O'Connor 102.
80. O'Connor 9.
81. O'Connor 10.
82. O'Connor 3.
83. O'Connor 74.
84. Jonathan Baumbach, "The Acid of God's Grace: The Fiction of Flannery O'Connor," *The Georgia Review* 17.3 (1963): 335.
85. O'Connor 12.
86. O'Connor 3.
87. O'Connor 86.
88. O'Connor 96.
89. O'Connor 65.
90. O'Connor 106.
91. O'Connor 72.
92. Robert Detweiler, "The Curse of Christ in Flannery O'Connor's Fiction," *Comparative Literature Studies* 3.2 (1966): 235.
93. O'Connor 120.
94. Mikhail Bakhtin, *Rabeleis and His World*, translated by Helene Iswolsky (Bloomington: Indiana University Press, 1984) 7.
95. Lockridge 360.
96. Lockridge 361.
97. Lockridge 576.
98. Lockridge 579.
99. Lockridge 585.
100. Lockridge 1007.
101. Lockridge 1008.
102. Tillich, *Courage* 184.
103. Lockridge 776.
104. Buechsel 17.
105. Lockridge 779.
106. Lockridge 55.
107. Buechsel 27.

Chapter Seven

1. Jeffrey Miller, *The Structures of Law and Literature* (Montreal: McGill-Queen's University Press, 2013) 18.
2. Miller 38.
3. James Gould Cozzens, *The Just and the Unjust* (New York: Harcourt, Brace 1942) 109.
4. Richard Weisberg, *Poethics and Other Strategies of Law and Literature* (New York: Columbia University Press, 1992) 55; italics original.
5. Cozzens 267–268.
6. Dwight Macdonald, "By Cozzens Possessed: A Review of Reviews," *Commentary Magazine*, 1 January 1958: 41.
7. Louis Coxe, "The Complex World of James Gould Cozzens," in *James Gould Cozzens: New Acquist of True Experience*, edited by Matthew J. Bruccoli (Carbondale: Southern Illinois University Press, 1979) 4.
8. Coxe 13.
9. Coxe 14.
10. Cozzens 361.
11. Cozzens 401.
12. Coxe 10.
13. Cozzens 433.
14. Cozzens 434.
15. Cozzens 434.
16. Cozzens 434.
17. Miller 165.
18. Eisinger 162.
19. Reinhold Niebuhr, *The Irony of American History* (Chicago: University of Chicago Press, 2008) 2.
20. Niebuhr, *Irony* 42.
21. Coxe 107.
22. Michael Wainwright, *Faulkner's Gambit: Chess and Literature* (New York: Palgrave Macmillan, 2011) 65.
23. Mick Gidley, "Elements of the Detective Story in William Faulkner's Fiction," in *Dimensions of Detective Fiction*, edited by Larry N. Landrum, Pat Browne, and Ray B. Browne (Bowling Green, OH: Popular Press, 1976) 242.
24. Faulkner, *Intruder* 165.
25. Faulkner, *Intruder* 120.
26. Faulkner, *Intruder* 164.
27. Faulkner, *Intruder* 166.
28. Faulkner, *Intruder* 95.
29. Peter J. Rabinowitz, "The Click of the Spring: The Detective Story as Parallel Structure in Dostoyevsky and Faulkner," *Modern Philology* 76.4 (1979): 364.
30. Rabinowitz 365.
31. Faulkner, *Intruder* 108.
32. Faulkner, *Intruder* 143.
33. J.K. Van Dover and John F. Jebb, *Isn't Justice Always Unfair? The Detective in Southern Literature* (Bowling Green, OH: Popular Press, 1996) 135; italics original.
34. Gidley 245.
35. Faulkner, *Intruder* 201.
36. Miller 12.
37. Cameron 50.
38. Cameron 44.
39. Cameron 46.
40. Cameron 48.
41. Cameron 50.
42. Metalious, *Peyton Place* 62.
43. Metalious, *Peyton Place* 136.
44. Metalious, *Peyton Place* 137.
45. Metalious, *Peyton Place* 305.
46. Metalious, *Peyton Place* 307.
47. Metalious, *Peyton Place* 309.
48. Metalious, *Peyton Place* 19.
49. Metalious, *Peyton Place* 20.
50. Otto Rank, *The Incest Theme in Literature*

and Legend (Baltimore: Johns Hopkins University Press, 1992) 301.
51. Metalious, *Peyton Place* 353.
52. Metalious, *Peyton Place* 361.
53. Metalious, *Peyton Place* 367; capitalized in original.
54. Cameron 50.
55. Metalious, *Peyton Place* 142.
56. Metalious, *Peyton Place* 2.
57. Mintz 286.
58. Metalious, *Peyton Place* 145; italics original.
59. Metalious, *Peyton Place* 154.
60. Metalious, *Peyton Place* 338.
61. Bellamann, *Kings Row* 53.
62. Bellamann, *Kings Row* 421.
63. Bellamann, *Kings Row* 441.
64. Rachel Devlin, *Relative Intimacy: Fathers, Adolescent Daughters, and Postwar American Culture* (Chapel Hill: University of North Carolina Press, 2006) 4.
65. Devlin 166; cf Bellamann *Kings Row* 507.
66. Bellamann, *Kings Row* 240.
67. Bellamann, *Kings Row* 247.
68. Bellamann, *Kings Row* 268.
69. Bellamann, *Kings Row* 270.
70. Bellamann, *Kings Row* 231.
71. Bellamann, *Kings Row* 531.
72. Bellamann, *Kings Row* 56.
73. Bellamann, *Kings Row* 59.
74. Bellamann, *Kings Row* 63.
75. Lockridge 259.
76. Lockridge 260.
77. Lockridge 260.
78. Lockridge 981.
79. Lockridge 1051; italics original.
80. Lockridge 1051.
81. Lockridge 1052.
82. Miller 71; italics original.
83. Miller 22.

Chapter Eight

1. Poll 50.
2. Orvell 1.
3. Page Smith, *As a City Upon a Hill: The Town in American History* (New York: Alfred A. Knopf, 1966) 200.
4. Smith, *City* 302.
5. Perrin. Loc. 999.
6. Perrin. Loc. 1015.
7. Poll 135.
8. Lewis A. Erenberg and Susan E Hirsch, *The War in American Culture: Society and Consciousness During World War II* (Chicago: University of Chicago Press, 1996) 1.
9. John G. Cawelti, *The Six-Gun Mystique Sequel* (Bowling Green, OH: Popular Press, 1999) 91.
10. Poll 93.
11. Poll 90.
12. Orvell 131.
13. Smith, *Strange Fruit* 88.
14. Slavoj Žižek, *The Sublime Object of Ideology* (London: Verso, 1989) 4.
15. Žižek, *Ideology* 5.
16. Fiedler 204.
17. Smith, *Strange Fruit* 43.
18. Johnson 13.
19. Johnson 11.
20. Fiedler 209.
21. Smith, *Strange Fruit* 201.
22. Smith, *Strange Fruit* 202.
23. Smith, *Strange Fruit* 342.
24. Smith, *Strange Fruit* 341.
25. Smith, *Strange Fruit* 342.
26. Perrin. Loc. 1235.
27. Smith, *Strange Fruit* 20.
28. Smith, *Strange Fruit* 269.
29. Van Dover and Jebb 154.
30. Van Dover and Jebb 155.
31. John Cullen Gruesser, *Race, Gender and Empire in American Detective Fiction* (Jefferson, NC: McFarland, 2013) 12.
32. Faulkner 18.
33. Ernest Mandel, *Delightful Murder: A Social History of the Crime Story* (London: Pluto, 1984) 46.
34. Faulkner 15.
35. Lewis 70.
36. Lewis 80.
37. Robert G. Lee, *Orientals: Asian Americans in Popular Culture* (Philadelphia: Temple University Press, 1999) 35.
38. John Trausbaugh, *Black Like You: Blackface, Whiteface, Insult & Imitation in American Popular Culture* (New York: Jeremy P. Tarcher, 2006) 24.
39. Qian Zhaoming, *Orientalism and Modernism* (Durham: Duke University Press, 1995) 2.
40. Qian 3.
41. Lockridge 45.
42. William Carlos Williams, *Paterson* (New York: New Directions, 1963) 244.
43. Inada xviii.
44. John W. Dower, "Race, Language, and War in Two Cultures: World War II in Asia," in Erenberg, 169.
45. Dower 170.
46. Dower 183.
47. Reed Ueda, "The Changing Path to Citizenship: Ethnicity and Naturalization during World War II," in Erenberg, 205.
48. Ueda 207.
49. Mori 20–21.
50. Inada xxii.
51. Mori 18.
52. Mori 19.

53. Frank Chin, "Come All Ye Asian American Writers of the Real and the Fake," in *The Big Aiiieeeee!* edited by Frank Chin et al. (New York: Plume, 1991) 22.
54. Ted Nakashima, "Concentration Camp: U.S. Style," in *Reporting World War II: Part One* (New York: Library of America, 1995) 354.
55. Inada xvii.
56. Metalious, *Peyton Place* 102.
57. Sally Hirsh-Dickinson, *Dirty Whites and Dark Secrets: Sex and Race in Peyton Place* (Lebanon: University of New Hampshire Press, 2011) 23.
58. Metalious, *Peyton Place* 23.
59. Metalious, *Peyton Place* 22.
60. Metalious, *Peyton Place* 317.
61. Cameron 50–51.
62. Metalious, *Peyton Place* 7.
63. Metalious, *Peyton Place* 29.
64. Metalious, *Peyton Place* 163.
65. Metalious, *Peyton Place* 335.
66. Metalious, *Peyton Place* 168.
67. Grace Metalious, *The Tight White Collar* (New York: Messner, 1960) 77.
68. Metalious, *Collar* 79.
69. Metalious, *Collar* 88–89.
70. Metalious, *Collar* 92.
71. Metalious, *Collar* 93.
72. Metalious, *Collar* 94.
73. Metalious, *Collar* 80.
74. Metalious, *Collar* 135.
75. Metalious, *Collar* 139.
76. Metalious, *Collar* 140–141.
77. Metalious, *Collar* 153.
78. Metalious, *Collar* 153.
79. Metalious, *Collar* 232.
80. Metalious, *Collar* 233.
81. Metalious, *Collar* 234; cf. Sherwood Anderson, *Winesburg, Ohio* (New York: The Modern Library, 1919) 11.
82. Metalious, *Collar* 235.
83. Metalious, *Collar* 236.
84. Metalious, *Collar* 238.
85. Metalious, *Collar* 243.
86. Metalious, *Collar* 237.
87. Metalious, *Collar* 233.
88. Metalious, *Collar* 241.
89. Metalious, *Collar* 241.
90. Metalious, *Collar* 241.
91. Bellamann, *Kings Row* 4.
92. Bellamann, *Kings Row* 308.
93. Harry McBrayer Bayne, "A Critical Study of Henry Bellamann's Life and Work" (dissertation, 1990) 17.
94. Bellamann, *Kings Row* 305.
95. Bellamann, *Kings Row* 305–306.
96. John Howard, *Men Like That: A Southern Queer History* (Chicago: University of Chicago Press, 1999) xv.
97. Howard 19.
98. Bellamann, *Kings Row* 306.
99. Bellamann, *Kings Row* 136.
100. Bellamann, *Kings Row* 162–3.
101. Bellamann, *Kings Row* 166.
102. Bellamann, *Kings Row* 307.
103. Bellamann, *Kings Row* 100–101.
104. Bellamann, *Kings Row* 313–314.
105. Bellamann, *Kings Row* 415.
106. Bellamann, *Kings Row* 416.
107. Bellamann, *Kings Row* 416.
108. Bellamann, *Kings Row* 185; italics original.
109. Bellamann, *Parris Mitchell* 125.
110. Bellamann, *Parris Mitchell* 126.
111. Bellamann, *Parris Mitchell* 127.
112. Bellamann, *Parris Mitchell* 132.
113. Bellamann, *Parris Mitchell* 133.
114. Bellamann, *Parris Mitchell* 135; italics original.
115. Bellamann, *Parris Mitchell* 136.
116. Bellamann, *Parris Mitchell* 138.
117. Bellamann, *Kings Row* 96.
118. Bellamann, *Kings Row* 415.
119. Bellamann, *Parris Mitchell* 322.

Chapter Nine

1. Rom. 6:23. KJV.
2. Westminster Confession of Faith (WCF) VI.III.
3. WCF VI.IV.
4. Sarah Webster Goodwin and Elizabeth Bronfen, "Introduction," in *Death and Representation*, edited by Godwin and Bronfen (Baltimore: Johns Hopkins University Press, 1993) 4.
5. Lawrence L. Langer, *The Age of Atrocity: Death in Modern Literature* (Boston: Beacon, 1978) 25.
6. Norman Mailer, "The White Negro," in *Advertisements for Myself* 277.
7. Poll 5.
8. Tillich, *Courage* 41.
9. Tillich, *Courage* 179.
10. Bellamann, *Kings Row* 261.
11. William Faulkner, "A Rose for Emily," in *The Collected Stories of William Faulkner* (New York: Vintage, 1995) 123.
12. Faulkner, "Rose" 124.
13. Faulkner, "Rose" 130.
14. Faulkner, "Rose" 127.
15. Faulkner, "Rose" 126.
16. Faulkner, "Rose" 121.
17. Faulkner, "Rose" 128.
18. John A. McDermott, "'Do You Love Mother, Norman?' Faulkner's 'A Rose for Emily' and Metalious's Peyton Place as Sources for Robert Bloch's Psycho," *The Journal of Popular Culture* 40.3 (2007): 461.
19. Bloch 112.

20. Bloch 183; italics original.
21. Bloch 216; italics original.
22. Žižek, *Looking* 97.
23. Žižek, *Looking* 99.
24. Bloch 14.
25. Brian Diemert, "Uncontainable Metaphor: George F. Kennan's 'X' Article and Cold War Discourse," *Canadian Review of American Studies/Revue Canadienne d'Etudes Américaines* 35.1 (2005): 34.
26. Michael Rogin, *Ronald Reagan the Movie: And Other Episodes in Political Demonology* (Berkeley: University of California Press, 1988) 266.
27. Lewis, *Main Street* 259.
28. Jack Finney, *The Body Snatchers* (Cutchogue, NY: Buccaneer, 1955) 153.
29. Finney 163-164.
30. Finney 162.
31. Finney 163.
32. Finney 109.
33. Bellamann, *Kings Row* 445.
34. Bellamann, *Kings Row* 445.
35. Finney 7.
36. Finney 20.
37. Finney 121.
38. Finney 183.
39. Finney 188; italics original.
40. Finney 189.
41. Finney 190.
42. Finney 190.
43. Lockridge 197.
44. Lockridge 103.
45. Buechsel 22.
46. Lockridge 210.
47. Lockridge 198.
48. Whitman 268.

Epilogue

1. Marx 4.
2. Lockridge 211.
3. Lockridge 293.
4. Lockridge 815.
5. Smith 278-279.
6. Lockridge 736.
7. Mijuskvic 134.
8. Erich Fromm, *Escape from Freedom* (New York: Avon, 1965) 135.
9. Whitman 192.

Bibliography

Anderson, Benedict. *Imagined Communities: Reflections on the Origin and Spread of Nationalism*. London: Verso, 1983. Print.
Bakhtin, Mikhail. *Rabelais and His World*. Trans. Helene Iswolsky. Bloomington: Indiana University Press, 1984. Print.
Baumbach, Jonathan. "The Acid of God's Grace: The Fiction of Flannery O'Connor." *The Georgia Review* 17.3 (1963): 334–346. Print.
Bayne, Harry McBrayer. "A Critical Study of Henry Bellamann's Life and Work." 1990. Print. Dissertation.
Beaty, Bart. *Twelve-Cent Archie*. New Brunswick: Rutgers University Press, 2015. Print.
Bedrosian, Margaret. "Toshio Mori's California Koans." *MELUS* 15.2 (1988): 47–55. Print.
Bellamann, Henry. *Kings Row*. Garden City, NY: Sun Dial, 1946. Print.
Bellamann, Katherine, and Henry. *Parris Mitchell of Kings Row*. New York: Simon & Schuster, 1948. Print.
Bloch, Robert. *Psycho*. New York: Tor, 1989. Print.
Bloom, Harold. *The American Religion*. New York: Chu Hartley, 2013. Kindle.
Bradbury, Ray. *Dandelion Wine*. New York: Bantam, 1976. Print.
Brevda, William. "'Is There Any Up or Down Left?' Noir and Existentialism." *Soundings: An Interdisciplinary Journal* 89.3/4 (2006): 321–346. Print.
Buechsel, Mark. *Sacred Land: Sherwood Anderson, Midwestern Modernism, and the Sacramental Vision of Nature*. Kent, OH: Kent State University Press, 2014. Print.
Burgum, Edwin Berry. "The Sociological Pattern of 'Strange Fruit.'" *Science & Society* 9.1 (1945): 77–82. Print.
Cacioppo, John T., and William Patrick. *Loneliness: Human Nature and the Need for Social Connection*. New York: W. W. Norton, 2008. Kindle.
Cameron, Ardis. *Unbuttoning America: A Biography of "Peyton Place."* Ithaca: Cornell University Press, 2015. Print.
Castronovo, David. *Beyond the Gray Flannel Suit: Books from the 1950s That Made American Culture*. London: Bloomsbury Academic, 2004. Print.
Cawelti, John G. *The Six-Gun Mystique Sequel*. Bowling Green, OH: Popular Press, 1999. Print.
Chin, Frank. "Come All Ye Asian American Writers of the Real and the Fake." In *The Big Aiiieeeee!* Ed. Frank Chin et al. New York: Plume, 1991. Print.
Columbus, Christopher. *The Four Voyages*. Trans. and ed. J.M. Cohen. New York: Penguin, 1969. Print.
Conkin, Paul K. *A Requiem for the American Village*. Lanham: Rowman & Littlefield, 2000. Print.
Cooke, Alistair. "William March: A Trial Balance." *Manchester Guardian* June 8, 1954, p. 4. Print.

Coxe, Louis. "The Complex World of James Gould Cozzens." In *James Gould Cozzens: New Acquist of True Experience*. Ed. Matthew J. Bruccoli. Carbondale: Southern Illinois University Press, 1979. 1–14. Print.
Cozzens, James Gould. *The Just and the Unjust*. New York: Harcourt, Brace 1942. Print.
Debord, Guy. "The Situationist International Text Library/Introduction to a Critique of Urban Geography." N.p., n.d. http://library.nothingness.org/ Web. 18 Aug. 2016.
Detweiler, Robert. "The Curse of Christ in Flannery O'Connor's Fiction." *Comparative Literature Studies* 3.2 (1966): 235–245. Print.
Devlin, Rachel. *Relative Intimacy: Fathers, Adolescent Daughters, and Postwar American Culture*. Chapel Hill: University of North Carolina Press, 2006. Print.
Diemert, Brian. "Uncontainable Metaphor: George F. Kennan's 'X' Article and Cold War Discourse." *Canadian Review of American Studies/Revue Canadienne d'Etudes Américaines* 35.1 (2005): 21–55. Print.
Dorman, Robert L. *Revolt of the Provinces: The Regionalist Movement in America, 1920–1945*. Chapel Hill: University of North Carolina Press, 1993. Print.
Dower, John W. "Race, Language, and War in Two Cultures: World War II in Asia." In Erenberg. 169–201. Print.
Eisinger, Chester E. *Fiction of the Forties*. Chicago: University of Chicago Press, 1963. Print.
Erenberg, Lewis A., and Susan E Hirsch. *The War in American Culture: Society and Consciousness During World War II*. Chicago: University of Chicago Press, 1996. Print.
Faulkner, William. *Intruder in the Dust*. New York: Vintage, 2011. Print.
———. "A Rose for Emily." In *The Collected Stories of William Faulkner*. New York: Vintage, 1995. Print.
Fiedler, Leslie. *Love and Death in the American Novel*. New York: Meridian, 1964. Print.
Finney, Jack. *The Body Snatchers*. Cutchogue, NY: Buccaneer, 1955. Print.
Francaviglia, Richard V. *Main Street Revisited: Time, Space, and Image Building in Small-Town America*. Iowa City: University of Iowa Press, 1996. Print.
Freud, Sigmund. *The Interpretation of Dreams*. New York: Macmillan, 1913. Print.
———. *Totem and Taboo*. Trans. A. A. Brill. Digireads.com, 2009. Print.
Fromm, Erich. *Escape from Freedom*. New York: Avon, 1965. Print.
Gidley, Mick. "Elements of the Detective Story in William Faulkner's Fiction." In *Dimensions of Detective Fiction*. Ed. Larry N. Landrum, Pat Browne, and Ray B. Browne. Bowling Green, OH: Popular Press, 1976. 228–246. Print.
Goodrich, Joseph. *Blood Relations: The Selected Letters of Ellery Queen, 1947–1950*. Lexington: Perfect Crime Books, 2012. Print.
Goodwin, Sarah Webster and Elizabeth Bronfen. "Introduction." In *Death and Representation*, Ed. Godwin and Bronfen. Baltimore: Johns Hopkins University Press, 1993. 3–28. Print.
Gruesser, John Cullen. *Race, Gender and Empire in American Detective Fiction*. Jefferson, NC: McFarland, 2013. Print.
Harbison, Robert. *Eccentric Spaces*. New York: Alfred A. Knopf, 1977. Print.
Herron, Ima Honaker. *The Small Town in American Literature*. Durham: Duke University Press, 1939. Print.
Hilfer, Anthony Channell. *The Revolt from the Village 1915–1930*. Chapel Hill: University of North Carolina Press, 1969. Print.
Hirsh-Dickinson, Sally. *Dirty Whites and Dark Secrets: Sex and Race in Peyton Place*. Lebanon: University of New Hampshire Press, 2011. Print.
Hoffman, Daniel G. "Fable as Reality." In *Pastoral and Romance: Modern Essays in Criticism*, Ed. Eleanor Terry Lincoln. Englewood Cliffs, NJ: Prentice-Hall, 1969. Print.
Howard, John. *Men Like That: A Southern Queer History*. Chicago: University of Chicago Press, 1999. Print.
Inada, Lawson Fusao. "Standing on Seventh Street: An Introduction to the 1985 Edition." In *Yokohama, California*. Seattle: University of Washington Press, 1985. v–xxvii. Print.
Jackson, Chuck. "Little, Violent, White: The Bad Seed and the Matter of Children." *The Journal of Popular Film & Television*. 28.2 (2000): 64–74. Print.

Jameson, Fredric. *Postmodernism, or, the Cultural Logic of Late Capitalism*. Durham: Duke University Press, 1991. Print.

Johnson, Cheryl L. "The Language of Sexuality and Silence in Lillian Smith's 'Strange Fruit.'" *Signs* 27.1 (2001): 1–22. Print.

Kenner, Hugh. *A Homemade World: The American Modernist Writers*. New York: Alfred A. Knopf, 1975. Print.

Kruse, Kevin. *One Nation Under God: How Corporate America Invented Christian America*. New York: Basic Books, 2015. Print.

Ladino, Jennifer K. *Reclaiming Nostalgia: Longing for Nature in American Literature*. Charlottesville: University of Virginia Press, 2012. Kindle.

Langer, Lawrence L. *The Age of Atrocity: Death in Modern Literature*. Boston: Beacon, 1978. Print.

Lee, Robert G. *Orientals: Asian Americans in Popular Culture*. Philadelphia: Temple University Press, 1999. Print.

Levy, Emmanuel. *Small-Town America in Film: The Decline of Community*. New York: Continuum, 1991. Print.

Lewis, R.W.B. *The American Adam: Innocence, Tragedy, and Tradition in the Nineteenth Century*. Chicago: University of Chicago Press, 1966. Print.

Lewis, Sinclair. "Introduction to Main Street." In *The Man from Main Street*. New York: Random House, 1953. 213–217. Print.

_____. "The Long Arm of the Small Town." In *The Man from Main Street*. New York: Random House, 1953. 271–272. Print.

_____. *Main Street*. New York: Signet, 1961. Print.

Lockridge, Ross. *Raintree County*. New York: Penguin, 1994. Print.

Lutz, Tom. *Cosmopolitan Vistas: American Regionalism and Literary Value*. Ithaca: Cornell University Press, 2004. Print.

Macdonald, Dwight. "By Cozzens Possessed: A Review of Reviews." *Commentary Magazine*. 36–4D7. 1 January 1958. Web. 6 May 2016.

Mailer, Norman. "The White Negro." In *Advertisements for Myself*. New York: Putnam, 1959. 337–359. Print.

Mandel, Ernest. *Delightful Murder: A Social History of the Crime Story*. London: Pluto, 1984. Print.

March, William. *The Bad Seed*. Hopewell, NJ: The Ecco Press, 1997. Print.

_____. Notes for *The Bad Seed*. No date. William March Campbell Papers. Hoole Special Collections, University of Alabama, Tuscaloosa.

Marcuse, Herbert. *One-Dimensional Man: Studies in the Ideology of Advanced Industrial Society*. London: Routledge, 2002. Print.

Marx, Leo. *The Machine in the Garden: Technology and the Pastoral Ideal in America*. Oxford: Oxford University Press, 2000. Print.

Mayer, David R. "Toshio Mori and Loneliness." *Nanzan Review of American Studies* 15 (1993): 20–32. Print.

McDermott, John A. "'Do You Love Mother, Norman?' Faulkner's 'A Rose for Emily' and Metalious's *Peyton Place* as Sources for Robert Bloch's *Psycho*." *The Journal of Popular Culture* 40.3 (2007): 454–67. Print.

Metalious. *Peyton Place*. Boston: Northeastern University Press, 1999. Print.

_____. *Return to Peyton Place*. New York: Dell, 1965. Print.

_____. *The Tight White Collar*. New York: Messner, 1960. Print.

Mijuskovic, Ben Lazare. *Loneliness in Philosophy, Psychology, and Literature*. Bloomington: iUniverse, 2012. Print.

Miller, Jeffrey. *The Structures of Law and Literature*. Montreal: McGill-Queen's University Press, 2013. Print.

Mintz, Steven. *Huck's Raft: A History of American Childhood*. Cambridge: Belknap Press, 2004. Print.

Moore, R. Laurence. *Selling God: American Religion in the Marketplace of Culture*. New York: Oxford University Press, 1994. Print.

More, Thomas. *More: Utopia*. Ed. George M. Logan. Trans. Robert M. Adams. Cambridge: Cambridge University Press, 2016. Print.
Moretti, Franco. *The Way of the World: The* Bildungsroman *in European Culture*. London: Verso, 1987. Print.
Mori, Toshio. *Yokohama, California*. Seattle: University of Washington Press, 1985. Print.
Nakashima, Ted. "Concentration Camp: U.S. Style." In *Reporting World War II: Part One*. New York: Library of America, 1995. 352–354. Print.
Nevins, Francis M. *Cornell Woolrich: First You Dream, Then You Die*. New York: Mysterious Press, 1988. Print.
Niebuhr, Reinhold. *The Irony of American History*. Chicago: University of Chicago Press, 2008. Print.
_____. *Moral Man and Immoral Society*. New York: Touchstone, 1995. Print.
_____. *Nature and Destiny of Man, Vol. 1: Human Nature*. New York: Scribner's, 1949. Print.
Nisbet, Robert. *The Quest for Community*. Intercollegiate Studies Institute, 2014. Kindle.
O'Connor, Flannery. *Wise Blood*. In *Three by Flannery O'Connor*. New York: Signet, 1983. Print.
Orvell, Miles. *The Death and Life of Main Street: Small Towns in American Memory, Space, and Community*. Chapel Hill: University of North Carolina Press, 2012. Print.
Palladino, Grace. *Teenagers: An American History*. New York: Basic Books, 1996. Print.
Palumbo-Liu, David. "Toshio Mori and the Attachments of Spirit: A Response to David R. Mayer." *Amerasia* 17.3 (1991): 41–47. Print.
Parthun, Paul. "Concord, Charles Ives, and Henry Bellamann." *Collected Work: Student musicologists at Minnesota. Centennial Ives Issue celebrating the USA's 200th Birthday*. University of Minnesota (Department of Music), 1975–1976. (AN: 1975–00297) 6 (1975): 66–86. Print.
Payne, Kenneth. "'This Dark Thing, This Other Self': Character and Self-Distantiation in Cornell Woolrich's *I Married a Dead Man* (1948)." *Papers on Language and Literature* 34.1 (1998): 94–105. Print.
Perrin, Tom. *The Aesthetics of Middlebrow Fiction: Popular US Novels, Modernism, and Form, 1945–75*. New York: Palgrave Macmillan, 2015. Kindle.
Poll, Ryan. *Main Street and Empire the Fictional Small Town in the Age of Globalization*. New Brunswick: Rutgers University Press, 2012. Print.
Qian, Zhaoming. *Orientalism and Modernism*. Durham: Duke University Press, 1995. Print.
Queen, Ellery. *Calamity Town*. Boston: Little, Brown 1942. Anthologized in *Wrightsville Murders*. Boston: Little, Brown, 1956. Print.
_____. *Double, Double*. Boston: Little, Brown, 1950. Print.
_____. *Ten Days' Wonder*. Boston: Little, Brown 1948. Print.
Rabinowitz, Peter J. "The Click of the Spring: The Detective Story as Parallel Structure in Dostoyevsky and Faulkner." *Modern Philology* 76:4 (1979). 355–369. Print.
Rank, Otto. *The Incest Theme in Literature and Legend*. Baltimore: Johns Hopkins University Press, 1992. Print.
Rauschenbusch, Walter. *The Righteousness of the Kingdom*. Ed. Max L. Stackhouse. Nashville: Abington, 1968. Print.
Rogin, Michael. *Ronald Reagan The Movie: And Other Episodes in Political Demonology*. Berkeley: University of California Press, 1988. Print.
Sandifer, Elizabeth. *TARDIS Eruditorum—An Unofficial Critical History of Doctor Who Volume 1: William Hartnell*. CreateSpace Independent Publishing Platform, 2014. Print.
Saroyan, William. *The Human Comedy*. New York: Dell, 1966. Print.
Scherer, Mark R. "Where's the Rest of 'Kings Row'? Hollywood's Emasculation of a 'Grand Yarn.'" *Literature/Film Quarterly* 27 4 (1999): 255–62. Print.
Smith, Lillian. *Strange Fruit*. Athens: University of Georgia Press, 1987. Print.
Smith, Page. *As a City Upon a Hill: The Town in American History*. New York: Alfred A. Knopf, 1966. Print.
Sterne, Laurence. *The Life and Opinions of Tristram Shandy, Gentleman*. New York: Macy, n.d. Print.

Stewart, Susan. *On Longing: Narratives of the Miniature, the Gigantic, the Souvenir, the Collection*. Durham: Duke University Press, 2012. Print.
Tanemura, Janice. "Race, Regionalism, and Biopower in 'Yokohama, California.'" *Discourse* 29.2/3 (2007): 303–329. Print.
Tillich, Paul. *The Courage to Be*. New Haven: Yale University Press, 1980. Print.
_____. "To Whom Much is Forgiven..." in *The New Being*. New York: Charles Scribner's Sons, 1955. Print.
Tocqueville, Alexis de. *Democracy in America and Two Essays on America*. New York: Penguin, 2003. Print.
Trausbaugh, John. *Black Like You: Blackface, Whiteface, Insult & Imitation in American Popular Culture*. New York: Jeremy P. Tarcher, 2006. Print.
Ueda, Reed. "The Changing Path to Citizenship: Ethnicity and Naturalization During World War II." In Erenberg. 202–216. Print.
Van Dover, J.K., and John F. Jebb. *Isn't Justice Always Unfair? The Detective in Southern Literature*. Bowling Green, OH: Popular Press, 1996. Print.
von Hassell, Malve. "Ethnography, Storytelling and the Fiction of Toshio Mori *Dialectical Anthropology* 19.4 (1994): 401–418. *JSTOR*. Web.
Wachhorst, Wyn. *The Best of Times: Motifs from Postwar America*. Bloomington: Author House, 2016. Print.
Wainwright, Michael. *Faulkner's Gambit: Chess and Literature*. New York: Palgrave Macmillan, 2011. Print.
Walker, Janet. "Textual Trauma in *Kings Row* and Freud." In *Endless Night: Cinema and Psychoanalysis, Parallel Histories*. Ed. Janet Bergstrom. Berkeley: University of California Press, 1999. 171–187. Print.
Weisberg, Richard. *Poethics and Other Strategies of Law and Literature*. New York: Columbia University Press, 1992. Print.
Whitman, Walt. *Complete Poetry and Collected Prose—Leaves of Grass (1855 & 1891–92), Complete Prose Works (1892), Supplementary Prose*. New York: Library of America, 1982. Print.
Williams, William Carlos. *Paterson*. New York: New Directions, 1963. Print.
Wolfe, Thomas. "The Lost Boy." In *The Complete Short Stories of Thomas Wolfe*. New York: Simon & Schuster, 1989. 359–380. Print.
Woodward, Kenneth L. *Getting Religion: Faith, Culture, and Politics from the Age of Eisenhower to the Era of Obama*. New York: Convergent Books, 2016. Print.
Woolrich, Cornell. *I Married a Dead Man*. New York: Penguin, 1994. Print.
Žižek, Slavoj. *Looking Awry: An Introduction to Jacques Lacan through Popular Culture*. Cambridge: MIT, 1995. Print.
_____. *The Sublime Object of Ideology*. London: Verso, 1989. Print.
_____. *Violence: Six Sideways Reflections*. London: Profile, 2009. Print.

Index

alienation *see* loneliness
Anderson, Benedict 7
Anderson, Sherwood 10, 11, 35, 38, 41, 83, 86–87, 90, 116, 153, 163, 169, 181
Archie Comics 7, 20, 61–62, 66, 67, 80–81
atomic bomb 11, 34, 65, 70, 114, 139–140, 176
automobiles 94–95, 130

The Bad Seed 43, 53–55
Bellamann, Henry 1, 2, 9, 16, 17, 20–22, 28, 43, 105, 107, 144, 151, 174, 188; *Kings Row* 67–72, 116–119, 148–149, 168–172, 181–182; *Kings Row* (film) 101–104; *Parris Mitchell of Kings Row* 72–74, 172–174
Bellamann, Katherine 22, 72, 114; *Parris Mitchell of Kings Row* 72–74, 172–174
blackmail 33, 37, 119, 166
Bloch, Robert 22; *Psycho* 84, 178–179
The Body Snatchers 179–183
Bradbury, Ray 9, 17, 18, 19, 43, 55, 58, 60; *Dandelion Wine* 47–49, 50–53; *Farewell Summer* 48; *Something Wicked This Way Comes* 48

Calamity Town 25–31, 83, 85, 94–96
capitalism 7, 20, 34, 35, 82, 83, 84–85, 86, 89, 90, 91, 97, 108, 121–122, 186
Chandler, Raymond 140, 160
"The Chessmen" 90–92
China 45, 160, 161, 180–181
the Cold War 61
Columbus, Christopher 5, 27, 29, 30, 39, 44, 45, 62, 76, 79, 161
corpses 32, 37, 134, 140, 144, 147, 178, 179
Cozzens, James Gould 2, 16, 21, 141; *The Just and the Unjust* 11, 135–140
crowds 73–74
cycle 30, 64, 66, 67, 76, 79, 83, 84, 96, 183

Dandelion Wine 47–49, 50–53
Debord, Guy 14
detective fiction 1, 2, 16, 25, 26, 140, 141
detectives 29, 136, 141–142, 159, 160
doctors 145–149, 182
Double, Double 31–32

Eden 11, 17, 19, 20, 21, 22, 26, 28–32, 34, 38–40, 42, 44–50, 56, 57, 62, 70, 76–79, 81, 91, 98, 107, 110, 114, 133–134, 135–137, 145, 149–151, 154, 156, 161, 170, 175, 176, 180, 182, 184, 186–188
"An Error in Chemistry" 141–142
euthanasia 68, 70, 102, 149
Existentialism 35–36, 115, 146

fall and redemption 11, 17, 28, 38
fallenness 9, 11, 18, 19, 20, 26, 29, 30, 38, 42–46, 47–50, 56, 57, 58, 72, 78, 79, 81, 97, 98, 114, 116, 117, 135, 137–139, 145, 149–151, 175–176, 186
Farewell Summer 48
Father-God 116, 119, 121–122, 129, 134
Faulkner, William 1, 22, 54, 151, 188; "An Error in Chemistry" 141–142; *Intruder in the Dust* 84, 140–141, 142–143, 159–160; "A Rose for Emily" 39, 55, 177–178
Fiedler, Leslie 46, 47, 156, 157, 165, 176
"The Finances Over at Doi's" 89–90
Finney, Jack 22, 188; *The Body Snatchers* 179–183

the garden 28, 32–33, 39–40, 69, 77, 81, 91, 93, 132, 162, 180, 182–184, 186–187
the Great Depression 10, 17, 85, 90, 124, 154
grotesque 87, 90, 153, 169

Hammett, Dashiell 140
Harbison, Robert 32

207

Index

hard-boiled 140, 159
Hawthorne, Nathaniel 33, 177
the Holocaust 114
homosexuality 43, 100, 101, 105, 144, 166–168, 169–173, 179
The Human Comedy 55–60

I Married a Dead Man 33–34, 35–38, 99
incarnation 19, 51, 52, 55, 63, 79, 80, 117, 131, 134, 137, 150, 151, 164, 173, 174, 179, 182
incest 43, 70, 71–72, 74, 100, 102, 112, 121, 143–145, 147–149, 169, 171
industrialization 32, 51, 84, 121, 122
innocence 6, 11, 19, 27, 31, 32, 42–44, 46, 48, 61, 62, 66, 78, 79, 81, 84, 85, 89, 138, 140, 142, 149, 159
Intruder in the Dust 84, 140–141, 142–143, 159–160
Invasion of the Body Snatchers see *The Body Snatchers*
It's a Wonderful Life (film) 86, 99, 108, 112, 154

Jameson, Frederic 12–13
Japanese Internment 38, 40, 96, 162, 163, 164
The Just and the Unjust 11, 135–140

Kings Row (book) 67–72, 116–119, 148–149, 168–172, 181–182
Kings Row (film) 101–104

lawbreaking 22, 98, 122, 135, 151
lawyers 135–141, 145
Lewis, R.W.B. 32, 44, 48
Lewis, Sinclair 11, 41, 84–85, 153; *Main Street* 10, 71, 85, 180–181
Lockridge, Ross, Jr. 19, 20, 21, 22, 63, 181; *Raintree County* 28, 34, 42, 45–47, 76–80, 131–134, 149–151, 183–184, 186–188; *Raintree County* (film) 108–112
loneliness 2, 11, 13, 17, 18, 19, 22, 28, 30, 38, 39, 43, 44, 47, 48, 49, 51–53, 55, 57–60, 62, 69, 70, 74, 82, 84, 87, 90–92, 97, 101, 112, 118, 119, 131, 136, 145, 150, 152, 169, 171, 173, 175–177, 179, 182–184, 187, 188
"The Lost Boy" 82–83

Magic Town (film) 5–7, 8, 10, 12, 19, 27, 29, 34
Mailer, Norman 65, 70, 176
Main Street 10, 71, 85, 180–181
March, William 19, 60; *The Bad Seed* 43, 53–55
Marx, Leo 32–33, 186
Masters, Edgar Lee 11, 176

Metalious, Grace 9, 20, 21, 22, 28, 101, 105, 106, 107, 151, 178, 188; *Peyton Place* 43, 143–148, 164–165; *Peyton Place* (film) 104–108; *Return to Peyton Place* 75–76; *The Tight White Collar* 165–168
More, Thomas 12–13, 14
Moretti, Franco 20, 62, 63, 70, 82
Mori, Toshio 19, 28, 30, 41, 85, 97, 160, 180, 182, 183; "The Chessmen" 90–92; "The Finances Over at Doi's" 89–90; "My Mother Stands on Her Head" 88–89; "Say It with Flowers" 92–93; "The Seventh Street Philosopher" 38; "The Six Rows of Pompoms" 93; "Slant-Eyed Americans" 39–40, 164; "Three Japanese Mothers" 93–94; "Tomorrow Is Coming, Children" 162–164; "Toshio Mori" (story) 39; *Yokohama, California* 86–88, 161–162
"My Mother Stands on Her Head" 88–89

nature 22, 28, 32–33, 40, 42, 45, 47, 62, 74, 77–79, 105, 115–116, 118, 133–134, 156, 184, 187
the New Deal 122
Niebuhr, Reinhold 50, 125, 139–140
nostalgia 6, 8–10, 16, 18, 19, 22, 25, 42–43, 50, 56, 174, 176, 188–189

O'Connor, Flannery 21, 134; *Wise Blood* 127–131

Parris Mitchell of Kings Row 72–74, 172–174
patriotism 44, 65
Pearl Harbor Attacks 39–40, 119, 161
Peyton Place (book) 43, 143–148, 164–165
Peyton Place (film) 104–108
poetic redescription 79–80, 173–174
Poll, Ryan 1, 7, 8, 12, 13, 14, 18, 20, 21, 23, 34–35, 63–64, 90, 74, 82–86, 94, 95, 99, 108, 112, 152, 154, 155, 176, 186, 187, 188
psychogeography 14–15

Queen, Ellery 1, 2, 16, 17, 19, 20, 21, 38, 40, 79, 123, 127, 188; *Calamity Town* 25–31, 83, 85, 94–96; *Double, Double* 31–32; *Ten Days' Wonder* 110–123

Raintree County 28, 34, 42, 45–47, 76–80, 131–134, 149–151, 183–184, 186–188
Raintree County (film) 108–112
rape 73, 102, 138, 143, 144, 146, 148, 149, 165
rebellion 20, 60–63, 66–67, 70–71, 76, 92, 98, 115, 149
Regionalism (movement) 10–11, 29, 50, 74, 95, 104, 182

Return to Peyton Place 75–76
revivalism 123–127, 131–134
Revolt from the Village 10–11, 17, 18, 28, 65, 67, 71, 84, 85, 87, 187
Riesman, David 8, 11, 73
"A Rose for Emily" 39, 55, 177–178

Sandifer, Elizabeth 14–15
Saroyan, William 19, 43; *The Human Comedy* 55–60
"Say It with Flowers" 92–93
"The Seventh Street Philosopher" 38
sex 29, 46, 62, 67, 69, 72, 76, 77, 78, 79, 100, 105–105, 111, 112, 121, 130, 131–134, 143, 149–151, 156–157, 166, 167, 168, 169–170, 176, 184
Shakespeare, William 46
Sherlock Holmes 140, 160
"The Six Rows of Pompoms" 93
"Slant-Eyed Americans" 39–40, 164
Smith, Lillian 21, 96, 163, 165, 188; *Strange Fruit* 124–127, 155–158
Something Wicked This Way Comes 48
Sterne, Laurence 15–16, 108
Strange Fruit 124–127, 155–158

Ten Days' Wonder 110–123
"Three Japanese Mothers" 93–94
The Tight White Collar 165–168
Tillich, Paul 2, 11, 115, 116, 117, 119, 128, 130, 133, 176–177, 183, 188

"Tomorrow Is Coming, Children" 162–164
"Toshio Mori" (story) 39
trains 5, 25, 32, 33–37, 49, 57, 58, 80, 94, 96, 106, 147, 186–188
transcendence 3, 6, 8, 9, 10, 14, 15, 17, 18, 19, 20, 21, 22, 31, 42, 43, 45, 47, 50, 53, 57, 58, 62, 63, 73, 76, 81, 97, 98, 99, 100, 107–108, 112, 113, 114, 115, 116, 118, 119, 128, 131, 133, 134, 135, 143, 144, 146, 148, 149, 150, 152, 156, 157, 160, 163, 173–174, 176, 181, 183, 188
The Twilight Zone 34, 86

Utopianism 12–13, 81, 143

Whitman, Walt 2, 22, 30, 44, 48, 70, 79, 94, 95, 96, 116, 133, 184, 188
Winesburg, Ohio 87
Wise Blood 127–131
Wolfe, Thomas 46; "The Lost Boy" 82–83
Woolrich, Cornell 19, 38, 40; *I Married a Dead Man* 33–34, 35–38, 99
World War I 96, 126, 158, 174
World War II 1, 3, 6, 8, 14, 17, 21, 23, 28, 33, 38–40, 44, 55–60, 64, 65–66, 70, 73, 83, 86, 96, 98, 100, 106, 112, 114, 115, 119, 122, 126, 130–131, 134, 138–139, 143, 144, 153, 154, 158, 161–162, 164, 174–176, 183, 189

Yokohama, California 86–88, 161–162

www.ingramcontent.com/pod-product-compliance
Lightning Source LLC
Chambersburg PA
CBHW032056300426
44116CB00007B/766